Melbourne Girls Grammar School
Centenary Essays 1893–1993

Melbourne Girls Grammar School
Centenary Essays
1893–1993

edited by
Rosslyn McCarthy and
Marjorie R. Theobald

HYLAND HOUSE

First published in 1993 by
Hyland House Publishing Pty Limited
10 Hyland Street
South Yarra
Melbourne
Victoria 3141

National Library of Australia
Cataloguing in publication data

McCarthy, Rosslyn, 1945- .
   Melbourne Girls Grammar centenary essays, 1893-1993.

   Includes index.
   ISBN 1 875657 03 7.

   1. Melbourne Church of England Girls' Grammar School—History.
   2. Church of England—Education—Victoria—Melbourne—History.
   3. Church Schools—Victoria—Melbourne—History. I. Theobald,
   Marjorie R. II. Title.

371.02099451

Edited by Lee White
Index by Kerry Herbstreit
Typeset by Solo Typesetting, South Australia
Printed in Australia by The Book Printer, Victoria

Contents

Abbreviations   ix
Acknowledgments   xi

Introduction
    Rosslyn McCarthy and Marjorie R. Theobald   1

1 Beginnings: 1893–1912
    Marjorie R. Theobald   11

2 A very Anglican arrangement: the Diocese of
  Melbourne and schools for girls, 1884–1920
    Stuart Blackler   31

3 The Gilman Jones era: 1916–38
    Ailsa G. Thomson Zainu'ddin   50

4 Merton Hall women and professional life: 1917–38
    Pip Nicholson   68

5 The school as a democratic community:
  the educational ideas of D. J. Ross
    W. F. Connell   88

6 The war years, 1939–45: an oral history
    Desma P. McDonald   110

7 Back into line
    Lyndsay Gardiner   128

8 MCEGGS in a time of change: the era of
  Edith Mountain, 1957–74
    Rosslyn McCarthy   147

9 Melbourne Girls Grammar School in 1993   170

Notes   187
Index   203

List of illustrations

Jacket   'View from the Hockey Field' by Arthur Streeton.
Endpaper (Front)   MCEGGS girls of the Edwardian era.
Endpaper (Back)   The school in the Gilman Jones era.

*facing
page*

Merton Hall in Domain Road, *c.* 1894.   20

The Morris family.   21
Merton Hall, *c.* 1907.

The staff, *c.* 1909.   52
Morris Hall, *c.* 1915.

Bishop James Moorhouse, by C. W. Walton.   53
Archbishop Henry Lowther Clarke.

Entrance hall, Merton Hall.   *between*
Dr Alexander Leeper, by Rupert Bunny.   *pages*
                                                                    68–69

Miss Kathleen Gilman Jones.
The Assembly Hall, 1917.

Dr Betty Wilmot.
Miss Lorna Mitchell.

Miss Mary Cameron.
Dr Jean Laby.
Dr Gwyneth Dow.

The building of new Merton Hall.   *between*
                                                           pages
Miss D. J. Ross, 1939.   100–101

Teachers and helpers, Mt Kitchener House, 1942.
Miss Alison Winfield and girls, Marysville, 1942.
Outside gymnastics, Doncaster, 1942.

Miss Edith Mountain, Michelle Allan and Sally
Anderson, with Bulfa, 1960.
Miss Edith Mountain and staff, 1968.

Grade Three classroom in the new Junior School.   *facing*
Dean Thomas taking communion in St Luke's Chapel.   *page*
The girls in the Mountain era.   148

Miss Nina Crone.   149
The Nina Crone Resource Centre.

Girls in the Garnsworthy Centre for Computer Studies.   180
Swimming team, 1990.

Rehearsing for 'Noye's Fludde', 1958.   181
Rehearsing for 'Professor Taranne', 1990.

                                                          page
The Organisation of MCEGGS in the Ross Era.   103

Portrait of Miss D. J. Ross, 1979, by Diana Mogensen.   109

Weg's view of 'the crisis'.   146

Abbreviations

ACER	Australian Council for Educational Research
ADB	*Australian Dictionary of Biography*
AEQ	*Australian Educational Quarterly*
AIF	Australian Imperial Forces
AMAV	Assistant Mistresses Association of Victoria
ARP	Air Raid Precautions
ATTI	Associated Teachers Training Institute
AWAS	Australian Women's Army Service
B.A.	Bachelor of Arts
B.Sc.	Bachelor of Science
CEGGS	Church of England Girls Grammar School
C. Mins	Council Minutes
C. of E. Mess.	*Church of England Messenger*
COS	Chief of Staff
C.P. Ed. Mins	Council of Public Education Minutes
CSIRO	Commonwealth Scientific and Industrial Research Organisation
D.Sc.	Doctor of Science
GPDST	Girls Public Day School Trust
HMAA	Headmistresses Association of Australia
HMA	Headmistresses Association
HM Mins	Headmistresses Association Minutes
HM Rep.	Headmistress's Report to Council
IARTV	Independent Association of Registered Teachers of Victoria
IASTV	Independent Association of Secondary Teachers of Victoria
IE	*Information Exchange*
JCH	Janet Clarke Hall

LCP	Liberal Country Party
LOTE	Language Other Than English
M.A.	Master of Arts
MBE	Member of the British Empire
MCEGGS	Melbourne Church of England Girls Grammar School
MGGS	Melbourne Girls Grammar School
MLA	Member of the Legislative Assembly
MLC	Methodist Ladies College
NCW	National Council of Women
NFRC	National Fund Raising Council
Ph.D.	Doctor of Philosophy
PLC	Presbyterian Ladies College
PSSC	Physical Science Study Committee
RAAF	Royal Australian Air Force
SEC	School Executive Council
SN	*School Notes*
UNESCO	United Nations Educational Scientific and Cultural Organization
VAD	Voluntary Aid Detachment
VCAB	Victorian Curriculum and Assessment Board
VCE	Victorian Certificate of Education
VISE	Victorian Institute of Secondary Education
VPRS	Victorian Public Record Series
WAAAF	Women's Australian Auxiliary Air Force
WRANS	Women's Royal Australian Navy Service

Acknowledgments

In the preparation and publication of this volume of essays the editors and authors owe a collective and individual debt to many people. The authors have chosen to make these acknowledgments in the end notes to their own chapters, and the many people who shared their memories, gave access to documents and photographs, and in other ways gave their support, will find themselves there. The encouragement and co-operation of many other people must be acknowledged. The School Council and the headmistress, Nina Crone, made the decision to publish the volume and extended to the editors and authors full professional control of the project and access to sources. In particular, the editors wish to thank the Council representative on the Centenary History Subcommittee, Dr Alan Gregory, for his constant support and for reading the manuscript. Bishop James Grant, deputy chairman of the School Council, also gave personal support and read the manuscript. The Old Grammarians' representative on the subcommittee, Lorna Mitchell, gave not only support but practical help at all stages.

The authors wish to acknowledge the unstinting help of the MGGS archivist, Rosslyn McCarthy, Old Grammarians, Margaret Clark (née Sanders) and Margaret Spring (née Colclough), who work in the archives as a labour of love, and the many members of the school community who have deposited material there over the years. Without this valuable collection this book could not have been written. The authors also wish to acknowledge the assistance of the archivists and librarians at the Public Record Office of Victoria, the State Library of Victoria, the La Trobe

Library, the Archives of the Diocese of Melbourne, the University of Melbourne, Janet Clarke Hall, Oxford, Nottingham and Putney Girls High Schools, the University of London, and Queen's and Westfield Colleges, London.

Artist and Old Grammarian, Diana Mogensen, gave permission to reproduce her portrait of Dorothy Ross; W. E. Green (Weg) and the *Herald and Weekly Times* gave permission to use the delightful cartoon on the 1958 crisis; the Arthur Streeton painting of the school was reproduced on the dust jacket with the permission of Mrs M. Streeton; the photograph of the Morris family was reproduced with the permission of Old Grammarian Meredith Bell (née Wade), daughter of Marcia Morris and granddaughter of William Morris; the Rupert Bunny portrait of Dr Leeper was reproduced with the permission of Nigel Buesst and Janet Clarke Hall; the organisational chart of MGGS was reproduced with the permission of the Australian Council for Educational Research from K. S. Cunningham and D. J. Ross, *An Australian School at Work*, ACER, Melbourne, 1967; and the portrait of Archbishop Lowther Clarke is from the collection of Stuart Blackler. The photograph of Betty Wilmot is reproduced with the permission of the *Age*; the photograph of Mary Cameron is reproduced with the permission of Mirror Australian Telegraph Publications; and the photographs of Jean Laby and Noye's Fludde are reproduced with the permission of the *Herald and Weekly Times*. Many of the photographs in the volume were taken or reproduced by MGGS photographer and staff member, Don Wirth. To all these people we are most grateful, and to those whom we have forgotten in the confusion which invariably envelops the last stages of publication, we most humbly apologise.

The editors wish to acknowledge the constant support and encouragement of their husbands, Shane McCarthy and John Theobald.

Rosslyn McCarthy and
Marjorie R. Theobald

Introduction

M ELBOURNE GIRLS GRAMMAR SCHOOL (MGGS) BEGAN IN 1893
as a privately owned ladies' school with nine students
in Domain Road, South Yarra. Its owner-principals
were Cambridge-educated Emily Hensley, who had been briefly
principal of Trinity Ladies' Hostel (later Janet Clarke Hall), and
her friend and fellow Englishwoman, Alice Taylor. Merton
Hall, as its founding principals chose to call it, had an early link
with the Church of England: two prominent Anglican families,
the Clarkes and the Grimwades, financed the venture on the
understanding that Merton Hall should be an unofficial 'Church
of England High School for Girls'.

This link with the Church was strengthened when, in 1898,
Merton Hall was purchased for Mary and Edith Morris by their
father, W. E. Morris, who served on the staff of the Diocesan
Registry under every bishop from Perry to Lowther Clarke, and
was registrar of the diocese from 1887 until 1910. In 1900 the
Morris family moved the school to the present Anderson Street
site and financed the original building, which they also named
Merton Hall. The school under the Morrises was indeed a family
affair: it was the family home and William Morris departed each
day for his office at St Paul's Cathedral; his wife Clara acted as
matron and housekeeper; several smaller Morris children grew
up there; and another sister, Gwynneth, was sports mistress.
W. E. Morris clearly intended that Merton Hall should become
Victoria's first diocesan girls' school, and in 1903, five decades
after the establishment of Melbourne Grammar School, the
Morris family school passed into the hands of the Church of
England. Mary and Edith Morris remained as principals until

1

their respective marriages in 1908 and 1912. To this day, MGGS remains the only Anglican girls' school in Victoria created by Act of Synod.

When Edith Morris left in 1912, Melbourne Church of England Girls' Grammar School, as it was then known, had an enrolment of almost 300 girls. The original 2-acre site purchased by W. E. Morris from the Cain family in 1900 had doubled in size with the acquisition of 'Old Fairlie' on the southern side. A series of red-brick extensions had been added behind Merton Hall in an easterly direction, and the original Morris Hall had arisen on the site of the 'Old Fairlie' bungalow. Yet Merton Hall had not quite outgrown its identity as a family school. When the beautiful and imperious Miss A. Tunnicliffe arrived from England in 1914 as the fifth headmistress, bringing in her cultural baggage strict notions of an English girls' Public school, the achievements of the Morris family and the Church were apparently invisible to her, for she was critical of almost every aspect of the school. The MGGS community did not accept her and in 1915 she was asked to resign. Thus it was that, shortly after the outbreak of the First World War, MGGS was again in search of a principal.

This time the search was successful, for the appointment of the Cambridge-educated and feminist Kathleen Gilman Jones in 1916 marked the beginning of a remarkable era of stability and achievement in the school's history. Though her principalship has been overshadowed by that of her more controversial successor, Dorothy Ross, Kathleen Gilman Jones fought against the tide of comfortable middle-age which engulfed Australia's Public schools between the wars, developing a unique blend of Public school traditions with progressive educational ideas concerning the unique development of every girl. Girls at school in those decades will remember the myriad ways in which those ideals shaped the day-to-day life of the school. Some Old Girls will also remember the opening in 1917 of the Assembly Hall between Merton Hall and Morris Hall, and the acquisition in 1927 of Phelia Grimwade House on the corner of Anderson and Clowes Streets. Miss Gilman Jones, whose greatest regret was that she could not persuade the Council to build a school chapel, was an inspiring and much-loved head.

The Australian-born Dorothy Ross was both protégée and disciple of Miss Gilman Jones, 'a natural successor . . . but not a mere continuer'. She had taught at MGGS in the 1920s, but came to the principalship in 1938 from the Associated Teachers Training Institute (ATTI) where she had been director since 1930. Miss Ross had been principal for barely two years when MGGS was required to evacuate its premises under wartime emergency legislation, and from March 1942 until August 1944 the school was scattered across three guest houses at Marysville and the Eastern Golf Club at Doncaster. This potentially disastrous disruption to the school's life in fact necessitated devolution of authority and a 'sink-or-swim' self-reliance on the part of staff and girls. These wartime exigencies accorded with Miss Ross's proclivity for less hierarchical ways, for co-operative rather than competitive endeavour, and for learning by doing. When the school was once more assembled on the Anderson Street site, she encouraged the more democratic relationships between staff and girls, and the enhanced self-reliance of the girls developed during the evacuation.

In the first half of the twentieth century MGGS was part of an aristocracy of girls' schools which espoused the rights of women to a rigorous, academic education leading to the University of Melbourne and the professions, and, more controversially, the possibility of an autonomous life. With its Protestant counterparts, Presbyterian Ladies' College (PLC) and Methodist Ladies' College (MLC), a handful of Catholic convent schools, and MacRobertson Girls' High School, MGGS stood out against the general decline of women's education into mediocrity in these decades.

A charismatic figure, Miss Ross inevitably aroused both fierce loyalty and subdued opposition. As her opponents charged, she was indeed more left-leaning than Miss Gilman Jones, as were many of her staff, and she was more thoroughgoing in her educational experimentation. More importantly, however, her ideas and practice at 'Grammar' flowered in the wrong decades when fear of Communism sent Progressivism and its ilk once again to wait in the wings. Such was her prestige within the school and in the wider educational community that D. J. Ross was invulnerable while she remained in office; after she resigned changes were inevitable. Did anyone foresee how cataclysmic that process of change would be?

Unaccountably, a suitable replacement for Miss Ross proved to be elusive. She resigned in 1955, and Mrs Sylvia Martin's interregnum as acting headmistress stretched on through 1956 to 1957. Finally, 38-year-old Englishwoman, Edith Mountain, was appointed principal in 1958. Not even her greatest supporters would describe Miss Mountain as charismatic, and she did not share the educational philosophy which underpinned Grammar in the Ross era. She did, however, have her own strengths and her own educational outlook. By the end of that year, the whole school community was involved in a very public brawl; at stake was nothing less than the future identity of MGGS. Nobody who knew the school at that time would want to argue that MGGS did not change dramatically after 1958; indeed Dorothy Ross herself predicted that the school would have to change. What is controversial, and will remain controversial, is the desirability of those changes. With the wisdom of hindsight we can see that Edith Mountain began her term of office when Australia's independent schools were facing great challenges: the state secondary system expanded rapidly, challenging for the first time the traditional independent school monopoly over places in prestigious university faculties; the independent school clientele itself began to stay at school longer, raising in ever more acute form the 'problem' of what to do with the less academically inclined girl; the role of women in society changed rapidly, bringing schools like MGGS under greater pressure to prepare girls for careers outside the home; and the renewal of state aid altered the entire landscape of possibilities for the independent schools. In the Mountain era the school was physically trans- formed: new science laboratories and a new library were opened in 1961; in 1962 Gilman Jones Hall was refurbished as a board- ing house; a separate junior school on the old Wildfell property was opened in 1966 and named Morris Hall; fulfilling a long- held dream at MGGS, St Luke's Chapel was consecrated in 1967: and, finally, the Edith Mountain Sixth Form Centre and the new Ross Hall were opened in 1973.

It is a vexed question as to where history ends and the present begins, bringing with it a veritable army of experts from the smallest girl to the most exalted member of Council, to plague the hapless historian of the modern era. In the end a decision was made to bring the process of historical analysis to an end in 1974 with the departure of Miss Mountain. The final chapter, which covers the era of the present headmistress, Miss Nina Crone, is a collaborative effort, and descriptive rather than analytical.

When the School Council decided to commission a book of historical essays to mark the centenary of MGGS in 1993, mem- bers broke with tradition in two ways. Firstly, they decided to take the 100th birthday of the school from the establishment of Merton Hall by Miss Hensley and Miss Taylor in 1893. All previous celebrations, although they had not ignored these early years, took as their reference point the acquisition of Merton Hall by the Church in 1903. The Silver Jubilee was celebrated in 1928, although Gwenda Kent Hughes's *MCEGGS: History of the School*, published in that year, took as its starting point 1893, perhaps in deference to the many Old Girls from that period still in robust middle age. Indeed, one of the founding headmistresses, Mrs Alice Craig (née Taylor) was an honoured guest at the celebrations. The Jubilee was celebrated in 1953, when the second school history, *Nisi Dominus Frustra*, appeared. The Diamond Jubilee, or 60th birthday, was celebrated in 1963 by a special edition of *MCEGGS Magazine*.

Yet there are sound historical reasons for breaking with the reference point of 1903. Close historical research has revealed the early links between the establishment of Merton Hall in 1893, the Trinity College Hostel affair in the previous year, and the Grimwade and Clarke families. In addition, the acquisition of the school by the Church of England in 1903 did not bring the Morris era to an abrupt end. Mary and Edith Morris remained as principals until their marriages; their mother, Clara, continued to run the boarding house; and their father, William, remained a powerful figure behind the scenes, not least in the financial affairs of the school. Girls at MGGS in 1903 would scarcely have noticed the difference in their everyday lives at school. This acquisition of a private ladies' school by the Church was not an isolated incident. Under Archbishop Lowther Clarke the purchase of existing schools, rather than the establishment of new schools, became policy. Firbank, Tintern, Korowa, Ivanhoe Girls' Grammar School, and Mentone Girls' Grammar School all began life as privately owned ladies' schools. Their part in the story of Anglican girls' education should not be diminished. Indeed, recent historical scholarship on these early ladies' schools has restored their reputation as providers of worthwhile secondary education for girls at a time when church and state saw little need to provide for the education of girls.

The second tradition which the MGGS School Council jettisoned when it commissioned this volume was the narrative tradition in the writing of school histories. Instead, the members commissioned nine authors to write about certain aspects of the school's history. Some readers will doubtless regret the loss of the narrative, although they will find that it has not been abandoned altogether. A collection of essays has certain advantages over a traditional school history. Authors may be selected for their expertise in the history of a certain era or in a certain aspect of educational history, whereas the historian who must traverse the whole century inevitably scrambles more hastily, and with lighter conceptual baggage, across some decades than others. Authors may also be selected for their differing relationships with the school: whereas a history written entirely by an Old Girl or a retired headmistress may lack perspective, certain aspects of the school's life lend themselves admirably to the insider's perspective. On the other hand, an academic historian, well versed in the nuances of this or that educational vogue, may fail to capture the essence of what it felt like to be there at the time. Perhaps most importantly, a collection of essays may accommodate differences of interpretation which in the single-authored volume are either absent or rendered in shades of grey. All of these considerations shaped the selection of authors and topics in this collection.

Marjorie Theobald is a senior lecturer on the staff of the Institute of Education at the University of Melbourne. She is a historian with a special interest in the education of women, author of *Ruyton Remembers 1878–1978*, and of other books and articles on the history of women's education. Her doctoral thesis was on the privately owned ladies' colleges of nineteenth-century Melbourne and their gradual transformation and decline as the churches and the state began to intrude into their domain. Her chapter on Merton Hall as a private ladies' school and its acquisition by the Church of England draws upon this research.

Stuart Blackler's chapter on the Church of England and its policy on the education of girls in the years 1884–1920 is also informed by his doctoral thesis on the educational policies of Archbishop Henry Lowther Clarke. As an Anglican priest and as school chaplain from 1971 to 1992 he has combined an insider's knowledge with scholarly insight to write with wry tolerance of the Church's stately progress towards the establishment of its first girls' school—fifty years after the establishment of Melbourne Grammar and thirty years after the establishment of PLC.

Ailsa Zainu'ddin has recently retired as a senior lecturer in the Faculty of Education at Monash University. She is Melbourne's most distinguished historian of its girls' Public schools and in her retirement she hopes to continue her study of those institutions. She is author of *They Dreamt of a School: A centenary history of Methodist Ladies' College, Kew: 1882–1982*, and many other books and articles.

When the decision was made to include an article on the achievements of past students from the Gilman Jones era it seemed appropriate to invite a distinguished Old Girl from a more recent era to write the chapter. Pip Nicholson attended MGGS from 1977 to 1982 and held the Boarder's scholarship from form three to form six. She was school captain in her final year. She studied Law/Arts at the University of Melbourne, graduating in 1988. At the time of writing her chapter she was working as a solicitor at the Legal Aid Commission of Victoria and tutoring in law at Ormond College. Pip Nicholson documents the lives and careers of five past students of the Gilman

Jones era, revealing strong links between their experiences at school and their success as career women at a time when marriage and the private world of home and family was the norm for Australian women.

W. F. Connell is Emeritus Professor of Education at the University of Sydney and Fellow of the Faculty of Education at Monash University. He is one of Australia's leading historians of education with many books and articles to his credit. His more recent books include *A History of Education in the Twentieth Century World* and *Remaking Australian Education 1960–1985*. Bill Connell first met Miss Ross in the 1930s when she taught his wife, Margaret, at the ATTI, and in 1948 he worked with her at a six-week UNESCO seminar in Paris. He maintained a close friendship with her for the remainder of her life and they spent many hours happily discussing education. Bill Connell regarded 'Grammar' in Dorothy Ross's time as one of Australia's few genuinely innovative schools. His biographical study, 'Innovative headmistress—D. J. Ross', appeared in C. Turney's *Pioneers of Australian Education 1900–1950* in 1983.

In her chapter on the wartime evacuation of MGGS, Desma McDonald also combines the intuitive understanding of the insider with the detachment of the scholar. As Desma Stephenson she attended the school from 1938 to 1942, a stint which embroiled her in the evacuation to Doncaster, and she is presently writing her Ph.D. thesis at Monash University on the history of MGGS. Desma McDonald's brief was to write an oral history of the evacuation from the perspective of the students and staff who took part, and the result is a lively account which debunks some of the myths surrounding these momentous years in the school's history.

When the School Council decided to publish a book of centenary essays the members were agreed that the events surrounding the arrival of Edith Mountain as principal in 1958 must be fully investigated by a reputable historian outside the school community. Lyndsay Gardiner is a professional historian with several commissioned histories to her credit, including *Tintern School and Anglican Girls' Education 1877–1977*, *The Free Kindergarten Union of Victoria, 1908–80*, and *Janet Clarke Hall, 1886–1986*. The decision to devote a full chapter to the momentous events of 1958 will not please everybody, nor will Lyndsay Gardiner's conclusions. Her chapter on 'the crisis' should be read in conjunction with Rosslyn McCarthy's chapter on the Mountain era, for it is here that the question of perspective is at its most intriguing. It was a deliberate editorial decision to allow a considerable degree of overlap between the two chapters, and it will be apparent to the reader that Mrs Gardiner and Mrs McCarthy do not always agree in their conclusions. Rosslyn McCarthy is convenor of history and archivist at MGGS and is writing her Master's thesis at the University of Melbourne on Jean Lawson, who was careers counsellor in the Mountain era. Writing on an era of the school's history which is in that 'no man's land' between history and the present when there are too many voices to comprehend, Mrs McCarthy chose to concentrate on disinterring the 'bones' of the story, leaving the oral history of the era to historians in the future.

While each author in the collection brings to the history of MGGS his or her distinctive style and interpretation, certain themes emerge with striking regularity. Every headmistress, from the Morris sisters to Nina Crone, has been pulled and pushed between the need to provide a generous curriculum for all girls in what has always been an academically 'open entry' school, and the need to ensure respectable academic 'results' for entry to university. The Victorian Certificate of Education (VCE), for all its problems, is the most recent attempt to provide a curriculum for all students in a society which promises secondary education for all but still does not know how to achieve that aim.

Across the century, enrolments have always outstripped accommodation and space. In this respect, two decisions have been crucial: the decision to remain a boarding school; and the decision to remain on the South Yarra site when, in the post-war years, other independent schools moved to the burgeoning outer suburbs. By and large, girls' schools do not receive major benefactions, and the beautiful inner city campus, now the school's most appealing physical asset, has been acquired painfully piece by piece from within the school's own resources: Old Fairlie in 1905; Phelia Grimwade House in 1927; Wildfell in 1941; Ross Hall in 1947; property in Caroline and Walsh Streets in 1957; and further property acquisitions in Walsh Street in the 1970s and 1980s. With the exception of MGGS in wartime, every headmistress has been a builder, and each generation of girls has gone to school to the cacophony of building and renovation. So constant has been the physical transformation of the school that to the oldest of Old Girls in the centenary year, only Merton Hall and its red-brick extensions to the east will remain from the Edwardian era. And the saga of the chapel runs through the essays, from its first mention by the hapless Miss Tunnicliffe to the opening of the Chapel of St Luke in 1967.

Perhaps most insistently, there emerges from this collection of essays the realisation that no school can remained walled off from the society which it serves. Change is both constant and inevitable, although the larger forces at work are sometimes not clearly understood in the school community at the time. In its first century MGGS has experienced two women's movements: the suffrage movement in the Edwardian era demanded political emancipation and a widening sphere of influence for women; the later movement, in the 1970s and 1980s, demanded their economic and personal liberation. Both changed profoundly the expectations of female education. Two world wars have impinged on the life of the school, again pushing back the barriers to women's participation in society and, in the case of the Second World War, forcing upon the school dramatic and lasting changes. Three times in its first hundred years severe economic recessions have impacted upon MGGS—the 1890s, the 1930s, and the 1990s. As the crisis of 1958 illustrates, MGGS has been a testing ground for conflicting philosophical and educational ideas, ideas which are themselves deeply embedded in the wider philosophical and political movements of the day. The policies of the state—regulations governing public examinations and tertiary entrance, the Class-A system, official regulation of teacher education and registration, state regulation of registered women teachers' salaries, the fortunes of the state's own high schools, and policies on state aid to independent schools—set parameters within which the school must pursue its own distinctive mission as a girls' school of excellence at the end of the twentieth century.

In the writing of an institution's history, innumerable editorial decisions have to be made, sometimes on little more than apocryphal grounds. Where nine authors are involved, many of them with decided opinions about these matters, the task becomes even more difficult. The editors are aware that some of their decisions will pass unnoticed by many readers but arouse considerable passion in others. Pre-eminent among these matters is the naming of the school itself. It began as Merton Hall, changed to Melbourne Church of England Girls Grammar School in 1903, and again to Melbourne Girls Grammar School in 1987. It was sometimes known colloquially as 'Grammar', and 'Merton Hall' is sometimes used synonymously with MGGS, although it is the name of the original building in the Senior School. Eventually, an editorial decision was made to use the name most appropriate to the period under discussion in each chapter.

In any publication dealing especially with the history of women the 'name' problem arises. Most girls who attended MGGS eventually married, as did many younger teachers. In cases where students or teachers subsequently married, but appear in the school history before they married, they are referred to in the text by their maiden names. In chapters where the author had an intimate connection with the school community, for example, in Desma McDonald's chapter on the evacuation, married names are used and maiden names given in brackets where possible. Where past students re-enter the story as adults, for example, as teachers or as Old Grammarians' representatives on Council, they are referred to by their married names with the maiden name given in the text or in brackets. Past students are referred to as 'Old Girls', but only those who are members of the Old Grammarians' Society are referred to as 'Old Grammarians'. As the amount of research required to render this system foolproof would have been daunting, the editors apologise if they have erred in individual cases.

Marjorie R. Theobald

1   Beginnings: 1893–1912

T HE SCHOOL WHICH WAS TO BECOME KNOWN AS MELBOURNE
Church of England Girls' Grammar School (MCEGGS)
began tentatively at the height of the Depression which
devastated Melbourne in the early 1890s. Although only nine
girls enrolled on the first day in February 1893, the owner-
principals, Emily Hensley and Alice Taylor, were 'humbly thank-
ful to have what in the circumstances seemed to us a very
promising start'.[1] As evidence about the years as a private ladies'
school is sparse, we cannot be sure of the names of the original
nine. The school register begins only in term four, 1898, when
the second owner-principals, Mary and Edith Morris, acquired
the school.[2] Merton Hall, as it was first known, was not established on the present Anderson Street site in South Yarra, but
nearby in a house which still stands at 249 Domain Road. That
Merton Hall survived to become one of Australia's leading
Public schools requires some explanation.

To begin with, the handsome, Cambridge-educated Emily
Marianne Hensley was no ordinary schoolmistress. The circumstances under which she and her partner, Alice Taylor, came to
be establishing a girls' school in Melbourne at this inauspicious
time were extraordinary and well-known to the city's Anglican
community. The preliminary advertisement for Merton Hall, in
the *Argus* on 4 January 1893, was headed 'Miss Hensley and Miss
Taylor, late Principal and Vice-Principal of Trinity College
Hostel, the University, Melbourne'. The advertisement has references from leading Anglican clergy, intelligentsia, and lay
families, and from England, Mrs Henry Sidgwick, principal of
Newnham College, Cambridge, and Miss Hensley's uncle, the

Reverend Canon Lewis Hensley of Hitchin, Herts. For Melburnians, the omissions would have been as interesting as the inclusions, for the Merton Hall story properly begins with the Trinity College Hostel affair which had rocked the inner circles of the Anglican community in the previous year.[3]

Emily Hensley was selected in England by the Irish-born classical scholar, Dr Alexander Leeper, as the fourth principal of his ailing Trinity College Ladies' Hostel (later Janet Clarke Hall). Leeper had been warden of Trinity College since 1876, and his decision to establish a hostel for university women, against considerable opposition, signalled a commitment to the education of women which also led to a lifelong association with MCEGGS as a Council member and father of MCEGGS students, Valentine and Mollie. The Trinity College Women's Hostel was established in 1886, and when Emily Hensley arrived from England in 1890 it was about to move to the present building in the Trinity grounds, financed largely by Janet Lady Clarke's donation of £5000.

Miss Hensley was among the new elite of educated women in England. Born on 17 November 1853, the third of eleven children to Dr Frederick Hensley and Mary Filleuil, she was one of the first five women at Newnham College, Cambridge, in the 1870s when it was housed at Merton Hall under the principalship of Anne Clough. In the intervening years she had acquired 'long, varied, and valuable experience' as a governess, teacher and headmistress at Plymouth High School and in Tavistock, Devon.[4] Her *curriculum vitae* bore an uncanny resemblance to that of her successor at MCEGGS between the wars, Kathleen Gilman Jones. Alice Taylor's previous career is more difficult to unravel. Writing to Jessie Bage in 1928 she said:

> To say that I taught English subjects and French at Merton Hall gives a very meagre idea of the extent of my qualifications for the teaching profession, and the high standard required to obtain my certificates. From 1878 to 1886 Newnham College correspondence classes gave me rich assistance, and I was in close association with Miss Hensley from 1878 to 1895, when I married. I was co-principal in partnership with Miss Hensley at Tavistock and also . . . at Merton Hall.[5]

Unlike Emily Hensley, Alice Taylor was never a student at Newnham College, and she may have arrived in Australia in 1890 as Emily Hensley's secretary. The party also included two servants, a reminder that the achievements of educated women rested upon the labour of other women.

The Gothic tale of Miss Hensley's two years as principal of the Trinity College Hostel is told by Lyndsay Gardiner in her history of Janet Clarke Hall. Matters quickly degenerated into a stand-off between Dr Leeper and Miss Hensley, who was backed by the Ladies' Committee. Like the Hensley-Taylor advertisement of January 1893, the Ladies' Committee read like a 'who's who' of Anglican society and many of the same names recur: Janet Lady Clarke, Mesdames Morris, à Beckett and Grimwade, and Miss Charlotte Macartney. Miss Hensley was over-qualified for the position and bitterly disappointed with her subordinate, semi-domestic status and with the tiny, struggling hostel. She resigned at the end of 1892, as did the Ladies' Committee, and, with Miss Taylor, prepared to return to England. The crucial point for the history of MCEGGS is that Dr Leeper had gone about things in the wrong order. What was needed was an Anglican girls' school, similar to PLC and MLC, which would ensure a supply of young women to an Anglican university women's college.

The labyrinthine paths taken by the Church towards that goal are described by Stuart Blackler in chapter 2. When in 1895 Sydney CEGGS was established under Edith Badhams, the *Church of England Messenger* remarked that 'whereas the Melbourne scheme has been managed by church *men*, the Sydney scheme has been managed by church *women*'.[6] In a sense, Miss Hensley and the Trinity Ladies' Committee anticipated the Sydney women by three years. At the last moment, Miss Hensley and Miss Taylor were persuaded to stay in Melbourne to open a 'high-class Church of England boarding and day school for girls', with financial backing from the Clarke and Grimwade families.[7] The choice of site, at the other end of Domain Road from Melbourne Grammar School, can hardly be coincidental. While there was no official link between the Church and Merton Hall in Miss Hensley's time, the school was born out of deep frustrations within an Anglican community which agreed that such a school was needed but lacked the collective will to bring it into existence.

Old Merton Hall, as it was sometimes known, has maintained a precarious toehold in the history of MCEGGS, appearing and disappearing like the Cheshire cat. Dr Leeper ignored it in his preface to the 1928 Silver Jubilee history.[8] One hundred years on, even the vague outlines of the school are difficult to recover. The original advertisement proposed 'to combine the best features of the High School system of teaching with the advantages of a well-conducted private school'. Merton Hall sent up eleven girls to the matriculation examinations of the University of Melbourne in the years 1895 to 1898.[9] From these records, from a speech day report in the *Australasian* in December 1893, and from the Morris roll of late 1898, we can get some idea of who attended the school. Seventeen-year-old Agnes Snodgrass, niece of Janet Lady Clarke, came as a boarder in the first year. As the niece of Melbourne's unofficial leading lady, her presence was no doubt intended to draw in the daughters of other leading families. The big pastoral families were well represented: Dorothy Staughton (Byron Moore) was the daughter of grazier and MLA, Samuel Staughton, and her city home, St Neot's, was across the road from Old Merton Hall. Olive Wragge (Lamb) was from another prominent grazing family. And there were two, perhaps three, younger Morris sisters enrolled with Miss Hensley— Marcia, Katie and Gwynneth.

In April 1895 Miss Taylor left the partnership to marry, but there is a hint that, in any case, all was not well between the co-principals. Miss Taylor recalled:

> When I relinquished my partnership we had just over 50 [girls] and Miss Hensley was resolved not to exceed that number, and I would not agree to this limitation, for that was not my idea of a Church of England High School for Girls, and I argued that we were not fulfilling the pledges given and implied on which we accepted the generous loans of the two gentlemen who approached us with the proposal that it should be the Church of England High School for Girls.[10]

Although she had maintained her rage about Dr Leeper, Miss Taylor was an honoured guest at the Silver Jubilee celebrations in 1928. After the dissolution of the partnership, Miss Hensley's younger sister, Florence, then teaching at Notting Hill High School in London, joined the staff, which seems to indicate that Miss Hensley intended to continue at Merton Hall. Instead, in 1898, the school passed into the hands of the Morris family.

Emily Hensley did not return immediately to England. She visited her brothers and sisters in India and the United States, where family history has it that she acted as governess to her nieces and nephews. The last five years of her life were spent as an invalid in a private hospital in London. There she died on 1 August 1916. Her biographical entry in the *Newnham College Register* does not mention Merton Hall.

Mary Elizabeth and Edith Nina Morris were born in Melbourne in 1876 and 1877 respectively. With Dorothy Ross, they were to be the only Australian-born headmistresses of MCEGGS.[11] At 22 and 21 years of age they were also the youngest and least experienced women ever to hold the position. Their father, W. E. Morris, played a crucial role in the survival of Merton Hall and its acquisition by the Church in 1903. He migrated to Victoria in 1852, and in 1854 joined the staff of the Diocesan Registry where he was to serve under every bishop from Perry to Lowther Clarke. A highly regarded figure, he became registrar in 1887, and his encyclopedic knowledge of the Church's triumphs and failures must have included the saga of the girls' high school.

In 1872 William Morris's wife, Mary, died of tuberculosis. Three years later, he married 27-year-old Clara Elizabeth French, stepdaughter of Dean William Cowper of Sydney. Mary and Edith Morris were the first-born of eleven children. A photograph of the Morris clan taken when Mary and Edith were young women depicts a family endowed with striking good looks and vitality. The photograph also encapsulates why William Morris was concerned for the education of women; at a time when most men were grandfathers, he had six daughters under the age of 20, all of them unmarried. While William lived at their city home in East Melbourne, walking each day to St Paul's Cathedral, Clara raised the children at the family's country retreat, Leintwardine, on 70 acres at Upper Beaconsfield. There the Morrises had a healthy, outdoors childhood and their brother William recalls: 'I was kept in my place by six sisters! . . . In that close communal life we learned responsibility, and we learned "give and take" . . . We became bushmen as well as townsmen very early in life.'[12]

Both family and MCEGGS records are disconcertingly silent about the formal education of the oldest Morris girls. Mary and Edith were, however, attending Ormiston Ladies' College, East Melbourne, when they sat for the matriculation examination in 1892 and 1893 respectively.[13] Whether they lived with their father or at nearby Ormiston is not clear. Mary Morris enrolled in Arts at the University of Melbourne, entering Trinity Ladies' Hostel in 1895 when Dr Leeper's enrolments had climbed to twelve. She graduated B.A.Hons in 1898 and M.A. in 1900. There are glimpses of Edith and Mary as teachers in private practice, as they brought at least one pupil, Adele Ingram, with them to Merton Hall in 1898.[14]

There is some evidence that W. E. Morris had a 'first refusal' understanding with Miss Hensley should she decide to sell Merton Hall.[15] When he purchased the 'goodwill' of the school in 1898 Miss Hensley was apparently able to prevail upon most of the girls to stay, for the Morris sisters listed twenty-seven names on the roll for the commencement of term four. Mary Morris's registration papers record that she was an assistant mistress with Miss Hensley at Merton Hall for one term in 1898 — perhaps an interim arrangement to smooth the transfer of the school to its inexperienced new principals.[16] Although there is no proof that the Morris family had any formal understanding with the Church as early as 1898, there is no doubt that they had ambitions beyond the modest enterprise in Domain Road. The 1900 school year began with sixty girls, ten of whom were boarders. Mary Morris later wrote:

> When the school opened [in 1900] every nook and corner was being utilised. The curtained recess of the drawing-room was the Principals' study, one room did duty as dining-room, form room and boarders' sitting-room by turns; Honour German classes were accommodated in the Principals' bedroom; an occasional mathematical demonstration was given in the bathroom.[17]

As if to underscore the point, a measles epidemic hit the school and the boarders who fell ill had to be carried off in cabs to a nearby house to be nursed.

In 1900 W. E. Morris purchased from William Cain, then living in what is now Phelia Grimwade House, a narrow strip of land which stretched from 82 Anderson Street to Walsh Street in the east, within walking distance of the Domain Road school. Although Mrs Cain was on the provisional council for MCEGGS and both husband and wife appear as referees in the early prospectuses, they were always uneasy about the proximity of the school, and retained a block of land as a buffer at 84 Anderson Street, upon which they placed a caveat that no school should be built. After negotiations broke down for the purchase of the land in 1917, it was sold to the Tye family who built Greyholm, and the property was not acquired by MCEGGS until 1947 when it became Ross Hall. Throughout the winter and spring of 1900 the original buildings, which were financed by W. E. Morris, rose on the Anderson Street property opposite the Botanical Gardens. The school, together with the entire Morris family, moved into the new Merton Hall for the beginning of 1901.

On the eve of its acquisition by the Anglican Church in 1903 Merton Hall was poised between two traditions in women's education, traditions which reflected a deep ambivalence about the role of women in Edwardian society. To Melburnian parents, MCEGGS was still identifiable as a nineteenth-century ladies' academy of the kind which spread rapidly throughout the British Empire in the baggage of well-educated, entrepreneurial British women. Often run by families such as the Morrises, these schools offered what were known as the female accomplishments: music, modern languages and art took the place of the classics and mathematics which dominated the male curriculum; there was a core curriculum of English language and literature, history, geography and arithmetic; and surprisingly, a considerable emphasis on natural sciences long before science became important in the education of boys. In the accomplishments curriculum may be discerned the enduring female preference for the humanities, the performing arts, and the 'soft' sciences. Ladies' schools were enormously popular with middle-class parents, who believed that their daughters should be well educated, but for life within the private sphere as wives and mothers. These parents saw no contradiction between a distinctively female form of education and the highest possible standards. Decades before Merton Hall began, there were excellent ladies' schools in Melbourne educating the sisters of the boys at Melbourne Grammar, and many, such as Ormiston, Tintern and Ruyton, had cultivated close links with the Anglican Church. In many respects, early Merton Hall was a superior ladies' academy.

In the Edwardian era, however, no middle-class girls' school could remain walled off from the reform movement which had swept through the education of Western women in the last quarter of the nineteenth century. Under the banner of the 'movement for the higher education of women', women had challenged their exclusion from the universities, from the professions, and from the masculine forms of secondary education. This challenge was closely linked with campaigns against the legal, economic and political disabilities suffered by women, culminating in the suffrage movements at the end of the century. Australian women gained the vote federally at the first Commonwealth election in 1901, and in Victoria in 1908. Women were admitted to the matriculation examination of the University of Melbourne in 1871, to the Arts Faculty in 1881, and to medicine in 1886. As we have seen, Janet Clarke Hall dates back to the same era, and PLC and MLC, established in 1875 and 1882 respectively, have their origins in attempts to reform the secondary education of girls. The Morris sisters publicly espoused the suffrage cause and women's right to enter the professions, and Mary was an early beneficiary of the educational reform movement in Australia.[18] Yet the link between the old and the new traditions in the history of MCEGGS was not, strictly speaking, the Morris sisters or the Anglican Church, but Emily Hensley, a link which she emphasised by naming the school Merton Hall.

The Morris sisters and the Anglican Church inherited these two traditions of female education at Edwardian MCEGGS, and it fell to the lot of the headmistresses to work out in the day-to-day life of the school what Edwardian society could not resolve in its attitude to the role of women. The consequences were immediate and profound. As early as 1901 the principals drew attention to the difficulties in catering for two distinct groups of senior students in the one school:

> So far it has not been easy to reconcile the sometimes conflicting needs of girls who are preparing for matriculation and University work and of those who do not propose entering for any University examinations. The former must devote most of their time to mathematics, classics and science; the latter would often very profitably with a view to their after-life devote most of theirs to English literature and history, modern languages and the subjects usually classed as accomplishments. It will be easily seen that quite distinct courses of work are required by these two classes of girls.[19]

The youthful MCEGGS had an urgent need to establish its academic credentials, and in the process the requirements of public examinations and university entrance for a minority of girls came to dominate the organisation of the school, casting as a 'problem' for the first time the majority of girls who continued to study traditional female subjects untroubled by ambitions to academic honours.

Achievement at public examinations and at university became a high priority for both the Morris sisters and the Council. When the heads reported their modest tally of two matriculated students in 1901, they pleaded the extreme youth of the school. One year later, the tally had risen to six, and they were urging the parents to keep their daughters at school for post-matriculation work in preparation for university entrance. In 1904 Eveline Syme became the first of many MCEGGS girls to be placed first on the class list at a Matriculation examination with Exhibitions in French and German. In 1903 the Morris sisters announced to Council that the first MCEGGS girls to proceed to university had successfully passed second-year Arts, and that three girls were to be enrolled at Trinity College in the next year, adding: 'Their careers will be watched with the keenest interest'. Twelve months later Stella Deakin, daughter of Alfred Deakin, three times prime minister of Australia, won the Biology Exhibition in first-year Science, and in first-year Arts Ruth Topp gained first-class honours in English and honours in Greek and Latin. In 1905 Madeline McConachie became the first MCEGGS girl to graduate from the University of Melbourne, with final honours in modern languages. By 1906 the number of MCEGGS girls at the university had grown to eight. After its inception in 1906 *School Notes* regularly listed results in the public examinations (renamed Junior and Senior Public in 1904) and at the university. It also published articles on university life—in 1909, 'In residence at Trinity' by Noela Gilbert. The article was frankly recruiting ('it is there that C.E.G.G.S. girls naturally go'), and not surprisingly, given that Dr Leeper still presided, omitted to mention Miss Hensley in its potted history of the Trinity College Hostel. By that time Theodora Sproule, Ruth Topp, Irene Dixson, Helen Kelsey, Noela Gilbert, Margery Herring and Enid Joske had all been 'hostiles'—resident women at Trinity College Hostel.[20] MCEGGS had considerable ground to make up: by 1906, a quarter of a century after women entered the University of Melbourne, PLC had fifty-nine graduates, MLC had sixteen and Ruyton, the most academically ambitious of the private ladies' schools, had seven.[21]

While Edwardian girls' schools like MCEGGS struggled to establish their academic credentials it is not surprising that *School Notes* and headmistresses' annual reports are skewed towards the doings of this minority of academically oriented girls. We are apt to overlook this fact because we read backwards into the past our own reality that most middle-class women will proceed to higher education and pursue careers, whether or not they marry. For the Morrises, however, the more pressing problem was what to do with the majority who had no such intention. The saga of the 'alternative fifth' began not with Miss Gilman Jones or Miss Ross, but virtually from the beginning.

In 1901 the Morrises proposed that the two distinct courses would be offered separately, 'if a sufficient number of classrooms can be . . . secured'. The new, 'non-academic' class began in 1902 with an enrolment of ten, and the Morrises reported that 'the advantages of having more time available for special subjects such as Dressmaking and Music have been very great. The standard of work in this form will become higher as its curriculum becomes less of an experiment.' The alternative class was sufficiently popular to warrant the formation in 1905 of an 'extra fifth', 'in which the course of Modern languages, Literature and History especially will be as advanced and scholarly as the attainments of the pupils will allow'. The acquisition of further property in 1905 provided much-needed space for practical subjects such as dressmaking and cooking, and the principals reported that 'we anticipate seeing the *Extra* side of the school greatly developed and strengthened'.[22]

The Morris sisters were never able to decide whether the alternative senior program was indeed for the less able or simply for those who did not wish to sit for public examinations.

We wish . . . to warn people against the false idea that the 'Extra' side of the school is maintained in order that some favourites of fortune may have an easy time. It is for those who, for various reasons, are not able to take a course of study leading to University examinations . . . parents should less readily concur in their children's too frequent wish to discontinue subjects that prove hard to master . . . But if after a fair trial a girl does not show herself fitted for a purely intellectual course of work, then let her join the Extra side of the school, and let her find her own special bent— something manual, something artistic, something domestic— whatever it may be.

What the conscientious and high-minded Morris sisters could not accept was that the alternative course might be for the more frivolous, regardless of their intellectual capacity. *All* of their girls were to be cast in their own image—devoutly religious, deeply intellectual and socially responsible, whatever their future in life—and this was to be achieved by disciplining the mind with solid, systematic study, regardless of the content. This was ever the stuff of headmistresses' dreams.[23]

If MCEGGS could not be walled off from reforms in the education of women, neither could it be walled off from events in the wider educational world. The partnership between the Morris family and the Church began in the very decade when the state began to intrude into the affairs of the church schools for the first time. The state in Victoria moved to establish control over secondary education in two ways: through the establishment of its own high schools; and through the *Teachers and Schools Registration Act* of 1905 which brought the non-government schools under a measure of official regulation for the first time.

As a high-class, fee-charging Anglican school, MCEGGS was not affected by the establishment of state high schools, although there was considerable opposition from the independent schools which in hindsight appears both elitist and alarmist. Nor did the independent schools disagree in principle with the notion of registration. Mary Morris herself welcomed the legislation in her speech day report of 1905, and she was an active member of the Independent Association of Secondary Teachers of Victoria (IASTV), the professional body founded in 1904 to safeguard the interests of schools such as MCEGGS in the volatile situation created by the state's entry into secondary education.[24]

Unexpectedly, however, registration posed a threat to Melbourne's independent girls' schools, and the nub of the matter was registration as a secondary school.[25] In a decision which we would now identify as male-centred, the Registration Board

Merton Hall in Domain Road, circa 1894. Miss Taylor and Miss Hensley seated third and fourth from the left in the second row.

The Family of William Edward and Clara Elizabeth Morris:
L. to R. standing, Katie, William Perry, Agnes, William Edward,
Marcia, Gwynneth.
L. to R. seated, Edith, Clara Elizabeth, Mary, Edward.
L. to R. in front, Basil, Arthur.

Merton Hall, circa 1907.

chose to define a secondary school as one with a proven record at the university matriculation examinations. Many of Melbourne's leading ladies' schools, including the Morris sisters' own school, Ormiston, were denied secondary registration on these grounds. Indeed, if MCEGGS had been obliged to apply for registration a few years earlier, it may have suffered the same fate. The requirements for secondary registration obliged the surviving girls' schools to conform to the requirements of public examinations, but they did not abandon their preference for the humanities.

The *Registration Act* also affected the independent girls' schools in the matter of staffing. Until that time anybody could teach and anybody could open a school. Edith Morris herself was co-principal of a prestigious girls' school with only the lowly matriculation certificate to her credit. In 1906, with thousands of other teachers outside the government sector, she gained registration by means of the 'loop-hole' clause, 'Teaching prior to the Act'.[26] After that time, however, stringent qualifications were laid down for registration as a teacher. The consequences for MCEGGS were twofold: it was obliged to recruit fully qualified staff at all levels, with predictable consequences for the salary bill; and MCEGGS girls wishing to become teachers had no option but to proceed through public examinations to university or teachers' college.

With the female graduate still a rare species in the early twentieth century, the staff which the Morris sisters had assembled by 1906 was remarkable.[27] The prospectus lists eleven full-time teachers, nine of whom were university graduates or completing degrees while teaching at the school. Most were young, and many went on to outstanding careers in related fields. One of the most outstanding was 30-year-old Susie Williams who taught at MCEGGS for most of the Morris era, leaving in 1913 among the alarming exodus of staff under the Morris sisters' successor, Miss Tunnicliffe. She was Annie Grice Scholar at Trinity in 1894, where, together with Mary Morris, she was a protégée of Dr Leeper's in the classics. She took the classical tripos at Newnham College, Cambridge, and returned to teach at MCEGGS in 1902. When Mary Morris resigned to marry in 1908 Susie Williams became 'head of teaching staff' on a salary of £300 per annum, the same salary paid jointly to the Morris sisters. She was classics tutor at Trinity College Hostel from 1914 to 1919, and was appointed second principal of the non-denominational Sydney Women's College in 1919.[28] A brilliant scholar and teacher, she was the natural successor to Edith Morris, but her appointment as acting-principal in 1911 was ruled unconstitutional as she was not a member of the Anglican Church.[29] The other obvious contender for what had quickly become a plum career position was the talented Elsie Morres who left MCEGGS at the end of 1905 to become founding principal of The Hermitage, a new Anglican venture in Geelong. She taught for seven years at MCEGGS, becoming joint acting head (with Sarah Anderson) in 1903, and was imbued with the Morris blend of family intimacy and high-minded service which she put into practice at The Hermitage during her twenty-seven years as principal.[30]

Another distinguished teacher of the Morris era was Dr Georgina Sweet, who taught physiology, botany and junior science. It comes as a surprise to find that science was listed in the prospectuses as an 'extra', and Dr Sweet as a visting teacher. She was also a demonstrator in biology at the university and a lecturer in biology at Queen's College.[31] An important aim of state intervention into secondary education was to force upon the university and the boys' Public schools a commitment to science in the interests of national prosperity, and the new state high schools led the way by privileging science from the outset. In the Edwardian era both boys' and girls' Public schools struggled to build and equip laboratories and to recruit qualified science staff. By and large the girls' schools settled the issue by building upon the accomplishments tradition of the 'soft' sciences— botany, physiology and later biology—and MCEGGS was no exception. Miss Tunnicliffe's judgement in her first report that the provision for science was 'entirely inadequate' was probably sound, if a little tactless in a headmistress newly arrived from England. One of the earliest Doctors of Science from the University of Melbourne, and the first woman, Georgina Sweet became Associate Professor in Zoology and a member of the University Council. She was regarded as Australia's foremost parasitologist.[32] Other women from Professor Baldwin Spencer's first group of female science graduates to teach at MCEGGS were Edith Muntz, who died while on the staff in 1911, Ada à Beckett (née Lambert), who taught on Miss Hensley's original staff, and Ethel Remfrey, who in 1905 married the oldest Morris brother and founder of the Church of England Grammar School, Brisbane, the Reverend W. P. F. Morris.

It would be unfair to give the impression that the only teachers of excellence at early MCEGGS were this advance guard of the 'movement for the higher education of women'. The point is nicely made by a photograph of the staff in 1909. Beside Edith Morris in the front row, surrounded by the youthful graduates with their small waistlines and academic gowns, is the French-born Madame Augustine Liet, doyen of visiting French teachers in Melbourne for over forty years, now grown somewhat stout, tightly laced, and resplendent in turban hat. As a member of the original staff in 1893, she was the longest serving teacher and quite able to match honours at the matriculation examinations with the new breed of graduate women. She was awarded the Légion d'Honneur for her services to the French language, and after her death in 1926 her former pupils endowed the Liet Prize at the University of Melbourne for matriculation French.[33] The MCEGGS staff in 1906 was the last generation of non-government teachers in Victoria who would be permitted to register without teacher qualifications. In that year only two staff members were qualified specifically as teachers: Elsie Hardie B.A., in charge of the Preparatory School, had completed her training as a primary teacher at what was then known as the Government Training College; Ethel Henderson, her assistant and an Old Girl, was a certificated kindergarten teacher.[34]

In 1903, on the eve of their full association with the Church, the Morris sisters took a sabbatical year to study educational institutions overseas; Edith went to England and the Continent, and Mary to the eastern United States of America. Their decision to make this trip is a revealing insight into their sense of themselves as professional women, but it is also frustrating, for they were surprisingly reticent upon their return as to where they went and what they saw.

They were outspoken in their judgement that the provision for sport in Australian girls' schools was markedly inferior to what they had seen overseas. Their decision to send their younger sister Gwynneth straight from her sixth year at MCEGGS to Madame Osterberg's Physical Training College in Kent, England, was one outcome of their trip. Upon her return in 1907 Miss Gwynneth, as she became known, took complete charge of physical education, drilling all classes in the Swedish gymnastics which she helped to pioneer in Melbourne, superintending all games played in the grounds, and coaching the hockey, cricket and basketball teams to innumerable triumphs. A fine athlete (she played for the first Victorian women's hockey team), Gwynneth conducted the sports program with unflagging enthusiasm; as she was also editor of *School Notes*, one could gain the impression that the girls also thought of little else — were it not for the occasional exhortations to backsliders which creep into her reports. Her lengthy descriptions of inter-school matches contained outspoken criticism of individual girls which strikes a discordant note in the modern ear. In these years physical activity, let alone fiercely competitive team games, was still suspect as 'mannish' and potentially harmful to the developing young woman. The need to tread warily comes through the

Morris sisters' manifesto that 'it is our firm belief that sports carefully directed by experienced people do very much to quicken the mind, build up the constitution and discipline the character'. Gwynneth Morris conducted a crusade to harness sport to the moral and physical well-being of the girls, and like all crusaders she was apt to swing the pendulum a little too far.[35]

Although we cannot with certainty trace the Morris sisters to any of the British or American Meccas of women's education, it is apparent that they returned to their new partnership with a greatly enhanced vision of what the school might become:

> We believe that its new connection with the Church has not merely given it a greater nominal dignity, but that all who belong to it — teaching staff and present and *past* students have felt a new stimulus, a new ambition, to make the Church of England Girls' Grammar School worthy of its name and worthy of the church to which it now so specially belongs.[36]

Enrolments expanded rapidly. At the end of 1901 there were just over one hundred girls, among them twenty boarders, and potential boarders had been turned away. By 1904 there were 161, including 22 boarders, and by the end of the Morris era, in 1912, there were 281 girls with 48 boarders. Throughout the period enrolments outstripped accommodation.

The original Merton Hall building, which was also the Morris family home, consisted of the boarding house, staff and boarders' common rooms, a principals' study, the large schoolroom and three smaller classrooms. The constraints of the original site dictated that the first extensions be built behind Merton Hall in an easterly direction, a pattern of development which is still clearly visible today. As early as 1902 Merton Hall was extensively remodelled and a new wing added with additional classrooms, a larger dining room, more bedrooms and bathrooms, and a new art studio.[37] The entrance was moved from the north to the west side of the house, signalling fading hopes of acquiring from the Cain family the land immediately to the north. As the agreement between the Morris family and the Church was not ratified until the following year, these extensions were presumably financed by W. E. Morris.

Soon after the ratification of the agreement, however, the principals began to push for more accommodation, announcing in their 1904 report that: 'The Council of the School is earnestly considering how this need may be met'.[38] W. E. Morris attended a Council meeting late in 1904 to present plans for a proposed new wing to cost £1000.[39] As the school had made a profit of £500 in

1904 and the same was anticipated for 1905, Council agreed to the proposal. With a speed and efficiency unimaginable at the end of the twentieth century, the new wing was habitable by Easter 1905—several new classrooms, additional music rooms, and a cloakroom and lavatory, all connected with the main building by bridges.

In a situation which was potentially fraught with difficulties, the Morris family and the School Council appear to have worked in reasonable harmony—except in the acquisition of Old Fairlie. The 2-acre property adjoined MCEGGS to the south and ran through to Walsh Street in the east. On the property was Old Fairlie, a single-storey, timber bungalow which had been imported prefabricated from India by Joseph Anderson. Old Fairlie appears in the 1907 prospectus as 'Miss Stretch's Boarding-house'.

If the school were to expand, the purchase of the property was crucial. Evidence that the School Council and the Morris family differed on the matter appears in the minutes of August 1905 when the Council, 'after considerable discussion', rejected an offer to purchase the property for £5820.[40] In the Church's defence, it was caught in a cleft stick between Archbishop Clarke's ambitious plans to expand into girls' secondary education (embodied in his 1906 Education Act put before Synod) and an embarrassing lack of funds.[41] After further futile negotiations, W. E. Morris offered to facilitate the purchase of Old Fairlie by buying a church property in Hotham Street, East Melbourne (the disposal of which had preoccupied the School Council for some time), and by writing down £3000 from the amount of £8067 still owed to him for the purchase of Merton Hall. He also offered to pay £100 per annum rent, presumably for Old Fairlie, and conveyed on behalf of his daughters an offer to forgo their bonuses for that year. At the same meeting, Council member F. S. Grimwade offered to give the school £500 'at any time that the land was purchased, on condition that a Scholarship be founded . . . to be called "The Jessie Grimwade Scholarship"'.[42] Under those conditions the Council agreed to buy the Old Fairlie property.

No hint of these backroom negotiations appeared in the principals' report for 1906, when they spoke of 'the event of supreme importance to the School's welfare' and the Council's wisdom in recognising that 'unless prompt action were taken an opportunity of adding to the school property might never again occur'. Old Fairlie was used temporarily as additional accommodation for boarders, for the 'alternative' practical classes, and for the Preparatory School. The prospectus for 1907 has photographs of the juniors, with their Alice-in-Wonderland hair and short smocks, posed somewhat self-consciously tending their flower gardens in the new grounds. The additional space also meant that two new tennis courts could be built, and these were opened by Mrs Deakin in Easter week 1906. A hockey field of sorts was established in Old Fairlie's front garden. In that year, six new classrooms were added to the 1905 wing at a cost of £1700, making the red-brick eastern wing with its 'severe, but not unbeautiful, lines' clearly visible to passengers travelling by train between the city and the southern and eastern suburbs.[43] The Council decreed that 'no further building will be entertained for six years', and the new buildings were opened by Archbishop Lowther Clarke in May 1907.

The exotic bungalow on the southern site was, however, on borrowed time. At the Council meeting in June 1910 plans were passed for the most ambitious building scheme to date—a new preparatory school for one hundred girls and a second boarding house for thirty girls on the site of Old Fairlie. A hockey field was to be constructed to the east of the new house. The difference in levels between Anderson and Walsh Streets made this an undertaking of some magnitude. As MCEGGS stands on stony ground, magnificent for foundations but resistant to the efforts of draught horses and scoops, the field was still incomplete when Edith Morris left in 1912. The plans of 1910 also included electric light for Merton Hall and the classroom blocks.[44] Completed at a cost of £6000, the new building, with its broad balconies, wide verandahs, and 'sleeping out' places, was named Morris Hall.

Susie Williams wrote an account of the dedication ceremony which took place in May 1911.[45] The girls arrived on Monday morning to find a huge marquee in place between Merton Hall and its new neighbour. Assembled in the tent by 3 p.m. were the archbishop and Professor T. G. Tucker, both in scarlet robes, the staff in their brightly coloured academic hoods, five hundred parents and friends, and nearly three hundred girls in white, massed on the verandah and steps of Morris Hall. The ceremony began with the school hymn, 'Oh God, our help in ages past'. The Reverend L. Townsend, vicar of the parish and member of the School Council, read the first verse of Psalm 127, which in Latin begins with the words 'Nisi Dominus Frustra'. Somewhat tactlessly, Professor Tucker had some harsh words to say about modern education for women—it would, in his view, 'produce no Harriet Martineau, no George Eliot, no Miss Mitford or Jane Austen'. Archbishop Lowther Clarke conveyed yet again to the empire-building Morris family that 'the School had almost reached the limits which our educational policy and circumstances were likely to place upon it'. The expense and inconvenience of the marquee were not lost upon him, however, for he urged that the school would not be complete until an assembly hall was built to dignify occasions such as this. The MCEGGS hall was built in 1917 on the spot where the marquee stood. Unthinkable as it would have been to anyone present at the time, Morris Hall was demolished in 1967.

When Susie Williams invited readers to visualise the three hundred girls in white as the 'background' to the opening of Morris Hall that day, she had already begun a process in the writing of school histories which relegates girls to the status of bit players, glimpsed here and there through the doings of more important people. In the pages of *School Notes* we are offered carefully selected vignettes of school life, framed by momentous events: Empire Day; the funeral of Edward VII; the Women's Exhibition of 1907; the marriages of the Morris sisters. We learn that many of the girls devoted themselves to Christian Union, and to charitable works for St Barnabas's parish, South Melbourne, where the youthful and idealistic Reverend W. P. Morris ministered to the waterside workers and their families. The interior photographs of the boarding house in the early prospectuses — the entrance hall, the drawing room, and the dining room — remind us, as indeed they were meant to do, that for fourteen years Mrs Clara Morris conducted it as a gracious and well-ordered Edwardian household. Again, we meet the boarders only on the way out the door: in 1906 to entertain forty girls from 'their new sister school at Geelong' with hockey (played at a private ground in Toorak lent by Mrs Armytage), tennis and a picnic lunch in the Botanical Gardens; in 1910 to visit the German cruiser *Condor* at the invitation of the German Consulate; in 1911 to hear de Sousa at the Glaciarium, and a few days later in a motor charabanc to see the city illuminations for the coronation of George V. But the texture of everyday life remains opaque.[46]

Yet in the formative years of MCEGGS life for the Australian schoolgirl was changing rapidly. The spectacular growth in enrolment at MCEGGS was not simply an artefact of church ownership, or new premises, or the passing of time. 'Going-to-school' itself began to encroach further into the lives of middle-class girls. Compulsory attendance had been visited on all the children of Victoria by the *Education Act* of 1872, but the promoters of that legislation did not have in mind middle-class daughters. Many girls continued to be educated at home, and typical attendance patterns at the ladies' academies had been spasmodic and largely confined to the 'finishing' years. Although dates of entry and exit are not entered on the MCEGGS roll, it is clear girls were coming to school at an earlier age and staying longer. So complete has been the triumph of regular school attendance in the twentieth century that we no longer comprehend the significance of this change for middle-class girls who had hitherto been closely protected in the family home. The nineteenth-century prejudice against the Public school for girls was precisely on the grounds that the social and psychic relationships inherent in a larger institution were not conducive to the formation of the modest and retiring female character. By the turn of the century it was apparent that life would be different for women in the new century, as newly enfranchised citizens and as independent women, at least in the years before marriage. In hindsight it may be disconcerting that the Morrises set about forming the character of the 'new woman' through competitive examinations, team sports, the prefect system, and uniformity of dress. Yet at the beginning of the century these innovations were still controversial and gave to the girls at MCEGGS opportunities for leadership, autonomy, pride in achievement, and above all, preparation for a presence in the world outside the home which had been considered inappropriate even in their mothers' time.

The growing demands of women for a legitimate presence outside the home in the Edwardian era also spurred the formation of past students' societies in the independent girls' schools of Melbourne. The National Council of Women, the Lyceum Club, the Free Kindergarten Union and many other women's societies made their appearance at this time, and for the same reasons. At MCEGGS the Old Grammarians' Society was formed in 1904.[47] Mary and Edith Morris were its presidents until 1909, when Adele Ingram, by then teaching at the school, became the first past student to hold the office. At the same meeting which installed Adele as president, Mary Morris unveiled the Old Grammarians' gift of a stained-glass window with the design of the school badge and motto in dark blue and gold.[48] In a more leisurely society, when fewer middle-class women were in the paid work force, the Old Grammarians' activities—sporting, cultural and philanthropic—were well supported. School Notes for December 1908 has a photograph of a group at Anniversary Day, newly returned from their annual service at the cathedral and a walk back along Alexandra Avenue through the gardens to lunch at the school.[49]

The first London meeting of the Old Grammarians was held in September of the same year in Mrs Syme's sitting room in the Lancaster Gate Hotel. Kathleen Oliver's letter from London recording the event has left a record of some Old Grammarians' doings between school and marriage: Marjorie Syme had just returned from a Mediterranean cruise; Hilda Gellatly was attending a domestic economy school in London; Adele Gellatly was nursing; Freda Oliver had been touring Scotland; Kathleen herself had recently visited the old Roman city of Calleva. Cecily Sharp, and Constance and Mildred Syme missed the meeting as they had left that morning for Paris. The first register of Old Grammarians, published in *School Notes* for December 1911, is a treasure trove of over 250 names, addresses (and marriages) of the girls who had left MCEGGS by that date.

The MCEGGS women singled out as 'Distinguished Old Grammarians' in a 1928 *Age* report of the Silver Jubilee were all at school in the Morris era. President of the Old Grammarians' Society in that year was Margaret Brown (McMahon). Enrolled in 1901, she became the first MCEGGS girl to study at Girton College, Cambridge, where she took the historical tripos. She also qualified as a nurse and served for four years with the AIF in Egypt, England and France. She was later appointed by Susie Williams to the staff of Sydney Women's College. We have already met Madeline McConachie M.A., as the first MCEGGS university graduate. She appears as student number ten on the 1898 roll, and in 1900 was appointed the first head prefect.[50] Dr Helen Frances Kelsey, who enrolled in 1901, was the first Old Grammarian to take a medical degree, with final honours after a brilliant degree. She also took the degree of Bachelor of Science and the Diploma of Public Health. In 1928 Dr Kelsey was bacteriologist at the Infectious Diseases Hospital, Fairfield. Margery Herring (1904) handed over the principalship of Janet Clarke Hall to Enid Joske (1901) in the Silver Jubilee year. The *Age* report singled out two talented artists, Ethel Louisa Spowers (1899), who had studied in Paris and at the Melbourne Gallery School, and Eveline Syme (1900), who was also the first MCEGGS girl to study at Newnham College, Cambridge, where she took the classical tripos in 1910. Eveline Syme also studied art in Paris and London, and exhibited regularly in Melbourne. She was a member of the first council of the National Gallery of Victoria, and of the University Women's College, Melbourne. Muriel Millicent Stott (1901), school captain in 1907 and a past president of the Old Grammarian's Society, was the first MCEGGS woman to practise architecture in Melbourne. Twenty-nine Old Grammarians from the Morris era signed the roll at the Diamond Jubilee celebrations in 1963.[51]

MCEGGS was born out of a bitter dispute within the Anglican community in a city at the depth of the worst economic depression in its short history. As a private ladies' school in

Domain Road it maintained a precarious toehold only because of the quality of its founding owner-principals, Emily Hensley and Alice Taylor, and because it had the imprimatur of the powerful Clarke and Grimwade families. As the Church's acquisition of Merton Hall pre-dates the arrival in Melbourne of the empire-building Archbishop Henry Lowther Clarke, the key to the survival of the school must surely be the remarkable Morris family.

In Victorian Melbourne the acquisition of an ailing ladies' school by a father with capital to invest, and talented and ambitious daughters to provide for, was by no means unique; what was unique about the Merton Hall episode was W. E. Morris's willingness to sink considerable capital in the construction and outfitting of a new school with the clear intention of handing it over to a church whose record in the education of women had become an embarrassment. The continuing presence of the Morris family ensured the success of MCEGGS in its vital first decade as a church school. As the episode of the Old Fairlie property illustrates, W. E. Morris remained a powerful figure behind the scenes. Clara, Mary, Edith and Gwynneth gave their lives to the school in a gruelling daily round of administration, teaching, extra-curricular activities and housekeeping. So quickly did the daily labours of the Morris women take on the appearance of the immutable order of things that the marriages of the two headmistresses, Mary to Thomas Stephen in 1908 and Edith to William Irwin in 1913, were greeted with incredulity by the Council, and dismay by the schoolgirls, whose affection and respect for the two young women survives the somewhat saccharine tributes which have been recycled down through the years. In 1912 the Morris family's legacy to the Anglican community was a thriving school of nearly three hundred girls, housed in modern buildings, in one of Melbourne's most beautiful inner suburbs. The partnership between the Morris family and the Anglican Church at Edwardian MCEGGS is surely a unique episode in the history of Australian women's education.

Stuart Blackler

2 A very Anglican arrangement: the Diocese of Melbourne and schools for girls, 1884–1920

I N 1903 THE PRINCIPALS' REPORT FOR MERTON HALL WAS written by Miss Elsie Morres and Miss Sarah Anderson, acting principals during the absence overseas of Edith and Mary Morris. The report has, for the first time, the superscription 'Church of England Girls' Grammar School'. The acting principals wrote: 'The most important event . . . during the year has been the ratification of the agreement entered into provisionally by the Bishop-in-Council to purchase the School Buildings and take over the financial responsibilities involved in carrying on the School. The resolution was carried almost unanimously.'[1] The following year the Misses Morris were back in their office. In their report for 1904 they stated, with family pride: 'The school is now at the close of its first year as a fully-fledged Church School'.[2]

This achievement deserved considerable fanfare, not only for its intrinsic significance but because it was achieved after two decades of struggle and disputation. The story properly begins in 1876 when Sheffield-born James Moorhouse was elected second Bishop of Melbourne. He had a distinguished background in English church life, including the prestigious Hulsean lectureship at Cambridge.[3] A man of intellectual stature, eloquence and strength of personality, in Melbourne he gave forceful leadership for the establishment of the Trinity College Theological School, the building of St Paul's Cathedral, and the movement to introduce Bible teaching into Victoria's state primary schools. In 1884 he was elected Chancellor of the University of Melbourne. Although he had given no support to the admission of women to that institution, in the same year that he became chancellor he initiated moves to establish an Anglican girls' secondary school to complement Melbourne Grammar School and Geelong Grammar School which had been established thirty years earlier.

The constitutional structure of the Diocese of Melbourne placed legal restrictions on the powers of its bishops, including the use of general diocesan funds. The Council of the Diocese—or Bishop-in-Council—had the responsibility of assisting the bishop in such matters. To enact legislation it was necessary for the Church Assembly, operating on broad parliamentary lines, to be involved. Each of these bodies had clerical and (elected) lay representation.

Thus, in 1884 Moorhouse initiated discussions in the Council of the Diocese for the establishment of a girls' school. At the meeting of the Church Assembly, the Dean of Melbourne (Hussey Burgh Macartney) brought the motion: 'That . . . this Assembly legislate for the promotion of a ladies' college on the site in East Melbourne in connection with the Church of England'.[4]

To prepare legislation, the Assembly appointed a committee consisting of the Reverend T. Garlick, the Reverend H. F. Tucker, Judge Hickman Molesworth, W. E. Morris and H. N. P. Wollaston. Tucker was the vicar of Christ Church, South Yarra, and was later to have a close relationship with MCEGGS which was eventually established in his parish. As we have seen, W. E. Morris was an indefatigable champion of the girls' high school cause. Judge Molesworth, however, was to become the most outspoken critic against an Anglican girls' school. His attacks were to continue unabated during Assembly debates of the 1880s, beginning from the first debate in 1885 when a Bill for 'The Establishment and Constitution of a Church of England Girls' High School' was brought to the Assembly by F. G. Moule.

In his address to the Assembly in support of the Bill, Bishop Moorhouse stated that: 'It is incumbent on us as a church to give religious education to our children as far as our means allow'.[5] Yet the qualification 'as far as our means allow' indicated that the diocese was in no position to outlay money for such a purpose. The diocese was not heavily endowed and had to look for alternative means to raise money for such a project. In the case of the girls' high school, the means proposed by the Bill was to raise £10 000 by issuing debentures (initially at £25, later at £100) returning an interest of 5 per cent. The interest was to be paid out of income derived from 'the proportion of St James' lands originally set apart for educational purposes in connection with the Church of England'.[6] This plan still involved some use of Church funds and it was on that basis that Judge Molesworth's attack was launched. In the course of the 1885 debate Molesworth deemed the proposal 'a misappropriation of Church funds . . . much more fittingly and profitably employed on legitimate Church work in country districts'.[7]

In his address Bishop Moorhouse tackled another argument against the girls' high school scheme which was to come to the fore in subsequent debates in his successor's episcopate: given the existence of Protestant girls' secondary schools, was an Anglican school needed? The references were, of course, to PLC and MLC. Moorhouse argued cogently for the establishment of an Anglican girls' school:

> We cannot, then, I think, dismiss this question lightly, as we might have done had no denominational colleges for girls existed. Such colleges have been founded. They are, I rejoice to hear, succeeding, . . . But I do not hope—and it would be hypocrisy to say that I hoped—that they may succeed at the expense of the Church of England . . . I cannot forget that one-third of the inhabitants of this colony call themselves members of the Church of England; and that it is my simple duty, as it is yours, to spare no pains and no expense in the endeavour to give religious education to as many of our declared members as circumstances enable us to reach. That is our plain duty.

One can imagine the satisfaction of Molesworth and other opponents of the girls' high school. The diocese did not have the resources to subsidise schools, state aid had been abolished in Victoria by the *Education Act* of 1872, and costs would have to be borne by parents through fees. Molesworth seized the opportunity to argue against the scheme on the grounds of its social exclusivity, describing the proposed institution as 'an aristocratic high school'. If Dissenters had set a bad example 'in using money for the benefit of the few which ought to have been devoted to the many', he argued, 'it was not for the Church of England to follow so pernicious an example'. Molesworth ridiculed the idea of bringing the 'principles of the Church of England into relation with the ordinary branches of a lady's school education, including dancing and calisthenics'.

Unease about Anglican daughters attending the colleges of Protestant denominations paled into insignificance before the undeniable truth that many middle-class Anglican families were sending their girls to Roman Catholic convents. Anti-Catholic feeling was threaded through the debates on Anglican girls' education throughout the period under discussion, from Moorhouse to Clarke. Roman Catholic Orders of Sisters had been singularly successful in establishing female secondary schools in

Australia. The first convent school to be established in Victoria was the Academy of Mary Immaculate in Fitzroy. It was opened in 1857 by the Mercy Sisters, and thereafter the Mercy convent schools spread rapidly. After the *Education Act* of 1872 cut off state aid to church schools, the Australian bishops recruited Religious, both sisters and brothers, in increasing numbers. The Irish and French sisters who came to Australia were 'ladies', highly educated in the female accomplishments, and in many localities offered the best middle-class female education available. Indeed, their intellectual accomplishments were matched only by their business acumen. In the very decades that the Anglican churchmen quarrelled about an Anglican girls' school, the Sisters of the Sacred Heart purchased land in Burke Road, Glen Iris, for £13 592, and three years later, in 1891, built a new convent at a cost of £32 000.[8]

The extent to which the debate had become a gladiatorial struggle between the eloquent Moorhouse and the mocking Molesworth is captured in the official report of the bishop's reply:

> The Church of England in this colony was losing hold of a most influential class of its members — the growing girls — a class that could do more good for the Church in the future than perhaps any other agency in their midst. The objection had been raised that they were about to found a school for aristocrats; but for his part he had never heard of aristocrats in this colony. Some men might be a little richer than others, but that was all. Dancing and calisthenics for the girls were no more incongruous with religious principles than football and cricket for the boys. It was, in his opinion, a moral certainty that their girls' high school would be self-supporting after the first two years.

Eventually the Bill passed, church land was set aside in Clarendon Street, East Melbourne, and debentures were called for. However, 1885 was to be Moorhouse's last Church Assembly. He was offered and accepted the Bishopric of Manchester and left Melbourne on 10 March 1886. The girls' high school scheme had lost its most powerful and eloquent champion. Bishop Moorhouse remained at Manchester until 1903 and died in Devon in 1915.

When the Church Assembly met again to debate the girls' school question there was a new Bishop of Melbourne. Field Flowers Goe was sympathetic, but not the man to take up the cause. Goe did not have the eloquence or the passion of his predecessor and suffered unfavourably by frequent comparison. And when the Assembly again took up the girls' school issue in

1887, Hickman Molesworth was still a member. The immediate cause of the renewed debate was the failure of the debenture scheme. Whereas £10 000 had been sought, only £4900 had been raised, and there was a proposal before the Assembly to increase the interest rate from 5 to 6 per cent.

Again the opposition was led by Judge Molesworth, who again raised the issue of elitism, describing the proposed school as a 'fashionable ladies' school'.[9] Molesworth also suggested to the Assembly that its earlier decision to found a girls' school had been made, not on the grounds of reason, but 'under the spell of the late bishop's eloquence'. The 1887 debate again centred on whether the offerings of the Protestant colleges would serve as well as an Anglican school. The Reverend W. C. Ford 'did not believe that harm would accrue through the daughters of Churchmen attending the Presbyterian or Methodist Colleges'. Not everyone agreed with him, including the president, Bishop Goe, who believed that girls attending those schools 'would get a Nonconformist tone'. Canon Vance, founding headmaster of Geelong Grammar School and later Dean of Melbourne, saw the issue as one of denominational pride. He asked: 'Why is it that alone of the leading denominations the Church of England was contented to forego the advantages of a school of their own? (Applause).'

In 1888 a further amending Bill was brought by F. G. Moule, a supporter of the scheme from the beginning.[10] Once again the same arguments were rehearsed by the same protagonists for and against the scheme. On this occasion there was considerable discussion concerning the possibility of a Church of England 'ethos' in a school. Not surprisingly, the Reverend Dr J. A. Wilson, headmaster of Melbourne Grammar School, brought what might be termed the 'Anglican ethos argument'—that is, that there is something as distinctive about Anglican education as there is about, for example, Roman Catholic education. The Reverend T. H. Armstrong disagreed. He believed that: 'In girls' schools in Melbourne there was just as good Church teaching as was likely to be got in any Church of England girls' school'. Both positions have credibility, as even today there is no general agreement on what constitutes an Anglican ethos in education.[11] After the customary legal haggling in which some members of the Assembly seemed to delight, and indeed still do, the Act of 1885 was set aside and a new Act passed in which the idea of debentures was given up and the land in Clarendon Street made available to the school.[12]

The next obstacle was the disastrous economic depression of the early 1890s. Middle-class boys and girls were withdrawn from all Melbourne's church schools at an alarming rate, including Melbourne Grammar School, PLC and MLC. With the economic collapse the Clarendon Street property, placed at the disposal of the girls' school scheme by the 1888 Act, plummeted in value. In 1895 another Act was passed to amend the constitution of the proposed school, permitting a school to be built on any site without selling the land in East Melbourne, but to no avail. In 1896 the existing Acts were suspended, and the Assembly passed the following resolution: 'That the Bishop be respectfully requested to take . . . steps to establish a Girls' High School, the object of which shall be to impart to girls a sound, liberal education, including daily instruction in Holy Scripture, in conformity with the principles of the Church of England'.[13] Finance had not been forthcoming; support for the proposal had aroused powerful and eloquent opposition; there was no Moorhouse at the helm; and the economic climate was unfavourable. An alternative would have to be sought if the resolution were to be given effect — and indeed it was.

When Merton Hall formally came under the control of the Diocese of Melbourne in 1903 the *Church of England Messenger* recorded the event somewhat cryptically:

> The Church of England Grammar School for girls is now an accomplished fact. The discussion of the Church Assembly was more on the details of an agreement between the principals and the Council of the Diocese rather than on the desirableness or otherwise of establishing a Girls' High School. The question was settled in the year 1885.[14]

The change in the fortunes of the girls' school came with the decision of the committee appointed by Bishop Goe in 1899 that 'the only practicable course was to make arrangements with some existing school'.[15] This was a crucial decision, for it was to set a pattern in the Church's acquisition of schools over the next decades. Both Melbourne Grammar School and Geelong Grammar School were established as Anglican foundations from the outset with a particular relationship with the diocese through the bishop. Financial troubles at each of these schools in their early days involved the diocese in what was regarded as a financially irresponsible way. This had been alluded to in the girls' school debates by Judge Molesworth in 1887.[16] Those speaking in favour of the girls' school over the years had constantly tried to assure the Assembly that there would be no financial risk for the Church.

The 1899 committee which recommended an arrangement with an existing private school approached Mary and Edith Morris of Merton Hall. The summary of events prepared for the Church Assembly by G. O. Vance in 1903 goes out of its way to convince members that the approach was from the diocese to the Morris family and not the other way around.[17] There were three compelling reasons why Merton Hall recommended itself to the diocese. Firstly, as a business proposition Merton Hall was flourishing; the ghosts of financial disasters with the boys' schools could be laid to rest. In the event, the Church of England purchased the school from W. E. Morris for £13 000, a bargain price which prompted F. S. Grimwade to remind the Church Assembly of 1903 that: 'They were getting a good school in a cheap way without responsibility'.[18] Secondly, the site in Anderson Street, South Yarra, close to Melborne Grammar School, was preferable to the East Melbourne site. The third important factor was the Morris family connection. In the Church Assembly debates of the late 1880s we find W. E. Morris speaking frequently in favour of the scheme, support which he was prepared to back with a financial commitment. At that time Morris considered the Clarendon Street site the most desirable, and if found to be too small he declared himself willing to 'give up his own house land adjoining it to make it large enough'.[19] Moreover, no layman is closer to the bishop or better known to all clergy and laity than the registrar of the diocese.

Doubtless there were many unofficial and undocumented negotiations in cathedral corridors before, in early 1900, the Council of the Diocese accepted a recommendation: 'to allow the name "Church of England Girls' High School" (or "Church of England Girls' Grammar School") to be used by the School known as "Merton Hall", provided the School be carried on under the general supervision of a Provisional Council approved by the Bishop'.[20] For some years an advertisement had appeared in the *Church of England Messenger* each month for 'Merton Hall, Domain Road, South Yarra, School for Girls'. From the issue of 1 April 1900 the advertisement read 'Merton Hall, Church of England Girls' Grammar School'. The Church had at last taken its first step towards the realisation of its girls' high school.

In the same year, Bishop Goe appointed the first Provisional Council.[21] Ten members were appointed, five of them women. From the outset, the girls' school was not under total male control; indeed the Provisional Council had a higher proportion of women than does the School Council in the centenary year. The chairman of the Council was the bishop, Field Flowers Goe.

When the provisional constitution of the school was passed in 1903 the bishop was appointed Council chairman, not president as has often been claimed, and not 'Visitor' as he is to most of the Anglican schools. Melbourne Girls Grammar School, like Melbourne and Geelong Grammar Schools, stands in a special relationship with the bishop of the diocese.

The Dean of Melbourne was a member of the Provisional Council, another ex-officio position affirmed in 1903. A third clerical member of the Provisional Council was the Reverend Horace Finn Tucker. Thus the vicar of Christ Church, South Yarra, was also affirmed as an ex-officio member, and MCEGGS began its long association with its parish church. Until St Luke's Chapel was built in 1967 Christ Church was the place for boarders' worship each Sunday, school confirmation services were held there, and the Old Grammarians (many of whom were married at Christ Church) held their annual corporate communion there. Until 1971 the vicar of Christ Church served as school chaplain, the first full-time priest licensed as chaplain to MCEGGS being appointed in that year.

Among the lay members of the Provisional Council was the warden of Trinity College, Dr Alexander Leeper, who has already entered the story of MCEGGS as Miss Hensley's nemesis at the Trinity College Women's Hostel. Dr Leeper had been a strong supporter of Bishop Moorhouse's scheme for a girls' high school and spoke frequently on the matter in Assembly debates. He is therefore rightly remembered as a founder of MCEGGS as an Anglican school. Dr Leeper provided the school with its motto, *Nisi Dominus Frustra*, from the Latin version of Psalm 127, and designed the new crest. Always a controversial figure, Dr Leeper had a deep commitment to the Anglican Church which was in inverse proportion to the respect he held for some of its bishops. He remained on the MCEGGS Council until 1933. Another lay member of the Provisional Council was the Hon. F. S. Grimwade who had helped to finance Miss Hensley and Miss Taylor at Merton Hall in 1893, and continued to be a generous benefactor to the school.

The first of the women listed on the Provisional Council was Mrs Elizabeth Goe, wife of the bishop. She was a member for a brief period only, as she died at Bishopscourt in July 1901. Brief as it was, Mrs Goe's membership set a precedent—she was followed by the wives of Archbishops Clarke, Head and Booth. Indeed Mrs Beryl Booth (née Bradshaw) was an Old Grammarian.

Another link with the Merton Hall-Trinity College Hostel episode was the presence on the Provisional Council of Janet Lady Clarke who had also advanced money in 1893. Lady

Clarke's membership gave the school the endorsement of one of Melbourne's most prestigious families. Both MCEGGS and Janet Clarke Hall stand witness to her support for the secondary and tertiary education of women.

Mrs Margaret Blanch, wife of George Ernest Blanch, headmaster of Melbourne Grammar School, was a member, as was Mrs Sarah Hindley, wife of the Reverend William George Hindley who, as Archdeacon of Melbourne from 1902, was closely involved with the establishment and recognition of many Anglican schools. Mrs Hindley taught needlework for some time at MCEGGS. The other woman listed on the Provisional Council was Mrs William Cain, whose presence added further social and Anglican acceptability. Her husband, William Cain, served as a member of the Councils of the Diocese and of Melbourne Grammar School, and was a lay canon of the Cathedral Church from 1887. He was a member of the Legislative Council of Victoria from 1903 to 1909. As Marjorie Theobald has outlined, the Cain family sold the Anderson Street site to W. E. Morris in 1900.

The Provisional Council met six times until its demise when Merton Hall became Church property and the School Council was constituted in 1903. At its first meeting, in June 1900, Mary Morris was asked to draw up rules for the school and to submit these to a subcommittee of Council consisting of the women members convened by Mrs Goe. These rules, many of them following closely the wording of the Melbourne Grammar School constitution of 1898, were accepted by the Council in October of that year and provided a provisional constitution which remained until it was replaced by an Act of Synod in 1909 'to provide a constitution for the Church of England Girls' Grammar School, Melbourne'.

The constitution of 1909 provided that 'The School shall be called "The Church of England Girls' Grammar School" Melbourne'. The object of the school was to 'provide for girls a sound classical mathematical and general modern education including regular religious instruction throughout the School in conformity with the principles and formularies of the Church of England'. Two points should be underlined here. Firstly, the statement of purpose is almost identical with that of the Melbourne Grammar constitution of 1898. There was a clear intention that the education of boys and girls provided under the aegis of the Church of England would be comparable. Nor is this surprising, given that the original draft of the constitution was drawn up by the Morris sisters. Writing in *School Notes* in 1907 Edith Morris claimed for her girls 'the right to compete . . . for

University distinctions, and the professional openings to which they lead, to earn a livelihood in mercantile or government offices, to have some share, whether direct or by representation, in the legislature of this country'.[22] Edith Morris's powerful assertion of the rights of women was far removed from the ideas of the patriarch of the girls' school scheme, Bishop Moorhouse. He supported the higher education of women because he believed that 'by developing to the greatest possible extent the mental, moral and physical qualities of women, you will make them better wives and mothers'.[23] Ironically, the churchmen, clerical and lay, who laboured long and hard to see the school come into being may have been more in sympathy with Bishop Moorhouse than with the Misses Morris.

The second matter which should be noted with respect to the proposed curriculum of the school is its insistence on religious education consistent with the principles of the Church of England. In a state with a secular system of education there were two distinguishing features about the church schools: their governance and their religious teaching. While the former was highly prized, the latter was formalised and often token.

The constitution of 1909 then turned from the curriculum to matters of ownership and governance. The school's trustee was to be the Church of England Trusts Corporation of the Diocese of Melbourne. The affairs of the school were to be managed by a Council of nineteen comprising the archbishop, the dean, the two senior archdeacons of the diocese, and the incumbent of Christ Church, South Yarra. There were to be fourteen lay members, six of whom were to be women, four appointed by the Archbishop-in-Council and two by the Old Grammarians. All were to be members of the Church of England. The School Council had powers to control and manage all the assets and property of the school, and to 'acquire by purchase or otherwise freehold or leasehold properties and to erect buildings thereon for the purposes of the School'. However, clause 6(3) stipulated that, at the discretion of the Archbishop-in-Council, school funds could be used for other educational establishments in the Diocese of Melbourne under the Board of Education. Council had the power to appoint the 'Head Master or Mistress of the School', to determine the number of the teaching staff and other employees, to fix their salaries and to fix tuition fees. The principal was to be a communicant of the Church of England 'or of some Church in communion therewith', and that proportion of the teaching staff needed for giving efficient religious instruction was also to be members of the Church of England. The principal, however, retained the right to appoint and dismiss staff, after consultation with the Council. It was the principal's duty to 'regulate the duties of the staff and . . . be responsible to the School Council for the performance of the same and for the general discipline and efficiency of the School'. Under the 1909 constitution the principal gained for the first time the right to a 'deliberative seat' on the Council.

In the first decade of its existence as a church school, MCEGGS remained very much a 'Morris family school'. Mary and Edith Morris remained joint principals until Mary's marriage in 1908, which brought about the first minor constitutional crisis in the school's history. The agreement had been drawn up on the assumption that the sisters would remain in office for life. Their mother, Clara, continued in charge of the domestic arrangements and the boarding house. William Morris, who remained registrar of the diocese until 1910, retained an active and generous involvement. Yet in fact and in ethos the school was a 'fully-fledged Church school', and what occurred in the Church Assembly in 1903 was like a marriage service: not the creation of but the recognition of a committed relationship already in existence.

The Church Assembly ratified the agreement between the diocese and Merton Hall in October 1903. On 3 March of the same year, the Right Reverend Henry Lowther Clarke was installed in St Paul's Cathedral as the fourth Bishop of Melbourne. The choice of the Board of Electors for the bishopric had been made on the recommendation of two familiar identities—F. S. Grimwade and W. E. Morris—who had been commissioned to visit England to find a successor to Bishop Goe.

With Clarke's accession to the See of Melbourne the whole tenor of the Church's educational enterprise changed dramatically and this is no surprise when his credentials are examined. The bishop-elect was introduced to his new diocese through the *Church of England Messenger*:

> The Right Reverend H. Lowther Clarke comes to his new diocese with special qualifications and training to deal with certain problems of education that wait for solution, not only in his own diocese, but throughout the whole State of Victoria. It is a happy providence for the State that the future Bishop of the metropolitan See should be one who has been for many years of his life closely associated with the methods of primary education in Church and Board schools, and of secondary education in some of the most successful schools in England. [24]

Henry Lowther Clarke was born in 1850 at Firbank Vicarage, Westmoreland. [25] He took his degree from St John's College,

Cambridge, where he was seventh wrangler in mathematics. Two of his predecessors, Charles Perry and James Moorhouse, were of the same college with a degree in the same discipline. Clarke was made a deacon in 1874 and ordained priest in 1875 by William Thomson, Archbishop of York. His first parish was Hedon, Yorkshire, where he served from 1876 to 1883. From Hedon, Clarke accepted the post of housemaster at St Peter's School, York, which his son later described as 'his one failure'. Other involvements in education were more successful: he was at various times a governor of Public schools of church foundation; he was involved with government schools as chairman of the School Board of the West Riding of Yorkshire; a member of the examining board of Church Training Colleges for Teachers; and active in investigations which led to the 1902 *Education Act* (Balfour Act) in Great Britain.

At his 1905 Synod (formerly known as the Church Assembly) a committee was established to review constitutions of existing schools and to bring them 'in closer relation with the Synod'. Endorsing the decision, Archbishop Clarke (as he was now titled) said that 'the church wanted an educational policy. Through the absence of one she had lost a great number of her children, and would continue to do so until she took up the question of education seriously'.[26] The committee led to legislation in the 1906 Synod to establish a Diocesan Board of Education and a 'Constitution under which all our schools in the diocese will be conducted'.[27] The Board was chaired by the archbishop and in its heyday — until Clarke's departure in 1920 — counted many educational notables among its membership, including Kathleen Gilman Jones of MCEGGS and Elsie Morres of The Hermitage. Alexander Leeper was also a member for many years.

The Board of Education had extremely broad responsibilities: promotion of the education of boys and girls; appointment of inspectors to evaluate religious instruction, general efficiency, financial condition and the state of buildings; the establishment of new Church schools and granting of the use of the name 'Church of England' to existing schools; and the development of teacher training. The Board had a particular concern with the teaching of religious education in schools subject to its control. It laid down syllabuses and conducted examinations taken by students in many of its schools. The first examination was held in 1908.[28]

The Diocesan Board of Education never established an inspectorial system nor did it establish training colleges; however, it was involved in the acquisition and recognition of schools.

The diocesan accounts show that the source of the Board's funds was the Educational Endowment Fund, derived from rents on Bourke Street properties, but the most it ever received was £300 in 1915 and 1916. Like the Israelites of old, it was expected to make bricks without straw![29] Lack of money was the major factor affecting the archbishop's plans and the Board's fulfilment of its tasks.

When Clarke spoke of 'children' lost to the Church he meant particularly girls, and the loss to which he referred was the Anglican girls sent to Roman Catholic convent schools. Clarke told his 1906 Synod: 'We have no right to blame our people for sending their girls to these schools, which are at once both cheap and efficient, so long as we do not provide an education, equally good and equally cheap, under the control and government of our own Church'.[30] One possible way around the diocesan Board's financial problems was to follow the example of the Roman Catholic Church where the answer to the containment of costs lay in the religious orders. On a number of occasions Clarke had proposed this solution. His proposal was for a teaching order 'to which ladies could give themselves for five years in return for a home and a modest salary', but the proposal came to nought.[31] In his 1918 address to Provincial Synod he explained:

> It has often been proposed that we should have teaching
> brotherhoods and sisterhoods. Most excellent things if you are able
> to obtain them; but this implies that you call upon certain men and
> women, for the Church's sake, to devote their lives to teaching as a
> religious vocation. We have at the present time a number of such
> teachers, and I could wish that their numbers were increased![32]

In the Diocese of Melbourne there were two religious orders to which the archbishop would have been referring: the English-based Community of the Sisters of the Church and the indigenous Community of the Holy Name. Founded in 1888, the Community of the Holy Name had as its chief responsibility the Mission to the Streets and Lanes, and although at various times it ran two schools — St George's in the city's east end and St John's in Latrobe Street — these were part of their mission to the poor. This was not the case with the educational work in Australia of the Community of the Sisters of the Church who arrived in Melbourne in 1892 and established a girls' school, St Michael's, in 1896. This remarkable, and neglected, group of women in the story of Australian Anglican education of girls also established schools at Hobart, Adelaide, Perth, Sydney and Canberra.[33]

The sisters at St Michael's had a miserable time under Clarke's evangelical predecessor who viewed the Anglican sisterhood as redolent of the Church of Rome. Archbishop Clarke changed the Church's attitude to the sisters by occupying the position of Visitor to St Michael's and presiding at the annual speech day. Yet in Australia, the establishment of religious orders was not a realistic solution to the problem of expensive secondary schools for girls. Another possibility was for the Church 'to provide an income to subsidise the school fee', as Clarke suggested in 1918.[34] This was an unrealistic hope: the diocese did not have endowments, and the lack of enthusiasm for the Girls' Grammar School debenture scheme in the 1880s also suggests that His Grace was chasing the unattainable.

Despite the dearth of funds for the establishment of Anglican schools, the question was kept before the diocese. While Henry Lowther Clarke's strong commitment was a dominant factor, there was a broader social context in the state's burgeoning involvement in secondary education. The first Victorian state secondary school, the Melbourne Continuation School (later known as Melbourne High School), was established in 1905.[35] The first Director of Education, Frank Tate, wrote in the *Church of England Messenger*:

> It is vain to think that Victoria can steadily remain reactionary . . .
> in this matter of continued education. Whether the Church of
> England opposes or not the end is certain, the State must in its own
> defence undertake the work. 'The people have to have it so; and
> what will ye do is the end thereof'.[36]

The state rapidly established secondary schools in provincial cities such as Geelong, Bendigo and Ballarat, as well as the University Practising School (later University High School). However, reports of the Minister of Public Instruction from 1906 to 1921 show that the non-government schools held their own in secondary school enrolments; indeed there was some slight increase until 1920 as the registered schools became larger, but fewer in number.[37]

Of more import in the present context is the fact that the state's secondary schools were co-educational. As the Reverend H. B. Hewett told Synod, the parents of boys may be well content to send their sons to the state's secondary schools, 'but parents who would allow this did not care to send their girls there. They could not pay the large fees asked at the big Grammar schools, and were tempted to send them to convent schools.'[38] The implication that co-education is good for boys but not for girls has a decidedly modern ring. As we have seen, the sectarian issue also had a long history in Melbourne. In spite of the friendship of the two expatriate archbishops, the Anglican Clarke and the Roman Catholic Carr, in 1907 new fuel was added to the sectarian fires with the promulgation of the *Ne Temere* decree, which stated that marriages between Roman Catholics and non-Roman Catholics—so-called 'mixed marriages'—were invalid unless celebrated by a Roman Catholic priest. This decree, together with the well-documented sectarian tensions centring on Carr's successor, Archbishop Daniel Mannix, especially in the war years, all served to underline the need for an alternative to the convents for Anglican families who did not wish their daughters to attend state high schools.

Archbishop Clarke's plan was to have Anglican schools strategically placed throughout the diocese, and the first girls' schools to be founded in accordance with this scheme were Geelong CEGGS in 1905 and Firbank CEGGS in 1909. The *Church of England Messenger* for 23 February 1906 reported that:

> On Tuesday 13th February, a new Girls' High School was opened at Geelong in connection with the Church of England. The Diocesan authorities, at the end of last year, acquired a property, known as 'The Hermitage', on very advantageous terms, for the purpose of meeting the needs of the secondary education of women in Geelong.

The founding headmistress was Elsie Morres, formerly on the staff of Merton Hall and, as already noted, joint acting principal in 1903.

Firbank was financed by a legacy of £1400 left to Archbishop Clarke. Clarke stipulated that it was to be used 'in the founding of the school at Brighton, upon the condition that it is replaced as soon as possible, when it can be used again for a like purpose'.[39] There is no record that the condition was complied with! The Firbank procedure is, however, worth particular attention because it illustrates the extent of Lowther Clarke's commitment (the legacy, it appears, was personal) and his direct role in the implementation of policy. H. A. Brooksbank, a cleric who was closely involved in the diocese's educational policy, recalled that Archbishop Clarke tended to act first and inform the appropriate church body afterwards.[40]

Named after the archbishop's birthplace and his father's parish, Firbank was established by the purchase of St Andrew's from Mary and Katherine Hart. In her autobiography, *Forerunners*,

Constance Tisdall states that as owner-principal of nearby Rosbercon she was approached directly by Dr Clarke who wished to amalgamate her school with another to establish Firbank. Miss Tisdall claims that when she refused the offer the archbishop warned that the new Church of England school would put her out of business within a year.[41] This direct, if not harsh, intervention of the archbishop was also to be seen in negotiations for the purchase of Earlsbrae, the property on which Lowther Hall was to be established in 1920.[42]

A high priority for Clarke was a girls' school in the eastern suburbs. As early as 1907 the Diocesan Board of Education conferred upon Tintern the right to use the prefix 'Church of England School', and monthly advertisements thereafter appeared in the *Church of England Messenger* promoting 'Tintern, Glenferrie Road, Hawthorn, Church of England School, recognised by the Diocesan Board of Education'.[43] In the following year, the octogenarian Mrs Emma Cook, who had established Tintern in 1877, offered to sell her school to the Diocesan Board but its funds were committed to Firbank. Tintern was eventually purchased by the diocese in 1918 on the recommendation of a subcommittee charged to find an eastern suburbs school; advertisements were altered to describe the school as: 'Church of England Girls' Grammar School for the eastern suburbs'.[44]

One major change for Tintern following the purchase was the termination of the appointment of the principal, Agnes Cross, an Old Girl to whom the school had been leased by the Cook family since 1911. Miss Cross was a Congregationalist and diocesan policy required the position to be filled by an Anglican. The new headmistress, Hilda Ball, a committed Anglican and a science graduate of the University of Melbourne, was formally introduced to the school by Archbishop Clarke in May 1918.

Three other schools sought diocesan ownership in the period; each was rejected on financial grounds. In 1910 the Board rejected the offer of Ruyton Girls' School, then owned by Eliza Bromby, for the sum of £4600, again giving financial commitments to Firbank as the reason.[45] In 1914 the hall built next to the parish church for St James' Grammar School, the nascent Ivanhoe Grammar School, was also designed to house a girls' grammar school to be established by the vestry of the parish by taking over Cooerwull Girls' School. In spite of the desire of the headmistress, Frances Lowe, to see her *de facto* Church of England school come into the diocesan fold, this gained little official support. Ivanhoe Girls' Grammar School was later incorporated by the vestry of the Parish of Ivanhoe in 1922.[46] In 1919 Mentone High School approached the Diocesan Board of

Education but was rejected because of the school's geographical proximity to Firbank and because diocesan funds were committed to the conversion of Earlbrae into Lowther Hall. The school did eventually become an Anglican school (as Mentone Girls' Grammar School) — in 1962![47]

More successful was the acquisition of Korowa in 1920.[48] There are two aspects of the Korowa purchase which merit attention. The first is the continuation in office of the principal, Miss Ethel Akehurst, daughter of the school's founder, Mrs Henrietta Akehurst. Unlike Miss Cross of Tintern, Miss Akehurst was an Anglican. In later years, especially in the 1960s, the condition that the principal of a diocesan school be an Anglican was occasionally waived, not from any ecumenical liberality but from a lack of suitably qualified applicants. The second aspect of the acquisition of Korowa which is noteworthy was the imperious and condescending way in which Miss Akehurst was treated by the archbishop. Letters written to her include terse summonses to appear for meetings at prescribed times and demands over aspects of the takeover by the Church.[49] One other private school to be acquired by the Church in the period under discussion was Adamsdown in Alma Road, Caulfield, which was bought from the Bruford sisters in 1918. It was renamed Lovell House in memory of the archbishop's wife, Alice Lovell Clarke, who had died the previous year. The fortunes of Lovell House are discussed in chapter 3.

Although the creation of diocesan secondary schools, especially girls' schools, in Clarke's episcopate was a considerable achievement, the constraints on the activities of the Board of Education were indeed frustrating. Attempts were made to reform the Board by a new Act brought to Synod in 1918. This Act enlarged the Board, instituted monthly meetings, and mandated the appointment of salaried and honorary officers and inspectors. It also provided for the setting up of hostels and involvement in religious instruction in state schools. The diocesan schools were required to submit attendance and balance sheets, and there was to be an annual conference.[50] This ambitious Act failed to find fulfilment in action — again for financial reasons. Perhaps, too, there was a reaction to increased diocesan bureaucracy, a reaction still easily aroused among the schools today. And the brusque, aloof, and uncompromising personality of Archbishop Clarke cannot be discounted as a reason for the failure of the Act.

All this considered, the achievements of the first two decades of the twentieth century should not be diminished. The formal acquisition of Merton Hall in 1903 ushered in a period of educational expansion without equal in the Diocese of Melbourne, or indeed in the Anglican Church in Australia. There were three factors at work in the establishment of the schools of the diocese — each of which can be seen in the foundation of MCEGGS — although the relative importance of these factors was to vary in individual cases. These factors were to be important in the continuing life of the schools.

Firstly, there was the personal role of the bishop. In spite of the constitutional limits to his power, the bishop (later the archbishop) of Melbourne was highly influential in the establishment of schools. Melbourne and Geelong Grammar Schools, for example, had their champion in Bishop Perry in the early years.[51] And it was Bishop Moorhouse who initially sponsored a secondary school for girls. The leadership of Henry Lowther Clarke was also pivotal, not only in the establishment of schools, but in his continuing endorsement of their importance. Since that time, the schools — and the school clergy — have not always enjoyed such support.

The second factor was the role of individual and local initiative independent of the diocese. W. E. Morris established a precedent which was to remain crucial. Although his position as registrar of the diocese gave him easy access to people and processes, it was his personal conviction and initiative which did so much to bring into existence a Church of England Girls' Grammar School. This pattern of personal initiative is seen again and again, both in schools which were initially established as Anglican diocesan schools and in those which established a relationship with the diocese. Indeed, the failure of the 1906 Act to give the Diocesan Board of Education financial teeth virtually ensured from the outset that local initiative would be important in the establishment of Anglican schools. The devolution of power from the diocese to individual schools became policy under Clarke's successor, Archbishop Harrington Clare Lees, who was enthroned in St Paul's Cathedral in February 1922. Speaking to Synod in 1924 he observed that:

> In earlier stages of the movement [to establish secondary schools] it was desirable and right that they should have [been] . . . launched from the centre by the Diocese in the name of the Church . . . But I do with equal conviction believe that personal initiative, local enterprise, and all that goes with school *esprit de corps*, need to be given a fuller opportunity than was perhaps possible in their earlier stages. Directly the needs of a school spread beyond those of its infancy, there is a stronger incentive where responsibility is felt and faced. When the opportunities occur for financial ambition and development there must, I am persuaded, be such a measure of

self-government made possible, as can, without endangering Diocesan stabilities, make for progressiveness and self-determination.[52]

Archbishop Lees's policy of devolution is closely related to the third factor at work in the establishment and continuing life of the schools—the role of the school councils. Even by the end of Clarke's episcopate responsibility for the administration, day-to-day operation, and policy had begun to rest very much with the school councils. This is an inevitable outcome of what is essentially a federation of schools, not a system of schools. Under the peculiarly Anglican solution to the establishment of secondary schools, no equivalent to a Catholic Education Office is possible or desirable.

The period from 1884 to 1920 was a remarkable one in the story of the Anglican Church in Melbourne and schools for girls. From a time of delay and dubiety of purpose, there developed a series of schools in every region of the metropolitan area. In formal ways (their links with the archbishop), and in less formal ways (their links with each other), the girls' schools are a living part of the Diocese of Melbourne. The plan of Archbishop Clarke for something more akin to a system of schools never came to fruition. What evolved was a very Anglican arrangement—a pragmatic compromise with a bond of fellowship.

Ailsa G. Thomson Zainu'ddin

3   The Gilman Jones Era: 1916–38

To set both Kathleen Gilman Jones and MCEGGS within the educational and social context of the inter-war years is to explore a neglected period in the history of women's education and women's affairs in Victoria. In retrospect the Gilman Jones era was a golden age in the life of the school, while her influence in the educational world of Melbourne was extensive and multi-faceted. Miss Gilman Jones consciously built upon and acknowledged the work of her predecessors. In her own time she was innovative and forward-looking, playing an important part in preparing both the school and her successor, Dorothy Ross, for the experiments which aroused so much interest among progressive educators in the years following the Second World War. Those who have written about the progressive post-war experiments at MCEGGS have tended to subsume the work and influence of Miss Gilman Jones under that of her more controversial successor.[1] This can be seen as one measure of her success.

Miss Tunnicliffe, her predecessor as headmistress, was a graduate of Durham University with a London University M.A. in classics, a teaching diploma from Trinity College, Dublin, and ten years' varied experience as a teacher in 'large schools of repute' in England. Both beautiful and imperious, she arrived in 1914 full of reforming zeal. Despite her popularity with many past and present students, friction soon arose between herself and the staff. Her trenchant criticism of the lack of a school chapel and assembly hall, and of the 'entirely inadequate' provision of science facilities, led several Council members to resent her as too openly 'out to enlighten the colonials'.[2]

50

Archbishop Clarke attempted to divert Council criticism of this Yorkshire woman appointed with his support but, to the regret of many students and Old Grammarians, Miss Tunnicliffe resigned in 1915. Returning to Britain, she continued her teaching career at St Leonard's School, a leading Public school in St Andrew's, Scotland.[3]

In its first twenty-three years MCEGGS had five headmistresses for periods of from three to fourteen years. In that time it moved from its original site and changed from private to corporate ownership. Each change—of site, of leadership, of ownership—was a risk for a young school. In the midst of the uncertainties of a world at war, the Council again began to search for a headmistress who intended to make education her life work. This time the search was successful. In selecting Miss Kathleen Annie Gilman Jones from twenty-three applicants, the Council was appointing the longest serving headmistress in the school's first century. She said later: 'When the opportunity of coming to Melbourne was offered I snatched it very greedily. My friends in Sydney . . . told me that it was 'the' School of Australia . . . I realized it then and I have always been grateful for the wonderful inheritance I received.'[4]

Miss Gilman Jones, like Miss Tunnicliffe, came from England as a beneficiary and promoter of the reforms in the higher education of women which were taking place there in the last quarter of the nineteenth century. New professional women teachers found employment in newly established corporate girls' secondary schools. Those Englishwomen who could adapt to life in the colonies could create there an autonomous life style, sometimes at a higher social level than 'at home'. When, through ill health, she had to retire at the end of 1938, Miss Gilman Jones had been headmistress for half the school's existence. A school in search of a headmistress had found a headmistress in search of a school.

There are few glimpses of Kathleen Gilman Jones before she entered Newnham College, Cambridge, in 1900. She was born on 30 September 1880 at Fazeley, Staffordshire, where her father, Charles Jones, was manager of a tape mill.[5] Educated at Hildersheim House, Tamworth, and from 1892 to 1899 at Wellington Ladies' College in Shropshire, by 1900 she was at Newnham College where she completed the mathematical tripos.[6] From Cambridge she went to Bedford College, London, and completed the Cambridge Certificate of Education.

In September 1904 she became mathematical mistress at Edgbaston High School for Girls, Birmingham, founded in 1876 as one of the new academic schools. Its strong scientific bias was appropriate to the locality but unusual for a girls' school at the time. Miss Gilman Jones came to a day school of 150 girls presided over by a Girton graduand, Miss Georgina Young.[7] In 1906 Miss Gilman Jones moved to Salford Municipal Secondary School for Girls near Manchester, which then had 450 girls. She was in charge of senior mathematics, gave classes in religious instruction and physical training, and taught mathematics and English to an evening certificate class for teachers.[8] In January 1911 she went overseas as vice-principal of Queenstown High School for Girls, Cape Province, South Africa, taking over almost immediately as acting principal when the principal's health broke down. She also taught mathematics, biology and English, and trained pupil teachers.[9]

In July 1914 she arrived in Sydney to become headmistress of Ascham, then a private school owned by H. J. Carter. In 1914 Miss Margaret Bailey also joined Ascham and the two women bought the school, becoming joint principals.[10] In October 1915 when MCEGGS advertised for a headmistress, Miss Gilman Jones's letter of application indicated that 'we find that it will be some time before we can make a satisfactory living out of the school for two people'.[11]

On 9 February 1916 the MCEGGS *School Notes* reported that 'Miss K. A. Gilman Jones met for the first time the assembled girls as their new Head Mistress. We hope that her association with us will be a long and happy one.'[12] *School Notes* also reported that at last a fine red-brick school hall was to be built between Merton Hall and Morris Hall, facing Anderson Street. This reference to new buildings gave Miss Gilman Jones the opportunity to speak for the first time of the need for a chapel which she, like Miss Tunnicliffe, saw as central to the school's spiritual autonomy. 'A beautiful chapel would make our morning prayers more real, more earnest and more helpful.'[13] The school hall was opened in 1917. During the ceremony the girls sang their new school anthem, Psalm 127, set to music by Dr A. E. Floyd, organist and choirmaster at St Paul's Cathedral, who was already teaching choral singing at the school. When it was clear that, despite the urging of the present headmistress and her predecessor, no chapel was included in the Council's building plans, Miss Gilman Jones proposed that it should be 'built by the girls, not the Council, as their gift to the school'. By May 1918 she had established a School Chapel Trust Fund.[14]

In most ways school life during the war continued as in normal times. As usual, Miss Gilman Jones entered fully into

The Staff, circa 1909. Edith Morris fourth from left, front row.
Madame Liet fifth from left, front row.

Morris Hall, circa 1915.

Bishop James Moorhouse, by C. W. Walton. Bishop Moorhouse first raised the question of a Church of England girls' school in Melbourne.

Archbishop Henry Lowther Clarke. Under his influence the Church greatly expanded its role in the education of girls.

the life of her new school. She was president of the Games Committee, the Student Christian Union Committee and on the Debating Society Committee. Like most revered heads of schools, she soon had a reputation for remembering each of her girls by name. In her first annual report she emphasised that the school was not a 'finishing' school, also distancing it from Education Department schools—'their ideals are different from ours, their circumstances are different'. She proposed co-operation while asserting that 'it is not possible for either to control the other'. Under her leadership MCEGGS would not become a Class-A school, subject to Departmental inspection, 'because school examinations and inspections should be conducted by the University co-operating . . . with organisations representing secondary schools'.[15]

In 1916 the school debate that 'The principle of conscription is a right one' was lost by seventeen votes to twenty-one. This foreshadowed the decision of the nation on Saturday 28 October 1916, when 'no boarders were allowed to go out because Miss Jones thought the streets would be very rough on account of the voting'. Instead they had a tennis tournament.[16] In 1917 the school welcomed the Frensham hockey team from Mittagong (NSW), entertaining them to a concert and dance with the boarders.[17] At the school dance in the new school hall in 1918 members of staff were 'greeted with an avalanche of girls, all eager to procure at least one dance'. The headmistress, although not able to dance because of a heavy cold, 'booked' her program for sitting out. Later that term a Salamagundy evening was given by the prefects and probationers for the boarders—all except for one hapless pair, sent to bed early for some misdemeanour.[18]

Peace was celebrated prematurely on 8 November 1918 when thanks were given and the school dismissed for the day. The boarders went on a picnic to Heidelberg. They had a second celebration after the official announcement of the Armistice. The boarders 'gave the maids a holiday' and did the work themselves before holding a tennis tournament, unfinished because the girls walked to the thanksgiving service at the cathedral in the afternoon. They prepared their own evening meal, then danced till 9 p.m.[19] The influenza epidemic, which came with the returning servicemen, delayed the start of the school year, caused the postponement of speech day until May and replaced dancing with gargling morning and evening. Hamilton Brown, a prep. student, died in February of pneumonic flu.[20] Because Miss Gilman Jones departed unexpectedly for England in mid-October, she gave her dance for the Upper School to celebrate the

Armistice at the end of second term 1920, inviting the girls of 1918 to return for the occasion. [21]

The building program continued in the immediate post-war years and, in spite of problems arising from strikes by builders' labourers and seamen, the old buildings were remodelled and enlarged by the addition of a new wing of classrooms, more cloakrooms, a gymnasium and a studio. In 1920 the headmistress reported that MCEGGS now had buildings 'of which any school could be proud'. [22]

In 1918 the Council purchased Adamsdown, a private school in Caulfield, to be the branch school, Lovell House. Its numbers grew rapidly to 170 and, by 1923, it was seeking registration as a secondary school. New classrooms were also needed and the Council faced an expenditure of £34 000 to put the school on a sound footing and to meet the increasingly stringent requirements of the Health Department and Council of Public Education for secondary registration. When the Council decided to sell, Miss Gilman Jones submitted her resignation. The Council stood firm but requested the bursar to write to the headmistress indicating its regret at any inconvenience or disappointment involved in the decision. It assured her that 'any expenditure or implied covenant to teachers will be carried out', foreshadowing a special Council meeting to consider her resignation 'unless as the Council hopes it will be withdrawn'. [23] She withdrew it. Had she not there would have been widespread dismay in Melbourne where, from her arrival, Miss Gilman Jones had been accepted as a leader in the educational community.

On her arrival Miss Gilman Jones had quickly joined the IASTV. On 19 October 1916 she was proposed for membership of the Headmistresses' Association (HMA). [24] In 1916 she also became a member of the National Council of Women where, with Miss Isobel Henderson, owner-principal of Clyde, and Miss Catherine Remington, also of Clyde, she was on the Education Committee. In 1917 Frank Tate, Director of Public Instruction, proposed Miss Gilman Jones as a member of the Council of Public Education and its Registration Board. She remained on both until she resigned early in 1938. [25]

Through the IASTV Miss Gilman Jones strongly supported moves to improve the salaries of women teachers. At a conference of heads of schools and representatives of councils held in 1919 she expressed concern that many women teachers were not receiving even half the male salary, although she accepted that four-fifths of the male salary was an appropriate initial claim. The salary scale already worked out at MCEGGS was used by the

IASTV as its model.[26] Miss Gilman Jones was also involved in the IASTV's move to establish the ATTI. In 1919 she supported Frank Shann of Trinity Grammar when he requested that the IASTV Council be asked 'to draw up a scheme . . . to promote in registered schools a more efficient system of training of teachers'. Miss Gilman Jones was appointed to the Executive Committee of ATTI, one of the last public offices she relinquished during the illness leading to her final resignation.[27]

In 1923, when Miss Gilman Jones was president of the HMA, it was unanimously agreed to affiliate with the Head Mistresses' Association of Great Britain, which must have gratified her considerably. She was also unanimously elected vice-president of the Council of Public Education, and to the University of Melbourne Schools Board, the body then responsible for public examinations, remaining a member until 1937.[28] Given this wide and prominent involvement in educational affairs, she may have been as relieved to withdraw her 1923 resignation from MCEGGS as was the Council to retain her services.

Influenced by the New Education Movement of the inter-war years, Miss Gilman Jones was already planning innovations in the Middle School curriculum. Educational innovators world-wide were concerned with the concept of freedom for children and the role of education in creating and maintaining world harmony and peace at the conclusion of the 'war to end war'. Dr M. O'Brien Harris, headmistress of the 'Howard' School, a secondary school for girls at Clapton, England, was one such innovator. She had attempted to carry out the Montessori method in a secondary school by presenting the curriculum material 'in a Montessori atmosphere of freedom'. When Dr Maria Montessori, the Italian educational innovator, visited London in 1919 Dr Harris had taken a training course under her. *Towards Freedom: the Howard plan of individual timetables*, published in 1923, was written to provide a handbook for practitioners.[29]

In 1924 Miss Gilman Jones was president of the Independent Association of Registered Teachers of Victoria (IARTV). In August the association published the first number of the *Australian Educational Quarterly*, co-edited by Miss Dorothy Ross, who had joined the MCEGGS staff in 1923. The first editorial discussed the Howard Plan and the warning by Professor John Adams that 'it takes . . . a dynamic personality to infuse life into a Dalton or a Howard Plan'. The editorial suggested that the scheme could best be judged by the extent to which it developed spontaneity and creativity.[30] In the second number Miss Gilman Jones summarised five lectures, 'Tendencies of modern education', given at the University of Melbourne by Professor Adams.

She found him 'the same whimsical, sane and altogether delightful person' who had lectured in her own student days in London.

On speech day that year Miss Gilman Jones foreshadowed the
reorganisation of the Middle School in 1925, referring to the
London experiment as 'almost the exact plan I have been working
towards'.[31] Instead of the usual horizontal forms there would be
vertical classification of mixed age groups into houses. Each of
these three houses of about sixty girls would be in the care of the
same house (or home) mistress for the three years preceding
Intermediate Certificate. The house subjects — English, scripture,
civics, current topics, singing, gymnastics and games — were to
be taken each year. Other subjects, including mathematics,
sciences and languages, were to be selected and taken in order by
each girl in five stages of a term each. Girls would not enter the
Intermediate year, the first public examination class, until they
had satisfactorily completed sufficient subjects. With advice
from their home mistress, they would work on individualised
timetables enabling them to proceed at their own pace in each
subject. Each girl could choose subjects, time, place and method
of study within the total curriculum.[32] The May *School Notes*
outlined the new house system (the Howard Plan) indicating
that 'The value of this system is that a girl can get on very
quickly . . . and not be kept back because the other girls in her
class are behind her in their work. It also gives girls a chance of
concentrating more on their weaker subjects.'[33] Miss Gilman
Jones had to point out to some parents that the plan did not
provide a short cut to the Intermediate Certificate, warning that
'it is not the policy of this . . . school, nor is it the intention of the
Schools Board that a girl's work should be limited to the actual
subjects taken in the Intermediate examination'. The introduction in 1926 of a senior home-making class and in 1927 of a
fifth form emphasising music, craft work and art appreciation
for girls not sitting for public examinations emphasised this.[34]

The three houses were named for women saints: the musician,
St Cecilia; the scholar, St Hilda; and the warrior, Joan of Arc.
Their lives stimulated curiosity and creativity among the girls at
MCEGGS: in 1927 Evelyn Quinlan wrote the three-act play,
'Cecilia'; in 1931 the school captain, Lorna Mitchell, a former
member of St Joan's, wrote and produced the play 'St Joan' to
commemorate the quincentenary of Joan of Arc.[35]

The first house reports in *School Notes* capture the initial
excitement and the 'confusion and noise between lessons' as
'girls could be seen rushing along the balconies peering anxiously
into every room looking for their lessons, only to find that they
had preps'. House badges were chosen; for St Cecilia's a silver

harp; for St Hilda's a shield of royal blue and gold; for St Joan's a white dove on an azure blue background.[36] More important for the plan's success was the choice of house mistresses: Miss Ross (St Cecilia's), who had chosen this new venture, with its emphasis on innovative learning, in preference to senior science; Miss Marjorie Friend (St Hilda's), wiry and energetic, one of a family of four teaching sisters, and at the school since 1908; and Miss Jane Farrell, a big, kindly woman educated in Dublin, who, like Miss Friend, had studied French and German in Europe. Teaching from choice and conviction, they were experienced teachers interested in new educational methods and able to introduce their students to self-directed study and to current affairs in the wider world.[37]

After ten years even the indefatigable Miss Gilman Jones needed rest and recreation beyond her usual annual holidays at Cowes or at Barwon Heads where her cottage, The Whale, was an acknowledgment that she knew her nickname was 'Jonah'. In August 1925 the Council granted her leave of absence from March to December 1926 but initially some reservations were expressed about her recommended replacement, Miss Eliza Davidson, the second mistress. The Council contained powerful members of the Anglican establishment, clerical and lay. Dr Leeper had been a member since the Council's inception, serving with renewed devotion after his retirement from Trinity College in 1918, and finally resigning shortly before his death.[38] Mrs Leeper, who had been appointed in 1912, resigned in 1939. Mrs Herbert Brookes (Ivy Deakin) was a member until 1935. For many years W. M. Buntine, headmaster of Caulfield Grammar School, and L. A. Adamson, headmaster of Wesley College, were members. Yet Miss Gilman Jones was again prepared to confront the Council in defence of her own judgement and of her staff member. Who opposed the second mistress and on what grounds went unrecorded but there had been a similar episode when Susie Williams was appointed acting headmistress in 1911.

Expressing bitter disappointment that 'after ten years conscientious service the Council have so little confidence in my judgement', she withdrew her request for leave. This time she did not resign but indicated that she would try to continue for two or three years and 'resign when I feel I cannot go on without a prolonged holiday'.[39] Once the matter was resolved to her satisfaction, she departed for England via Canada. Miss Davidson, in her annual report, expressed her appreciation of Miss Gilman Jones's 'system of making individual members of the staff responsible for the different departments of the School work [which] rendered my task an easier one than it would otherwise have been'.[40]

Miss Gilman Jones returned with renewed energy and enthusiasm. She was welcomed by the Old Grammarians in March 1927 and in June she gave a short talk on her travels to a parent-teacher conference. The substance of her comparisons between Australian and English girls' schools was summarised in the *Australian Educational Quarterly*. The curriculum was much the same but, while English sixth form girls did more independent intellectual work, Australian girls were better at practical affairs such as organising a school dance or play. Sports were run on healthier social and physical lines in England. 'Here there is too much publicity, too much competition and rivalry, too strong a bent towards professionalism', a theme also taken up by heads of other girls' schools. She was impressed by the extent to which subjects previously regarded as 'frills' were 'an integrated part of the garment, a serious and necessary element in school life', encouraging increased respect for music and other arts.[41]

At MCEGGS she introduced musical appreciation classes throughout the school. Music was one of her recreations and she had already made provision for choral singing in 1917 by arranging for Dr A. E. Floyd to give classes.[42] Short lunchtime concerts had been held since 1920. Now the headmistress was keen to introduce special music classes throughout the school as soon as possible. The Council agreed to provide £100 a year with an extra £30 to purchase stringed instruments, enabling her to buy a gramophone, two violins, a viola and a cello! In common with the other girls' Public schools, she was anxious to begin a school orchestra. In 1928 the Music Club was formed 'to study the lives and works of great composers [and] to give opportunities for music pupils to play before their fellows'.[43] As in the Morris era, plans were made to introduce at the senior level a fifth form 'for those older girls who, for various reasons, do not intend to sit for public examinations'.[44]

In March 1927 Miss Gilman Jones suggested to the Council an anniversary festival in the following year to mark the twenty-fifth year since the school became the Church of England Girls' Grammar School, Melbourne. The question of reverting to Merton Hall, the name of the original school, was raised but failed to gain support from the Old Grammarians. Melbourne Church of England Girls' Grammar School was officially endorsed as the name for the school as a corporate body and Merton Hall applied to the residential house only.[45]

The birthday was celebrated in the first week of May 1928. The garden party, despite windy weather, was the most successful event, with over 1300 people present. The cathedral service at 3 p.m. on Sunday was considered the most impressive occasion. The collection went to the school chapel fund which reached £1146 by the end of the year, exceeding the £1000 target originally set before tenders could be called and raising hope that at last the chapel might be built. The history of the school, compiled by Gwenda Kent Hughes, was published in an edition of 1500.[46] The week concluded with an open day which even the wet weather could not spoil, and a dinner for Old Grammarians and parents at Scott's Hotel. The Parents' Association was established with Dr L. Mitchell, a Council member since 1925, as its first president. At his suggestion, parties were provided for the girls after the public celebrations. The Council and headmistress gave a dance for the senior girls and for the prep. children, the final party, complete with cake and candles, was held on Wednesday 16 May, a beautiful Autumn day.

In August that year the Council agreed to raise Miss Gilman Jones's salary to £800 per annum from February 1929 and to abolish capitation fees. It also considered plans to extend and remodel the school buildings. At speech day in 1928 the headmistress warned her listeners that, because a diocesan school lacked local backing, it needed continuous material support. 'We have so far managed to jog along and pay our way', she told them, 'but this becomes increasingly more difficult . . . a really first rate education is bound to be expensive, whether that expense is met by the parents or by the State or by endowments'.[47] The outstanding event of 1929 was the purchase of Yarra House on the corner of Anderson and Clowes Streets at less than market price from E. Norton Grimwade, a member of a family 'always generous to the Church and educational institutions'. Renamed Phelia Grimwade House after his wife, it was extensively remodelled and enlarged to provide extra boarding facilities. A common kitchen and dining room, more accommodation and playground space for the Preparatory School, extra tennis courts and a reference library room, which the Old Grammarians had offered to equip as their birthday gift to the school, were also provided in that year. At the 1930 speech day, which was combined with the dedication and opening of Phelia Grimwade House, Miss Gilman Jones directly confronted those 'quite sincere well-wishers of the School who do not yet see the need for a School Chapel'. She asked them to re-read the prophet Haggai, who wrote in times comparable to the Depression years which were clearly affecting Melbourne by the 1930s.[48]

The Council's first reference to troubled times in the surrounding community was in 1930. It suggested a patrol round the school at lunch time 'on account of so many undesirable men loitering about'.[49] Miss Gilman Jones, by now more confident than she had been during the conscription referendum in her first year, felt sure the school handymen would provide any protection required. Indeed, by then she was so much at home that she confided to Margaret Darling, whose brother was headmaster of Geelong Grammar School, that only on a north wind day or during Test matches was she really conscious of being English.[50] Commending the proceeds of over £1300 towards the school's extension fund from the very successful Early Melbourne Fete that year, Miss Gilman Jones commented that 'the great majority of our friends are not wealthy people . . . and others who in normal times do not have to consider their expenditure, are finding things difficult now'. She regarded the amount as 'very special evidence of the earnest desire to put education before other less important things' and reminded Council members that the school was committed to raising £1000 for each of the next five years. She found it 'encouraging, as evidence of the changed outlook with regard to the education of girls' that 'in this time of stress, when all classes in the community are reviewing their expenditure . . . education is not interrupted until all other avenues of retrenchment have been explored'.[51]

In 1931, as the Depression deepened, boarding fees were reduced by 10 per cent and consideration given to reducing all fees and salaries. Nevertheless, the headmistress reported that, with the 'conspicuous exception of the School Chapel', MCEGGS was now a well-equipped school for a maximum of 350 in the Big School and 150 in the Preparatory School. She was also glad to report that, after seven years of the Howard Plan, all girls who gained high honours had gone through the school under this plan.[52] In 1927 she had noted that school captain, Margaret Blackwood began there when she was six—on Miss Gilman Jones's first enrolment day—and that 'of the 12 Captains of the School during my Head Mistressship, 7 began in the Preparatory School'.[53] Although boarding numbers declined slightly in 1931 to 1932, by 1932 the 'definite maximum', particularly in the Big School, had already been exceeded.[54] Even so, a 10 per cent reduction in tuition fees and salaries accompanied the reduction in boarding fees. Miss Gilman Jones suggested that, as teachers had generously accepted a reduction in salary, 'it seems only fair to ask parents to allow their girls to take a share in the sacrifice . . . to be content with much less pocket money . . . [and] to have fewer and less expensive clothes and entertainments'.[55]

In 1930 Miss Gilman Jones submitted an entry to *Who's Who*

in the World of Women. Resident at Merton Hall in Anderson Street, South Yarra, she lived in the 'Yarraside' heartland of the women included. Over 50 per cent who gave a Melbourne address lived either in Toorak or South Yarra, including a number of Old Grammarians, mothers of her girls, and fellow worshippers at Christ Church, South Yarra. While the majority were the wives, mothers or daughters of the Melbourne establishment, she was one of nine headmistresses of 'leading girls' schools'. Her list of committees is the longest of any under that heading. It included the Victorian Women Citizens' Movement, of which she was president in 1928, and the Business and Professional Women's Club, of which she was vice-president. This choice of club emphasised her career orientation. Committees formed a large part of her out-of-school activities, extending her educational, religious and professional networks. Prepared to provide leadership, she held executive positions in each organisation at various times. The entry concluded succinctly that 'Miss Gilman Jones has by her unceasing efforts brought the school to its present standard of high efficiency, both educational and artistic'.[56]

In 1933 Miss Gilman Jones farewelled Dr Leeper on his retirement from the Council in his eighty-fifth year, one of its 'most active and enthusiastic members'. She referred also to the death of J. J. Raw, already a Council member when she arrived, and took the opportunity to reflect on the kind of school those churchmen sought to establish—one with a Christian environment, providing sound learning and giving an education for life—and to ask whether, thirty years later, the school was fulfilling their ideals. She could not refrain from remarking that 'curiously they do not seem to have considered the necessity for a Chapel as the centre of School life'. She spoke also of another concern dear to her, the need for trained women in the work of the Church, remarking that 'women are unfortunately not yet admitted to the Priesthood in our Church'. She announced her gift of an honour board for the hall, to hang beside those recording university successes, in honour of Old Grammarians serving as missionaries, sisters or deaconesses.[57] Presumably, were the time to come, she would also have wished to include ordained clergy. She expressed her views publicly on this in 1925 on the Executive Committee of the Sixth Annual Church congress, 'The Church and the New Age', held in Melbourne that May. In discussion on 'The ministry of women' she said:

> men are so apt to forget that women were human beings as well as themselves. In the Councils of the Church and in the diaconate, women should be given equal opportunity with men for serving

the Church. Why should they raise artificial barriers against women? The natural barriers were quite sufficient. No sensible woman wanted to do things she was not fitted for.[58]

She linked her view of the place of women with the changing concept of a modern girl's education. She reminded her 1933 audience that

> thirty-three years ago it was still unusual for girls of the middle-class to earn their own living, though in this new country the doors of the various professions opened more readily to them than in the older countries; during and after the war it became the accepted thing for girls to be trained for some career; to-day when there is a good deal of unemployment, some are beginning to say again: 'Women's place is the Home' . . . this is true; happy marriage and motherhood is the best career for the majority, but what about those who do not marry? . . . we feel that all girls as well as boys should have some real aim in life. Economic independence is desirable but this should not be the main objective—rather, what form of useful work will give the girl the greatest opportunity of finding happiness through service?

She believed that the most fruitful avenues for those without any special vocation for medicine, research or the creative arts might be in the traditional women's occupations: teaching, nursing, almoners' work, home-making or gardening.[59]

In 1934 financial recovery was sufficient for the Council to restore fees to their former level although staff received only a 5 per cent restitution of salary with full restoration to be considered in the light of the 1934 balance sheet. Salaries returned to pre-Depression levels in 1935.[60] With the introduction of a superannuation scheme in 1933, retirement age was set at fifty-five although individuals could be invited to remain a few years longer. In 1935 the headmistress reminded Council that she would reach retiring age that September. In April the Council congratulated her 'on the splendid manner in which she had carried on during a specially heavy year' and unanimously requested her to remain for another five years.[61]

In 1936, her twentieth year as headmistress, Miss Gilman Jones reported that the chapel fund had passed £2000, and proposed a comprehensive scheme of alterations and additions which included a chapel. When completed, the extended boarding accommodation could house 112 boarders. The school gained a senior and junior reference library, a prefects' room, six large classrooms, a physics laboratory, common rooms, better cloakrooms and administrative offices.[62] Her own study was 'smaller than the old one (but in a much better position for knowing what is going on in the School)'.[63] Conspicuously absent was the chapel although the chapel fund was, by then, over £2500. In her final report she expressed her great disappointment, commenting that 'perhaps I have been, like David, a man of war and only allowed to collect the wherewithal, and my successor will be the Solomon, who builds the House of God'.[64] Even this was unduly optimistic!

This complex building program in 1937 added further stress to a very difficult year. The infantile paralysis epidemic involved the organisation and supervision of correspondence work for girls living in quarantined areas.[65] Miss Gilman Jones reported 'an exceptional number of absences on the part of the Staff (wherein I set a very bad example)', her oblique reference to the heart trouble which had kept her from school until Easter and which led to her letter of resignation the following March.[66] This was the last report she was to present. She was not well enough to attend the opening of the New Merton Hall (since named Gilman Jones Hall) nor could she face the final speech day. 'I shall leave everything ready — my Report etc. — and Miss Waddell will carry on for the last fortnight', she wrote.[67] The Gilman Jones era was drawing to a close.

Her final report acknowledged that:

It has been a great privilege to guide the destiny of this great School for twenty-three years, which is more than half its life to date, and I carry away with me many happy memories. A Public School is essentially a co-operative affair, and I think with gratitude of all who have helped in building on the very sound foundations laid by my predecessors — Council, Parents, Old Grammarians, Staff, Prefects and girls (should I have arranged these in alphabetical order? There surely is no last nor first.)

She expressed satisfaction that 'the School will have a strong, healthy woman as Headmistress next year' but warned Miss Ross that she would find the school a full-time job, requiring all her strength and energy. She warned the Council that her successor would be 'though perhaps more tactful, as insistent as I have been on the need for constant additions to buildings and equipment'.[68] Miss Gilman Jones, as she departed, was able to congratulate the school 'in having as Headmistress a woman of such brilliant gifts as Miss Ross, who moreover knows the School well'.[69]

Miss Gilman Jones returned to England early in 1939, bought

a house in Etchingham, Sussex, which she named Merton Cottage, and entered fully into English village life, 'teaching Scripture in the village school two mornings a week, collecting from house to house for War Savings and all sorts of odds and ends'. In 1941 she offered hospitality to London war workers, 'all quite nice, but completely uneducated and "h"-less'. She also took her turn at fire-watching, in a village 'anxious lest incendiaries should be dropped in dry weather amongst the corn'.[70] The following year, the accidental overturning of a small primus stove in her own kitchen led, after a month of stoic endurance, to her death on 17 September 1942 from burns, within a fortnight of her sixty-second birthday. The school community, fragmented by evacuation, gave praise and thanksgiving for her life and work at a service in Christ Church, South Yarra, attended by hundreds of Old Grammarians and friends of the school.[71]

Miss Gilman Jones had come to MCEGGS as a young woman after ten years of varied and enthusiastic teaching experience, a born leader and organiser, who enjoyed a game of golf and vigorous surfing. Until her serious illness at the end of 1936 she had always enjoyed good health. Muriel Berry, a newly appointed probationer in 1917 and, as Mrs Muriel Maxwell, a staff member by 1938, remembered her best 'on many a holiday, sturdy and cheerful, hat a little on one side and hair escaping from it, never out of temper and never beaten by the longest and hardest walk'. To Muriel Maxwell the secret of her greatness as a headmistress lay in her vitality. 'No task ever daunted her and no detail was ever too trivial for her interest.' Her vigorous, humorous and matter-of-fact attitude to life, her sanity and her directness, were fundamental to her character and to her influence on students, staff, parents and Council members.[72] Miss Rigg saw her as the type of headmistress who 'trusts her subordinates with responsibilities and gives a free hand in developing their ideas to those who possess enthusiasm and ability . . . inspiring enthusiasm and initiative, and . . . teaching the self-distrustful confidence in attacking their work'.[73]

She valued communication between parents and staff, encouraging the creation of a parents' association well in advance of other girls' Public schools, an association involved with educational innovation, not primarily with raising additional finance. She was equally involved with the Old Grammarians and appreciative of their support and co-operation. Miss Mary Eltringham, the secretary appointed part-time when the Council finally acceded to her request for secretarial assistance, has given some idea of the tasks which the headmistress had handled unaided before 1933:

Can you imagine answering between 40 and 50 letters by hand every weekend!—letters to parents about their daughters, letters from parents . . . Letters from the University, from applicants for staff positions, from Old Girls seeking advice on their futures. All this after a busy week organising, teaching, interviewing, attending meetings . . . and also being available to boarders and their parents in the weekends, attending sports or other functions on Saturdays and always at 8 a.m. and 11 a.m. services on a Sunday at Christ Church South Yarra.[74]

Miss Gilman Jones shared with many other newly professional women a 'moral earnestness, an almost missionary zeal for educational work, and concern for each child as an individual'. She regarded liberal education as preparing girls for service in the community when school days were finished.[75] While she took her mission seriously, her earnestness was tempered by her 'great appreciation of the comic or naughty side of her pupils' and the nice touch, leavened with humour, which 'guided and checked without crushing'.[76]

Miss Gilman Jones maintained strong links with the Church: through her work on the Diocesan Board of Education; through friendship with archbishops and their wives, especially Mrs Edith Head who had also taught at Edgbaston Girls' High School.[77] The school was possibly more distinctively Anglican in those years than in any time before or since. Her biggest disappointment was her failure to persuade the Council to build a school chapel. Edith Head commented that 'She had never let the School wall her in and bound her horizon, but has seen the School always in its setting as a Church School, pledged to send out girls ready to serve their generation'.[78] She fostered links with the wider world through the school's membership of the Junior Red Cross, the Student Christian Movement and the League of Nations.

She maintained strong links with the University of Melbourne. Her reluctance to seek Class-A registration for the school and her willingness to serve on the Schools Board of the university also emphasised her support of the university's role as regulator of secondary education. The Gilman Jones Scholarship, established by the Old Grammarians in her honour to provide a residential scholarship at the University of Melbourne, was a continuing link with Janet Clarke Hall.[79] During most of her era its principals were Miss Margery Herring and Miss Enid Joske, both Old Grammarians, as were a high proportion of its residents. Yet she also supported the appeal for the establishment of the autonomous Women's College, commenting that women needed 'an independent college, not hostels tacked on to the men's colleges'.[80]

She emphasised the links, dating back to Miss Hensley's establishment of Merton Hall, between the school and her own
Newnham College, and rejoiced when Old Grammarians, such
as Adele Ogilvy, continued their studies there. She emphasised
other links with the past—the continuity essential to the Public
school and the growth of its traditions—welcoming visits from
earlier headmistresses, reminding the school of those policies in
which she was continuing the work of her predecessors.

Martha Vicinus, in her study of independent single women in
Great Britain, concludes that the inter-war years saw the decline
of teaching as an 'honourable choice, not a place of last resort
[and] the demise of the large feminist movement that had given
many a support group and had validated their lives'.[81] This
seems less true in Victoria. Perhaps the time-lag between Melbourne and 'home' enabled Miss Gilman Jones to find here a
sustaining network of feminists. She forged bonds with a variety
of women—other headmistresses, her teaching staff, the mothers
of her students, her own Old Girls, other professional and
business women, other women active as citizens—and she also
sought, as part of her own feminist program, to counter 'the
profound sexism that makes men's occupations more important
and more valuable' than those traditional to women.[82] 'Like
many other enthusiastic feminists, she insisted on the right of
women to enter the professions . . . yet she never forgot . . . that
marriage is, or should be, a profession requiring intelligence and
training, and not merely the common fate of those not capable of
taking a degree.'[83]

The Melbourne to which Miss Gilman Jones had come in
1916 was a city whose social leaders believed that the British were
the instruments of Divine Providence, that there was no need for
any change in society, that 'the industrious, the talented and the
frugal could rise to the top in . . . a New Britannia'. Industrious,
talented and frugal herself, she rose to the top of her profession
in a city which 'might have been one of the cities of the British
Isles'.[84] She departed in 1939 at the end of an era. After the
Second World War the old certainties were undermined.

Although she received 'admiration and respect and indeed
great affection' from girls who were in her classes or junior staff
who shared activities with her, many were in awe of her. The era
to which she belonged and in which she was acknowledged by
her peers as having been 'a great Headmistress', was passing as
she reached retirement.[85] It was also perhaps the last period in
which an Englishwoman could expect any automatic advantage
in applying for such a position. The aura of headship which set
its possessor apart was becoming an anachronism in a more

egalitarian world. On the other hand, as one Old Grammarian perceived on the eve of Kathleen Gilman Jones's departure, 'theories and ideas expounded and described as new and progressive [have] been in practice here ten years . . . or more. Most of us are apt to take for granted the things with which we are familiar.'[86]

Pip Nicholson

4   Merton Hall women and professional life: 1917–38

The idea that a woman should be a mother and nothing else was ridiculous.

> Kathleen Gilman Jones, headmistress, 1917–38.[1]

THE YOUNG WOMEN OF MERTON HALL IN KATHLEEN GILMAN Jones's time were taught to consider alternatives to domestic duty, motherhood and marriage. Did they always appreciate their exposure to models of economic independence? And what was it that the students took with them into the world beyond Anderson Street, South Yarra? What do these women recall about their education? And most importantly what did they become?

This chapter attempts to answer some of these questions by following the paths taken by a group of girls who left Merton Hall between 1917 and 1938. The study is also an opportunity to document the experiences of this group of women while their histories are still available orally. Australian histories of women frequently focus on the changes occasioned by the women's suffrage movement of the late nineteenth century or the impact of modern feminism in the 1970s and 1980s. The women in this study document the presence of women in the workplace in the years when feminism is assumed to have weakened. Indeed in many cases, the biographies portray women at work in areas dominated by men.

The cross-section of career women interviewed included a doctor, a teacher, a lawyer and two academics, one in science and the other in education. These examples illustrate that full-time remunerated employment was pursued by ex-students of Merton Hall in very diverse fields.

There is a pervasive myth that Merton Hall specialised in science teaching in the inter-war years, encouraging girls to enter non-traditional areas of study and careers. Yet those inter-

Rupert Bunny's portrait of Dr Alexander Leeper. Leeper played an important role in the establishment of the school as a Church of England school and was a founding member of the Council.

The entrance hall of Merton Hall as it was in the early years.

Miss Kathleen Gilman Jones
innovative Headmistress from 1916
to 1939 and advocate of women's
rights.

The Assembly Hall, 1917.

Miss Lorna Mitchell completed a distinguished career in teaching as Head of the English Department at MCEGGS.

Dr Betty Wilmot had a significant career in medicine.

Dr Jean Laby became a physicist at the University of Melbourne.

Dr Gwyneth Dow became a noted educationist and author.

Miss Mary Cameron, one of the early female undergraduates to enrol in Law at the University of Melbourne in 1935, entered private practice as a solicitor.

viewed did not state that science subjects were well taught at the school. In fact, mention was made of science being poorly taught. This is in marked contrast to the praise given by those interviewed to the teaching of mathematics. Neither is the myth about science supported by the empirical evidence. Enrolments of Merton Hall students in the Faculties of Science and Medicine at the University of Melbourne did not greatly increase during the period. For example, in 1919 and 1920 three Merton Hall women enrolled in science, and in 1930 and 1932 the number was still only four for each year. Similarly, in 1919, 1924, 1936 and 1937 two ex-Merton Hall students enrolled in each year in medicine at the University of Melbourne.[2] This is not to argue that women students who enrolled in science or medicine did not face particular difficulties associated with studying and working in areas traditionally dominated by men. However, it does indicate that there was no particular encouragement which caused the numbers studying in these areas at tertiary level to increase.

While I have elected to focus on women who went on to university, other women from Merton Hall who did not attend university had remarkable careers. For example, Alice Anderson, born in 1897, owned and ran a garage in Cotham Road, Kew.[3] In 1919 it was advertised as 'Miss Anderson's Motor Service'. This business offered, among other things, driving lessons, mechanical repairs, motor tours and specialised chauffeuring. Lorna Mitchell recalled that Kathleen Gilman Jones said 'Marriage is a career, and if that is what the girls want to do, then that is their career'. There is not sufficient scope in this chapter to consider the ex-students who devoted their adult lives to marriage and child-rearing, or the role played by these women in the public sphere in part-time work and service to the community. Similarly, many other women left Merton Hall and completed tertiary study and also continued to work full-time. The five biographies in this chapter serve as examples of women working full-time in the public sphere. I do not seek to create 'tall poppies' of the women who so modestly told me their history.

I have interviewed five women who went on to the University of Melbourne between 1917 and 1938. These women are not of the same age, come from different family backgrounds, undertook various studies at the university and subsequently worked in diverse fields. Their similarity is that each attended the university and worked in the public sphere for most, if not all, of their professional lives. Their similarity as women is that they used their education in the public sphere. All agreed that the school presented positive models for young women, fostered self-expression and promoted individual excellence in both academic studies and extra-curricular activities.

Born on 15 February 1912, Alice Elizabeth (Betty) Wilmot was the youngest of three surviving children. She had another brother who did not live beyond eighteen months. Her father was a pharmacist in Corowa, NSW, and all the children came to Melbourne for their secondary education. She described both parents as very much in favour of education and noted that both her siblings went on to the College of Pharmacy. Betty ultimately became a doctor specialising in maternal and child health.

In 1924 Betty Wilmot was awarded the Boarder's scholarship to attend Merton Hall where she commenced in 1925. She left Corowa Public School at the age of twelve and commenced life at Merton Hall as one of fifteen boarders. She recalled 'the companionship of being a boarder' and painted a picture of challenges and a sense of community that influenced her for the rest of her life. Betty commented particularly on the difference between the public school she attended and her experiences at Merton Hall. She enjoyed the innovative teaching in the school which included civics, current affairs, general science and music.

The value of the education Betty Wilmot described was not only in its formal teaching, but also in the government of the school which included the school prefects (student councillors) who were given various responsibilities. In her senior years Betty was a prefect and in her last year shared the position of school captain with Joan Ferguson. Self-government was a vital training ground. Her memories of League of Nations meetings, debating, taking part in the governing of the school, and discussing the matters raised in civics and current affairs classes, evoke a rich and vital environment.

With this broad education came the 'undoubted encouragement to go on to further education', an attitude which was very much endorsed in Betty Wilmot's home. Her mother was an early graduate from the Faculty of Arts at the University of Melbourne, completing her degree in 1899. Trained as a teacher, her mother ran a private school in Beechworth before joining the staff at Merton Hall for two years, commencing in 1902. Her mother believed it was very important for women to avail themselves of the developing opportunities for further education.

In 1930 Betty won a Trinity College scholarship to Janet Clarke Hall which enabled her to commence study for a science degree at the University of Melbourne. She described her social life at the university as centred at Janet Clarke Hall. She was the secretary of the Janet Clarke Hall Students' Council and in her last year was elected president—a position she was unable to hold due to restrictions on funding for scientific research precluding her return to the university.

Between 1935 and 1938 Betty Wilmot worked as the dietician and welfare officer at the Victorian Railways. The dietician's job, the first of its kind outside a hospital, included the study of meal quality provided in the railways workshop for 1200 men. The job also involved the production of nutrition education literature and posters for display on railway stations to improve public awareness of food value.

The University of Melbourne first awarded the Diploma of Dietetics in 1938 and the two recipients were Betty Wilmot and Audrey Osborne (née Cahn). Betty Wilmot was seconded for a year to the Commonwealth Department of Health commencing at the end of 1938. In Canberra Betty worked with Dr Frederick Clements who was the director of the newly created Nutrition Institute. After a year with him, producing nutrition education material and working on Vitamin B estimation in foods, the Second World War broke out and Dr Frederick Clements advised Betty to return to the university and study medicine. Betty Wilmot graduated from the Faculty of Medicine in 1945. On recommencing study she noticed the higher percentage of women enrolled in undergraduate degrees and identified this as a direct consequence of the onset of the war. She proceeded to do her first-year residency at the Alfred Hospital, Melbourne, and in her second year went to the Childrens Hospital in Perth.

Betty then took up the position of school medical officer for the north-west of Tasmania. In mid-1948 she was granted leave of absence to accept a British Council scholarship to study child health in the United Kingdom. She went first to the Institute of Child Health at Great Ormond Street Hospital for Children, where she completed a Diploma of Child Health before visiting other institutes of child health in England and Scotland.

On Betty Wilmot's return to Australia she was seconded from the Tasmanian Department of Health to work at the Bonegilla Migrant Hospital in north-eastern Victoria. In 1950, after a further time in Tasmania, Betty Wilmot became the assistant director of maternal, infant, and pre-school welfare in the Victorian Department of Health. After two years in that position she was seconded for three years to the World Health Organisation to the position of regional adviser on maternal and child health for the western Pacific region. This involved extensive travel in the region, including visits to Japan, Laos, Cambodia, Vietnam and Singapore to ascertain and report on health services for mothers and children. Between excursions, Betty Wilmot returned to Manila. She talked of the international perspective on maternal and child welfare she acquired at this time, as well as an understanding about the operations of United Nations agencies. Betty described this as exhausting work and she recalled that it was with some relief that she returned to the Victorian Department of Health towards the end of 1955. In 1960 she became the director of maternal, infant and pre-school welfare and held this position for the next fifteen years.

In 1966–67, Betty Wilmot was awarded a National Health and Medical Research Council fellowship in public health. She elected to go to the University of California, Berkeley, where she completed a master's degree in public health. Betty remembers these as 'traumatic' days at Berkeley with the anti-Vietnam rallies and the three-hour speech by Martin Luther King to a group 'not missing a word he said'.

Having returned to the Victorian Department of Health, in 1976 Betty was promoted to become the first woman to hold the position of assistant chief health officer (maternal and child health) in Victoria. In addition to her responsibilities for maternal, infant and pre-school welfare she was responsible for the Division of School Health. In February 1977 Betty reached the age of sixty-five and had to retire. In 1978 she was awarded the Order of the British Empire for her 'medical work, particularly in the field of maternal and child health'.

Since her retirement she has continued to work on the councils and committees of various voluntary organisations concerned with the health and welfare of families. She has played an active part in professional associations such as the Victorian Paediatric Society and the Victorian Medical Womens Society of which she has been president. Betty Wilmot has at different times been the delegate of both the Medical Womens Society and the Old Grammarians Society to the National Council of Women. In March 1992 Betty Wilmot was one of three women who was honoured by the National Council of Women (Victoria) at an 'appreciation dinner'.

Betty Wilmot spoke enthusiastically of the opportunities Merton Hall gave her, particularly its preparation for community service. She was a highly motivated and caring professional who devoted her working life to developing and encouraging others to develop policies and health-care initiatives for the benefit of women and children. Betty Wilmot was continually involved in the promotion and management of health-care systems, not only the treatment of disease.

Lorna Mitchell is the eldest of five children. She grew up with two sisters and two brothers and she remembers a family where reading and learning were encouraged. She explained that her early schooling was with Miss Mary Fison who ran what was in many ways an unofficial 'feeder' school for Merton Hall by teaching the children of several families in private homes. For example, Miss Fison taught for a time at the Sewell home. Lorna described these classes as small and extremely well taught. From this introduction to schooling she moved to Merton Hall in 1923. The Mitchell family was active in the life of the school. All three daughters, Lorna, Stephanie and Honor attended Merton Hall and Dr Leonard Mitchell, Lorna Mitchell's father, was the first president of the Parents' Association which was established in 1928. Lorna was also to return to the school to teach at a time when it was very much in need of continuity in its staff.

Lorna Mitchell was a serious student who applied herself energetically to her studies and who had a very full life as a girl at Morris Hall and then Merton Hall, completing three years Leaving Honours in 1931. She remembers especially the teaching ability of Kathleen Gilman Jones, Gwenda Lloyd, Mona Nugent, Ada Mackay, Elisabeth Lothian and Winifred Waddell. She commented: 'I was very lucky. I had a broad education.' Her only regret is that, apart from mathematics, she did not study science subjects. 'I think it was the teachers we had. They inspired my interest in the humanities', she explained. Lorna recalled that her school days were long and filled with activity: there was sport nearly every day, and often on Saturdays; debates and dramatic performances; and editing the school magazine.

The great encouragement she received at school was significant in her choice of a career. Her family was very much in favour of tertiary education, and her mother, father and grandfather were very keen and active supporters of women's education. Lorna recalled that she owed her love of learning and intellectual curiosity especially to the example set at home by her parents. She remembers her mother as a woman who 'always wanted to learn something new'. However, Lorna recalled, 'my mother could never understand that I wanted to teach. I do not know what she thought I should do'. She speculated that her mother probably wanted her to marry as her two younger sisters did. Honor Simpson (née Mitchell) was an art teacher; Stephanie Cullen (née Mitchell) was one of the early graduates from Invergowrie and went on to work as an almoner.

Lorna Mitchell went to the University of Melbourne and completed a master's degree in English. She then completed a Diploma in Education before going with her parents to the United Kingdom in 1936. She spent the first part of that year travelling, then went on to Oxford University and completed a further master's degree in English Language and Literature. She spoke of the privilege of having some of the world's greatest poets and authors as teachers—classes were given by J. R. R. Tolkien, C. S. Lewis, Edmund Blunden, Lascelles Abercrombie and Nevil Coghill. The tutorial system, where tutor and student met to talk together, was very stimulating to the young Australian.

From Oxford she and a Scottish colleague travelled to the Rhine area in Germany in 1938. Lorna Mitchell had been given a small travelling grant by Professor George Browne of the Faculty of Education at the University of Melbourne to complete a report on education in Germany but, with the onset of war, she found it very difficult to write a meaningful report. As she explained, war changed the entire context of her research.

On her return to Australia in 1939 Lorna Mitchell took the place of Margaret Kiddle, teaching at St Margaret's, Toorak. When the school closed she joined the teaching staff at MLC, Kew, where she remained for eighteen years. A student at MLC recalled that Lorna Mitchell 'placed the subject before either formal discipline or personal teacher-pupil relationships. Her sensitivity and patience were foreign to us . . . She presented the possibility of learning at an adult level, of mutual respect and detachment.'[4]

Through Lorna Mitchell's involvement with the Student Christian Movement she was encouraged by Dr Edward Gault and Dr Edna Gault to apply for a position in the Women's Christian College, Madras, where Miss Eleanor Rivett was principal. She arrived just after the first Indian principal had been appointed at the college and explained how she and a group of teachers from Europe and America worked with the local staff to create a very diverse and stimulating curriculum. Lorna described history excursions with staff and students by train to places far from Madras: Mahabalipuram, Agra, Delhi and villages in the foothills of the Himalayas. With other staff and students she helped with Sunday-school classes for the children of railway workers. Each Sunday one hundred children would arrive for Christian instruction.

After eighteen years at MLC, which included a year in Madras, Lorna Mitchell joined the staff at Merton Hall, a decision which had not been easy to make. However, with the resignation of so many members of staff at the school in 1958, she believed that there was a need for teachers at Merton Hall if the school was to survive the crisis which developed in that year (see chapter 7). She was not alone in moving to Merton Hall to provide the new headmistress, Miss Edith Mountain, with some experienced staff. Lorna Mitchell recalled that Dora Pike (née Whitelaw), Florence

Vasey (née Faul), Elaine Lovett (née Speed) and Mary Branigan (née Sewell) all took up positions at Merton Hall for the same reasons.

Lorna Mitchell described some of her post-1960s students as inclined to be 'rebellious and self-assertive'. She confessed: 'I do not know how married women with children teach. Teaching seemed to take up every moment of my life.' She discussed the unique relationship that exists between a teacher and student and concluded: 'It is an intensely personal job. There is no shutting the office door. I would teach all day, attempt to help students after class, discuss syallabuses and exam papers with staff, mark mountains of essays, prepare lessons, and then snatch a few hours sleep.'

Lorna Mitchell's love of literature was obvious as she sat in her library. She explained that when she commenced as a teacher she taught in several disciplines, but later specialised in English, teaching students of different ages and from diverse backgrounds. She continued to tutor in English until 1991. Now in retirement, she is both a teacher and a student of various courses at the University of the Third Age. As I left Lorna she was asking me what I felt about Elizabeth Jolley's work. It was 9.15 p.m. on a week night and we had talked for some time, but Lorna had to prepare for a summer-school paper and had begun, already, to work on it.

Lorna Mitchell's reticence in speaking of her contribution to teaching is marked. She consistently played down her own academic success, except where she praised those who taught her. However, Lorna is clearly a woman who equally loves learning and work as a teacher.

Mary Cameron arrived at Merton Hall in 1930 from The Hermitage, Geelong, where she was a boarder. She was the younger of the two Cameron daughters. Careful in describing her schooling, she frequently censored what she said. It was not clear whether this stemmed from her legal training and work as a lawyer, or a naturally cautious nature. Her observations were succinct. It took her some time to settle into her new school, where greater independence was encouraged by staff and practised by students. She identified that the students at Merton Hall were expected to display more initiative.

Describing herself as shy, Mary Cameron stated that she did not easily take the stage. Of debating at school she commented, 'I joined the Debating Society whose members were required to take part in at least one debate. I was too terrified to open my mouth and managed to avoid being called upon.' She particularly remembered Mona Nugent as both teacher and mentor. She recalled her first English lesson with Mona Nugent who said, 'Would someone please shut the door?'. When the door was closed, Mona Nugent proceeded to read a poem to the class. Mary recalled that 'you could have heard a pin drop'. She remembered that the poem Mona Nugent read was John Drinkwater's 'The Midlands'.

> Black in the summer night my Cotswold hill
> A slant my window sleeps, beneath a sky
> Deep as the bedded violets that fill
> March woods with dusky passion.

Mary Cameron wanted to go to the university and undertake an arts degree. She recalled that her father 'actively discouraged my enrolment' believing, as he did at that time, that the university was 'a hotbed of communism'. Her father had served in three wars and had been on the land in Kenya and appeared distrustful of higher education for women. In contrast, her mother, who had matriculated at a time when it was still rare for women to do so, supported her going on to the university. Her father insisted that if she did go to the university she should do something 'useful'. It was at school, particularly through discussion with Gwenda Lloyd, that she received encouragement to study law at the University of Melbourne. In 1935 Mary became one of four female undergraduates enrolled in first-year law. Like Betty Wilmot, her social network at the university was based at Janet Clarke Hall, where she found peers with whom she shared her undergraduate days. Together, they attended classes, went to seminars, studied and spoke about their interests.

Mary Cameron commented on the gradual inclusion of women in the law tutorials at Trinity College which were given by the warden, Dr John Behan. At this time there was only one female student of law from Janet Clarke Hall seeking tutorials in any one year but, in the ensuing years, their presence was more accepted. Sir John and Lady Behan hosted formal dinners. When the port was brought in Lady Behan would 'with a nod gather up the four women students present and retire with them to the drawing room where the men would subsequently "join the ladies"'. In her final year, when the senior students of Janet Clarke Hall were invited for dinner, Sir John insisted that the ladies 'stay for port'. Mary remembered the invitation as a 'great landmark'.

Mary Cameron also recalled that her sense of independence,

developed at school, helped her at the university. She described it as 'minimising the cultural shock' of campus life. At school she had become accustomed to assuming responsibility for her studies. At both Merton Hall and the university Mary was a conscientious student. She described herself as 'loving the study of law' and the intellectual and social life offered at Janet Clarke Hall. She recalled a brilliant student of French at Janet Clarke Hall who would read a French novel regularly before lunch, and then regale her fellow students with the plot at lunch. Mary Cameron explained that as a result of college life residents were in close contact with students of other disciplines and thus had the benefit of the exchange of ideas and a broader cultural background than would otherwise have been possible.

On the completion of her Bachelor of Laws degree in 1938 Mary Cameron went as an articled clerk to the firm of Rylah and Anderson, and remained there during the war years, nearly all the men of the firm being on military service. In late 1944 the Crown Solicitor's Office advertised a position for a conveyancing solicitor at £8 a week. Mary Cameron applied. Many months later, her application unanswered and seemingly forgotten, she was invited to an interview for the position and offered the job at a salary of £6 a week. As the reduction in wage was a consequence of her sex, she declined the offer. It was then arranged that the Public Service Board would offer her the position at the male rate of pay. However, by this time men were being de-mobilised and Mary was requested to resign in favour of returned servicemen. Mary decided she had no alternative but to agree and determined to remain in private practice, working for the firm of solicitors, Kiddle, Briggs and Willox.

In 1951 Mary Cameron advertised in the *Law Institute Journal* under the name of 'Lochiel' for a partnership. She recounted with humour her first conversation with a Mr Stedman, who had not realised the 'Lochiel' of the advertisement was a woman. Colin Stedman nevertheless admitted Mary to partnership and it lasted twenty years and only ended with Colin Stedman's retirement from practice. Mary Cameron developed a practice in common law whilst Colin Stedman specialised in conveyancing. As a result of a close working relationship with barrister, Joan Rosanove, she expanded her practice in family law. Stedman Cameron is now a firm of thirty-six partners and staff. Mary believes that, having established the practice, her sex was not of consequence to her working life as a solicitor.

Mary Cameron questioned why she was being interviewed and not others of her peers whom she considered brilliant. She seemed to underestimate the example she provides as one who developed her own private legal practice at a time when that was relatively unusual for a woman.

Jean Laby was born on 4 November 1915 in Melbourne. She completed all her schooling at Merton Hall before going on to study science at the University of Melbourne in 1935. Now in retirement, she recalled with a quiet sense of humour her time at school and her ensuing career. Not an outgoing student, her recollections of Merton Hall were reserved. This attitude contrasted with the warmth and vitality with which she described her life as a physicist from the 1940s until her retirement from the University of Melbourne teaching staff in 1980.

Jean Laby's anecdotes of school were set in the context of her life as one of the children who lived in the university precinct and journeyed daily to Merton Hall. She and her younger sister, Betty Laby, were two of a group of children who were ferried from the University of Melbourne to South Yarra by parents who lived on the University of Melbourne campus and rostered the driving of their offspring to the school. Jean described trips made with Dr Ethel Osborne in her 'Tin Lizzie', the old Ford with its open top. The Laby sisters, Betty and Jean, Yrsa Osborne and possibly some of the others would pile in and be taken across the Yarra. Before being set down, Dr Ethel Osborne sometimes took them for a spin around the hockey field.

At school Jean Laby was, by her own account, a shy girl. Betty Laby explains that Jean Laby was 'never one to blow her own trumpet'. She played baseball and received a pocket for her efforts. She described herself as the tenth player in a team of nine who was nonetheless decorated for her endeavours. She also played tennis sporadically. Jean confessed that she 'could not stand Shakespeare and had great trouble getting through English'. But her love of science subjects is clear. She recalled that Winifred Waddell was outspoken and would accuse students of 'committing a crime' when they erred at mathematics. Alleged crimes were 'such things as dividing by nought or using the wrong sign'. She explained that students tended either to enjoy good rapport with Winifred Waddell or feel excluded. She indicated that Winifred Waddell had a very strong personality.

In 1935 Jean Laby enrolled in science at the University of Melbourne where her studies were interrupted by poor health and an overseas trip. She recounted that the university took the view that she ought not undertake applied mathematics, a decision made on the grounds that for a young woman it would be too foreign. She was advised to enrol in graphics which was taught in the Engineering Faculty. She described this subject as a 'harrowing experience'. She found herself the only female student and was expected to enjoy and learn from 'locating and drawing bits of ironmongery'. Jean discontinued this subject. In 1939 she completed her science degree.

Whilst at the University of Melbourne Jean Laby's social life was frequently based around Dorothy Gawler's tennis court and her peers who, as children of university and college personnel, remained her friends after school days. Her sole long-term link with the school was with a group of women, some of whom came from Merton Hall, who formed the 'Old Grammarian Baseball Team'. The team had to select a new name when Valentine Leeper heard of it and discovered that not all of them were ex-Merton Hall.

On completion of her degree Jean Laby was told by her father that she should obtain work. She applied for several positions and was offered one at the Weather Bureau. She ultimately took up a part-time demonstrating position at the University of Melbourne as the pay offered by the Weather Bureau for full-time work was no more than the pay offered at the university for part-time employment. This decision placed Jean in the Physics Department where she continued researching and teaching until her retirement. She explained that her father did not directly encourage her to become an academic; his priority was that she should work. Jean's father, Thomas Laby, was a leading Melbourne physicist who was described by his daughters as having 'quite a high profile on campus'. Jean noted that her mother had never worked. She recalled that, when attending a graduation ceremony, her mother commented that 'Women look so "frumpy" in academic gowns'.

Jean Laby was more forthcoming as she talked about physics and the scarcity of women as colleagues during her working life. During the war the Natural Philosophy Department of the University of Melbourne established an optical munitions unit. This was part of a nationwide scheme to develop and produce much needed optical equipment for the war effort. Both Laby sisters worked on the project as did a great many staff and recent graduates in physics. In 1959 Jean became the first woman to graduate as a Doctor of Philosophy in physics at the University of Melbourne.

Jean Laby was involved in research which included using balloon tests to determine the flux of cosmic rays. She also worked extensively on research techniques enabling the study of stratospheric winds, aerosols and radioactivity in the atmosphere. Her studies took her to various parts of the world. Six months were spent in South Africa 'chasing balloons' in 1960 with

Professor Victor Hopper. This research involved international co-operation and resulted in a greater understanding of atmospheric conditions in the southern hemisphere. Between 1972 and 1981 Jean Laby worked in collaboration with the University of Wyoming in the United States of America on the Climatic Impact Assessment Program. The aim of the program was to produce a global study of the effect of supersonic aircraft on the environment. In addition to research assignments, Jean Laby was the first women to teach at the Royal Australian Air Force (RAAF) Academy at Point Cook. She remembered 'all those cadets marching around and saluting me and calling me "Sir"'. She taught at the RAAF Academy for twenty-one years with very little professional contact with women throughout the period: 'I had an occasional female student visting the academy from the University of Melbourne and secretaries as female colleagues'. Despite the solitariness of her position as a woman in science at this time, particularly in physics, Jean did not feel it an issue that she was a female pioneer.

Jean Laby spent all her working life in scientific research and teaching. She was first and foremost a scientist. For generations of women to follow, she and other female academics challenged the presumption that women were not well-suited to careers in science.

'I was a rebel at home and I suppose I was a rebel at school. I was always in trouble.' Gwyneth Dow (née Terry) was born on 14 August 1920, and completed eight years schooling at Merton Hall, three in the primary school and five in secondary school, commencing in the Junior School in 1929. In her first three years as a Prep. School student, she spent a great deal of time under the stairs. Not only was she frequently banished from the classroom, but she was also a delicate child, so she was frequently absent.

Gwyn said that in the Middle School she was probably even cheekier, more restless and more frivolous. As she said and others interviewed suggested, 'the teaching in the Middle School was very uneven'. It was only at the senior level that she began to take an interest in Mona Nugent's English, Margaret Davies's French, and above all Gwenda Lloyd's history. She was lucky in that her first examination failure was not until her final year when she failed in biology, and so she left school in 1939 without completing her Leaving Certificate.

Still very young, Gwyn Dow took the advice of the head of the Board of Social Studies at the University of Melbourne and worked for a year, among others things as an apprentice hairdresser at Myers, as well as studying biology at Taylor's College. In 1938 she enrolled at the University of Melbourne in the Arts Faculty to do a combined arts and social studies degree. Her parents were not intellectuals and their home had very few books. Her father, although he had supported his more diligent daughter, Mollie, refused to finance Gwyn's university course until reluctantly persuaded by Mollie who had recently finished her Master of Arts. It was her sister and friends who encouraged Gwyn to enrol. Gwyn explained that her father, who was much older than her mother, lived on his inherited capital. Her historical study, *Samuel Terry: The Botany Rothschild*, is an account of her convict ancestor who established the family fortunes in Australia.[5] She recalled that her father was an authoritarian figure whose attitudes conflicted with the values she had acquired at school. On the other hand, Gwyn recalled that her mother, while never pushing her children at school, was inordinately proud of any of her daughters' successes, and very tolerant and enlightened. She excelled at croquet and was the first woman Australian champion and the first to be selected in a test team when she won the doubles against England in 1935.

Gwyn Dow fulfilled her father's predictions by passing only five university subjects in two years, when she married journalist Rohan Rivett in January 1940. As a result of this marriage she left full-time study, moved to Sydney and then returned to Melbourne at the end of 1941 when her husband went with the BBC to Singapore. Gwyn explained that the period from the end of 1941 until mid-1942 was one of the most formative in her life. During that time her husband was missing after the fall of Singapore and later became a prisoner of war, she lost a child, and she had no income whatsoever. In mid-1942 she applied for and obtained a scholarship to undertake a six months' emergency training course in industrial welfare being offered at the University of Sydney by the Commonwealth Department of Labour and National Service. This scholarship paid her the basic wage.

On completion of the course, she returned to Melbourne and worked for two years as the industrial welfare officer at Maribyrnong in the explosives factory and then the ordnance factory. From this position she moved in early 1944 into private industry, initially working as a welfare officer which broadened into personnel management. She was one of the first women in Melbourne to work in this area. At this time she completed her arts degree part-time at the University of Melbourne. Gwyn recalled that the personal traumas and losses she suffered during this war period changed her. After the war ended she lost another child, and her marriage broke up. She settled into full-time work and described herself as becoming more mature and more studious.

In 1949 she obtained a Diploma of Education and then commenced teaching, first at Merton Hall and the Kindergarten Teachers' Training College, before moving to London in 1951 with her second husband, Hume Dow. There she taught at Peckham, one of the first five experimental comprehensive schools in London. On her return to Melbourne in 1953 she taught at MacRobertson Girls' High School for four years. During this time Gwyn actively — and successfully — campaigned for permanency for married women teachers. In addition, she returned to the University of Melbourne and enrolled part-time in a Bachelor of Education course in which she shared the Exhibition in History of Australian Education in 1955.

In 1956 Gwyn Dow was seconded to the Education Faculty at the University of Melbourne and was transferred to University High School to teach one day a week. She thought the segregation of the sexes within the school nonsensical and made a joking protest by always walking up the staircase reserved for men and boys. In 1957 she obtained permanency at the University of Melbourne and ceased teaching on a regular basis in schools. Her first publication was *Uncommon Common Sense*,[6] which she was commissioned to write for the clear-thinking program in senior school courses in English Expression. It had immense sales for many years, and was, she says, the only book from which she made any money. In the 1960s Gwyn was very much involved with the setting up of the Victorian Curriculum Advisory Board which kept her closely in touch with schools experimenting with curriculum reform. Later, her innovative approach to education involved her in an experimental school-based course for teacher education which still continues at the University of Melbourne. Her work in the school-based teacher education program formed the basis of her book, *Learning to Teach: Teaching to Learn*.[7]

Her working life was a balance of research, teaching in schools and universities and active involvement in contemporary educational issues. In 1962 Gwyn Dow obtained a master's degree in education from the University of Melbourne and won the Freda Cohen prize for the best thesis of that year. The thesis was published as *George Higinbotham: Church and State*.[8] In 1982 she was a Fulbright senior scholar. She elected to travel in the United States of America, visiting several universities to look at their teaching of popular culture and history of childhood. In 1984 Gwyn received a doctorate on an examination of her published work.

Of her working life Gwyn Dow said that as a woman 'it was much harder to get anywhere'. She also noted that her second husband provided ceaseless support for her work both academically and domestically. It is paradoxical, she suggested, that a woman who confessed to sloth and indifference during her school days should become a teacher of teachers. 'It was the realisation that I was unqualified and helpless that really pulled me up sharply.' She said that school did not put her off learning but it was the appreciation of her powerlessness—'that I had nothing'—which was the real catalyst to her assuming a serious approach to her work. As a teacher she thinks she has a special understanding of 'reluctant learners'. She continues to write and her latest book is *Australian Childhood: An Anthology*, edited with June Factor.[9]

These five biographical accounts of women who attended Merton Hall during the inter-war years suggest that each responded differently to what the school offered. With the exception of Gwyn Dow, each woman remembers her secondary schooling as producing an educated young person who was well-equipped to face the wider community of the University of Melbourne and a working life beyond. Each woman drew clear links between the experience of school at Merton Hall and her professional success in later life. They recall a stimulating and intellectual head-mistress, some excellent staff, rewarding academic study and extra-curricular activities, and a challenging environment which encouraged independence.

The headmistress, Kathleen Gilman Jones, is remembered for her own academic achievement. Many of those interviewed referred to the fact that Kathleen Gilman Jones had obtained final honours in the mathematical tripos at Cambridge. Betty Wilmot recalled the rigour of Kathleen Gilman Jones's divinity classes. 'Bible studies was a history' and taught with breadth and clarity: 'the bloodiness of the kings' wars was not omitted'. Nor was it only the headmistress who was recalled as a scholar. Memories of scholarly and stimulating teachers, particularly in the Senior School, are vivid. Members of staff such as Winifred Waddell and Gwenda Lloyd are recalled as creating an atmosphere in which respect for scholarship was fundamental and academic curiosity was aroused. Ada Mackay's Friday afternoon poetry readings were an example of the approach to learning that the students recalled.

The teachers are remembered for presenting scholarship as the natural course for young women. The women experienced an ambience of learning for its own sake and did not identify high grades as the primary aim. Success at public examinations was not emphasised. Of her education Lorna Mitchell recalled that 'there was no coercing or pressure'. There was an expectation that the girls would be able to pass their examinations and go on to complete further study in whatever area interested them. Mary Cameron recounted that as a student she felt a responsibility for her own work. Uncertain if this was the result of the Howard Plan of teaching, Mary was clear that teaching staff and girls shared a common pursuit of learning and scholarship.

Most of the women recalled their Senior School teachers with warm feeling and deep respect. They described an intimacy with their teachers which provided a secure base for the sharing of values and extra-curricular activities. Gwyn Dow's enthusiasm for Winifred Waddell, Gwenda Lloyd and Kathleen Gilman Jones came from an interest in their subjects and an appreciation for the manner and sensitivity with which they taught. She recalled that Winifred Waddell described her as 'the sort of girl who looks as though she is wearing nail polish even though she isn't'. However, Winifred Waddell and Gwenda Lloyd knew how to motivate the hitherto troublesome child without recourse to punishments such as detentions. Betty Wilmot talked of the intimacy of Winifred Waddell's mathematics classes where 'we talked a lot'. She described Winifred Waddell as very interested in people and also in painting. Lorna Mitchell talked of Ada Mackay's generous lending of books. She also recalled that she used to visit Ada Mackay, Winifred Waddell and Mona Nugent in their retirement. These memories are of staff who were available to their students and with whom their students felt very comfortable.

There are positive memories, too, of extra-curricular activities. For the annual Shakespeare's day each form would do a scene from a Shakespearian play and learn to appreciate not only the literature but the art of production. Betty Wilmot recalled that the Outdoor Club went walking at weekends at Werribee Gorge, among other places. These outings were occasions when the staff and students met on an informal basis to observe, discuss and experience the world beyond the classroom. There are memories of an outdoor production of Robin Hood complete with archery and horses, girls taught to ride, shoot a bow and arrow and to work together to produce an ambitious piece of theatre. From these extra-curricular activities, devised and implemented by staff who took great pride in the overall development of their students, the adult women remembered a sense of achievement and pride in accomplishment.

The women interviewed all identified a pervasive moral framework at Merton Hall during the inter-war years. Gwyn Dow recalled that the school had a 'very strong sense of social injustice', an attitude which she believed was 'caught rather than taught'. She believed that the school also fostered a 'high moral tone'. Gwyn said that many girls came from very 'snobbish' families and indeed, in socio-economic terms the school was, and remains, exclusive. Yet she felt that whilst at school the idea of an elite was frequently challenged. Instead, there was an emphasis on the worth of the individual and not on a class of people. Gwyn Dow recalled with warmth that the school encouraged the girls to reject 'anything that was authoritarian', an ethos which fostered freedom of expression and created the space in which to challenge 'anything that did not seem rational to you'. She commented that such liberty was extraordinary; it permeated her attitude to life.

Betty Wilmot recalled that the school fostered a sense of civic duty and commitment to the betterment of society. She reflected that these values and interests influenced her later life and career. She recalled that Kathleen Gilman Jones 'believed we should not become an elite' and engendered 'an interest in welfare work'. She also recalled Gwenda Lloyd's teaching of current affairs, where the roles of federal, state and local governments were explained and an interest in public policy was fostered. She also remembered that in civics classes examples of women working in local government were drawn on as models. She felt that the classes in civics, although very general, did encourage women to 'take their place'. Yet, in the five interviews this was the sole reference to teaching which explicitly referred to the role of women in the paid work force.

It emerges strongly from the interviews that the girls continued to receive conflicting messages from family, school and society about women's role in the inter-war years. Each woman interviewed acknowledged that Kathleen Gilman Jones, through her employment of married women, challenged the perception that a woman had to chose between a life in the home and a career beyond the home. Further, pregnant women were able to teach throughout what would once have been regarded as an appropriate period of confinement. Yet the women acknowledged that, at an early age, they had understood that to be married and working in paid employment was a rare practice. Jean Laby commented that many of her colleagues 'evaporated into married life' and confirmed that most women 'certainly did not continue working once married', at least not on a full-time and remunerated basis. Lorna Mitchell recalled that she was shocked when she met women who were both married and teaching. She remembered that, despite the presence of married teachers at Merton Hall, it was still very unusual in the early 1940s to work with married women. As four of the five women interviewed did not marry, it was still clearly a case of choosing between work in the public and private spheres.

One element perceived as lacking for students at Merton Hall at this time was social interaction with boys. Betty Wilmot felt that the school 'lacked something in preparation for co-education at the university'. This was manifest 'in a slight awkwardness and lack of confidence in a mixed society for some time after I left school'. Yet no such reserve was evident when both Betty Wilmot and Mary Cameron talked of their friends at Janet Clarke Hall. Further, Betty was clear that her reserved nature with men was only social; there was no such shyness in her working life. Lorna Mitchell and Jean Laby commented similarly. On the other hand, unlike the women who recalled their shyness and reserve, Gwyn Dow spent a large amount of time with men socially; she did not refer to any inhibitions with the young men of the period. Despite their reserve with men, the women interviewed did not remain with other ex-students of Merton Hall whilst at the university, quickly developing new friends and interests. In effect, the pattern of learning and informal association that had begun at school was continued at university and beyond.

The stories of the five women demonstrate that the education they received at Merton Hall played a large part in producing competent and confident professional people. But they remember the prevailing philosophy of the school as encouraging excellence in whatever its students undertook. The students of Merton Hall in the inter-war years did not receive particular encouragement in any one discipline or field of study to go on to further education.

In what sense then, are these women remarkable in their own generation? Jean Blackburn writes: 'Putting major emphasis on individual breakthroughs by girls and women as "role models" ignores the essentially political nature of the accommodations to be made, and the importance of structures'.[10] This is true. Nonetheless, those women who did achieve in the male-dominated workplace, commencing in the first half of this century, played a vital role by contributing to the acceptability of female professionals.

There are very few women who began a professional life in the 1930s and 1940s and continued in uninterrupted employment in the public sphere until retirement. It cannot be a coincidence that four of the five women did not marry and none had parenting responsibilities. The only married woman, Gwyn Dow, commented particularly on the support she received from her husband, Hume Dow, in her career and in the home. Consistent application to their careers was possible but, with the single exception of Lorna Mitchell, they still had to make their way in a male-dominated world. The fact that most do not recall this as a major factor is the result of their working in a period that pre-dated greater awareness among women of gender politics. The significance of this generation of professional women who completed their education at Merton Hall before 1936 lies in their life-time commitment to careers in the public sphere.

With the advent of principles of equal employment opportunity and affirmative action in the workplace the contribution of these unwilling female pioneers can easily be forgotten. It ought not to be so.

W. F. Connell

5 *The school as a democratic community: the educational ideas of D. J. Ross*

DOROTHY ROSS WAS HEADMISTRESS OF MCEGGS FROM 1939 to 1955. She was a natural successor to Miss Gilman Jones but not a mere continuer. She had similar ideas and the desire to build on the contribution which Miss Gilman Jones had made. She had a 'great admiration' for her predecessor and wished to 'develop further some of the ideas that she had put into practice'.[1] At the time of her appointment she was a skilled, practical teacher and a thoughtful and discerning educator who had made a serious study of educational ideas and practices, had discussed them with leading and innovative educators overseas and dissected them in teacher education courses with her own students.

A product of the cultivated and prosperous middle-class world, D. J. Ross, as she preferred to be known, grew up in the educated society of late Victorian and Edwardian Melbourne. Born in 1891, she was the only child of Alfred Ross and Charlotte (Lottie) Walden, a handsome and talented couple who encouraged her intellectual and physical development to a remarkable degree. She spent much of her time in Geelong where her grandmother, Ellen Walden, had an interesting and intellectual group of friends centred round the Morrisons of Geelong College. D. J. knew from a very early age that she wanted to be a teacher. She went to various private schools, including The Priory in Alma Road, St Kilda, and in 1910 when she was eighteen, entered the University of Melbourne. There she began a law course and moved into arts where in 1913 she completed an honours course with majors in French, German and English. She won a university blue for tennis and played the flute at concert parties. Five years later, she began to study part-time for a B.Sc. Hons degree in the biological sciences which she completed in 1922.

Dorothy Ross's first teaching experience was with the Victorian Education Department at Coburg Higher Elementary School in 1914. She also taught briefly at Trinity Grammar School and, in 1915, joined the staff of Oberwyl, a private girls' school in St Kilda, where she stayed for the next six years. Then, after a brief spell at St Catherine's School and a full-time year on her science course at the university, she joined the staff of MCEGGS in 1923. There she remained until 1928. By the end of that period she had become a skilled secondary school teacher of twelve years' experience mainly in middle school language work. Dame Margaret Blackwood, then a student at MCEGGS, recalls D. J. as a teacher:

> She had us fascinated with genetics—a very new subject just ten
> years old. She had brought Mendel's Law from England that year.
> We would greet her arrival in the classroom with searching
> questions on the inheritance of blue eyes and brown eyes and the
> like and she would expand for most of the lesson, with us rivetted.
> Then she would say, 'Well, you side-tracked me again, didn't you?
> You had better double up on your homework for next time![2]

D. J. had also developed in other significant ways.

From Miss Gilman Jones she learned something of the revolution in ideas and practices which had been transforming education during the past two decades. 'I think', she later recalled, 'that all the educational ideas that seeped into me then . . . emanated from Miss Gilman Jones.'[3] With Miss Gilman Jones she attended John Adams's lectures on the New Education in Melbourne in 1924 and found reinforcement for those ideas and a great stimulus to her thinking along progressive lines. At that time, as Ailsa Zainu'ddin has indicated, the Howard Plan was introduced to MCEGGS. Miss Ross was put in charge of the new arrangements for the Middle School. In the process of organising the vertical houses and the individual work she acquired considerable administrative skill and built up a capacity to deal patiently with misunderstandings and resistance to change. Those traits were to be characteristic of her later work as headmistress.

In addition, she developed an abiding interest in studying individual differences and methods of catering for them. Her interest led her to the study of individual psychology, and she was attracted by the 'nature-nurture' controversy then prominent in biological and educational circles. Above all, her experience with the Middle School at Merton Hall developed in her a curiosity and a desire to learn about what was then being termed the New Education. Before that time she seems to have been little aware that overseas an important educational revolution had been under way, producing important practical proposals which were being tested in the progressive schools of Europe and America.

At that point in her career Miss Ross was offered the position of supervisor of the ATTI. Before taking up the position in 1930 she spent a rich and stimulating year in Europe during which she completed a teacher education course at the University of London, took a course of lectures with Maria Montessori, and attended a New Education Fellowship conference at Elsinore in Denmark where many of the world's leading educators had gathered. After the conference she went on to Vienna to visit Cizek who was teaching art in his celebrated Children's Studio. For the rest of her life she remembered that inspirational year and she kept in touch with the progress of educational thinking and practice.

In 1935 Miss Ross returned to the University of London Institute of Education to study child development with Susan Isaacs who reinforced her views on the importance of the intellectual and social education of young children. Throughout her career she had insisted on the importance of each pupil's individuality and recent movements in education and psychology had strengthened her view. Montessori, Cizek and Isaacs studied and cultivated individual differences in their pupils, and their views were supported by Adler's psychoanalytic approach to individual psychology which was widely read in the 1930s. Another psychoanalyst, I. D. Suttie, also attracted Miss Ross's attention. In studying human development he emphasised the importance of love and companionship in an individual's growth. For Miss Ross, that was the means to reconcile both individual and social growth. Many progressives were interested as much in a pupil's growth into caring, democratic behaviour as in the cultivation of individuality. That linkage became the basis of her approach in education. Democracy, she thought, was concerned with providing opportunity for sharing and caring as well as with individual expression and advancement. Education in a democracy, therefore, should be centrally concerned with encouraging individuals to develop not through competition but in co-operation with each other.

Miss Ross's nine years in charge of ATTI helped to consolidate her thinking, brought her into contact with a wide range of experienced and beginning teachers, and provided her with an opportunity to observe the quality of most of Melbourne's independent schools.

In social background, academic training, sporting and musical interests, and in teaching experience, Miss Ross was admirably suited to a school such as MCEGGS. Towards the end of her term as headmistress, on speech day 1953, the school's Jubilee Year, she spoke at length on 'the essential unity of aim running like a thread through the years of the school's history'.[4] Of that continuity she was always very conscious, and she regarded her work as building on to an existing tradition in a way which would make it appropriate to a mid twentieth-century democratic culture. She wanted, she said 'to run a school where children were persons', learning to participate fully in the development of the school community.

D. J. Ross began her period as headmistress at the beginning of 1939; by the end of that year Australia was at war. For the next two years the school was little affected by the war situation and was able to adjust quietly to the new headmistress. By July she had taken the first formal step towards more democratic procedures through which staff and girls could discuss matters of general organisation. After meetings with the staff and prefects, she inaugurated a modest, elective School Advisory Council representative of all sections of the school. 'The opinion of the School', she wrote, 'is obtainable through this body and [has] already proved helpful in the making of probationers and other matters of organisation.' It consisted of seventeen members from the staff, prefects, sports committee, boarders, and all school groups, and never failed to have a mass of business to consider. 'Through the work of this body', she wrote, 'an appreciation is being gained by the whole school of the relation between freedom and responsibility, and the very delicate balance between freedom and security.'[5] In 1942 a further step towards self-government was taken. The prefects, appointed by the headmistress, elected their own head prefect who became the school captain, and they met as a body known as the Prefects' Executive Committee. After 1945 the prefects were elected by the Senior and Middle School girls. Those moves were a foretaste of the School Executive Council which grew up slowly in the 1940s after the school had returned from its wartime evacuation.

In her first year Miss Ross spent much time studying the work of the Junior School. She considered the curriculum, textbooks, timetables, and methods of teaching; she had several long staff meetings in which she hoped to make clear the fundamental activity principles on which she felt primary school work should be based. In the end she was thoroughly dissatisfied. In her view, the primary school teaching in Morris Hall was deficient and outmoded. She dismissed the staff, advertised the positions, brought in new teachers, and made Mary Davis, then teaching in the Middle School, headmistress of Morris Hall. Miss Davis remained in that position until 1949 when she was appointed headmistress of St Catherine's School. In the following year, 1940, Wildfell, a property in Domain Road, was purchased and developed into a boarding house for junior girls.

The changing nature of the Junior School was explained in Miss Davis's report for 1940. She referred to the 'splendid co-operation during the year between the parents and staff', the improvement in the physical work and general posture of the girls, and the emphasis in physical education on music and interpretive dancing. For the very youngest children the building of 'an ideal garden nursery school' in the Phelia Grimwade House garden had been an important addition to the school. The principal movement in educational style from nursery school through Junior School was towards an activity curriculum. 'The teaching methods of today', Miss Davis reported,

> do not call for a silent class trying to digest the interesting information dealt out by a teacher. School life must be part of real life, with the children learning by their experiences through their centres of interest . . . The results of such a curriculum should appear in the form of better self-control, a greater degree of intelligent co-operation in the group, a satisfactory amount of useful information, and an increased command of the useful skills.

Her comment summed up the message of the New Education Fellowship conference held at the University of Melbourne, for which Miss Gilman Jones had closed the school to enable her whole staff to attend and profit from the ideas of some of the world's leading progressive educators.

D. J.'s action in reorganising the Junior School must have been cataclysmic for many long-serving members of staff, anticipating in some respects the 'crisis' which was to befall the school at the end of 1958. Her drastic solution to the Junior School problem was out of character, for she believed in democratic consultation and procedures, but it arose out of sheer exasperation. For the past decade she had spent her time teaching teachers up-to-date methods for primary schools. Yet on arriving at MCEGGS she found that all the Junior School work was entrenched in outmoded methods seemingly impossible to change. She felt she could not re-educate her Junior School staff.

Several further changes to the school curriculum were made in 1940. Miss Ross informed the School Council that she intended to extend the school day by one period. The extra time would be used for physical education and in the Middle School for supervised homework. She thought that too much emphasis was placed on competition among senior sporting teams and too little effort was put into broader work in physical education for all girls. She also thought that many girls were going home from school 'to empty flats too early in the afternoon'; it would be wiser to keep them usefully occupied at school.

Another significant development in the school's curriculum was the establishment in 1940 of the two new non-examination forms which became known as the School Certificate group. After sub-Intermediate, girls could take a two-year course of general education designed for those who did not wish to proceed to the Leaving Certificate and the university. The two-year course, apart from its value as a general education, was designed to prepare girls for such work as nursing, mothercraft, applied art, interior decoration, commercial activities, and further education at the Homecraft Hostel, Emily McPherson College, and the Kindergarten Training College. In the School Certificate course girls were required to take English, social studies, arithmetic, biology, art, and domestic science, and could choose one or more subjects from French, German, botany, typing and shorthand. In addition, some co-operative, social service project was carried out; in 1940 the girls adopted the Boroondara Kindergarten. The School Certificate course was the forerunner of the practical fifth form which developed at the end of the 1940s.

In 1940 no prizes were awarded at the school. The School Advisory Council suggested that the money saved should be spent on patriotic purposes such as a bursary for a girl evacuated from England or for the daughter of a person on active service. Miss Ross let it be known that she doubted the desirability of prize-giving; the practice was long-standing but perhaps set the 'wrong sort of value on things which are able to be marked'. She invited the school and parents to think about the matter and let her have their views.[6]

The story of the school's evacuation during the Second World War is told by Desma McDonald in the following chapter. The dislocation of MCEGGS during the years 1942—44 had important consequences for the later development of the school. During the exile at Marysville and Doncaster relationships throughout the school became less formal and more mutually helpful. Closer bonds were forged between the girls and the staff, and many of the girls came to accept responsibilities for the welfare of their companions and the good conduct of the school which they had not previously taken. The experience shook the school out of some of its settled ways. It had never been a thoroughly conventional school like its male counterpart in Domain Road, but it had still retained various traditional practices such as a prefect system, school prize-giving, the award of school colours for athletic performance, class lists in order of performance, and various other devices to stimulate competition. The wartime experience of the staff and the girls was a powerful catalyst to modify traditional competitive elements and to affirm more strongly the importance of co-operation and curiosity as more significant elements in learning and in democratic life.

Another important outcome of the evacuation experience arose from the significant role played by the headmistress throughout that period. Miss Ross was responsible for the basic planning and organisation of the various moves, and she was the only vital, constant, and visible link between the various parts of the divided school. Mrs Sylvia Martin (Reilly), acting headmistress for two years after Miss Ross's retirement and Old Girl of MCEGGS, graphically described the activity of the peripatetic headmistress: 'Right through the evacuation period, from March 1942 to August 1944, she sped around (ever wrestling with the 'gas-producer') from one centre to another, encouraging and cheering all, and making each section feel very important but most definitely part of the whole'.[7] Miss Ross provided a unique quality of leadership, a concern for the personal development of the staff and the girls, and a determination, despite the adverse conditions, to maintain and develop the school as a viable and interesting educational community. In those years she became the school's headmistress not merely by position but by virtue of her competence, intellectual capacity, and obvious concern for the school as a living whole.

In her speech day reports for 1948 and 1949, Miss Ross took the opportunity to explain the aims of the school and the ways in which school life was directed towards their fulfilment. Since it was a church school, the basis of all activities must be found in Christian principles, especially the belief in the 'uniqueness and wholeness of personality and the importance of seeing life as a whole and as purposeful'. In consequence, the school's task was to arrange programs so that each girl could develop best along her own individual line within a group of her contemporaries. The school, therefore, did not have a single curriculum but a range of offerings from which individual programs could be constructed suitable to the interests and abilities of each girl. In that situation material incentives such as traditional prizes had no value. The girls were encouraged 'to work for work's sake, to develop an attitude of service, to do the thing that is right for righteousness sake, and not through fear of punishment or hope of reward'. The activity of every girl in the school was important, and 'not just that of the academic or athletic'. The school must develop a balanced program in which the work and the interests of all girls were valued and cultivated.

To Dorothy Ross, the content of the curriculum, however, was not as important as the approach towards learning embodied in it. The aim of the school was not merely to cover a prescribed syllabus but to help individuals to use materials critically, to learn to think as clearly as possible, to build up a body of defensible opinions, and not to rush into precipitate judgements. In her opinion there was no place in the school for social, political, or economic propaganda; only the Christian propaganda which teaches a student respect for personality, responsibility for the whole life of the person, and the need to use all her faculties in every situation. In short, the aim of the school was

> to help immature young people to come to maturity, to help them
> build solid foundations and develop the desire to serve the
> community best in whatever way may lie before them in the future.
> Education, to be worthy of the name, must encourage a disciplined
> sense of obligation and the unfettered development of the
> individual's capacities.

Some who listened to the headmistress's exposition in 1948 apparently found difficulty in reconciling 'a disciplined sense of obligation' with 'the unfettered development of each individual's capacities'. For in her next annual report, she referred to the apparent contradiction between 'disciplined' and 'unfettered'. 'I have heard it said that girls can do what they like in this school, but that can only be thought by those who confuse discipline in the real sense with imposed external authority which brings quick results but diminishing returns.' She pointed out that a girl's freedom must be conditional on her obligations of fellowship at home, at school, and subsequently in the wider community. 'Self-expression unlimited' was socially irresponsible.[8]

By the end of the 1940s the school went from nursery level for three- and four-year-olds to sixth form which girls should complete at the age of seventeen and eighteen. It was divided into six sub-schools. The Senior School consisted of the fifth and sixth year secondary classes, in two sections. One led to the matriculation examination and entry to tertiary level courses; the other, the non-academic, provided a general education for a variety of vocations such as nursing, kindergarten teaching, and others in business and industry. By taking an extra year, it was possible to transfer through the transition sixth to the other stream.

The Middle School, third and fourth forms, and the Junior Secondary School, first and second forms, together formed the first four years of secondary education. A number of students from preparatory schools elsewhere and from state primary schools began at MCEGGS in forms one or three, substantially increasing the size of the school at the secondary level. The Primary School, grades four to six, was fed by a sub-primary group covering the preparatory grade and grades one to three, and by a kindergarten which had been given new premises in the Phelia Grimwade House garden in 1940. When Greyholm on the northern boundary was acquired in 1948, it housed the Sub-Primary School, and in 1951 was renamed Ross Hall. The primary and junior secondary classes were in Morris Hall, and the Middle and Senior School classes in Merton Hall. In 1953 the new Merton Hall was renamed Gilman Jones Hall and became the Junior Secondary School.

Each of the six divisions of the school had a teacher in charge, who was responsible to the school's headmistress, who in turn was responsible to the School Council. The Council met once a term, received a report from the headmistress, made decisions on the school's financial affairs, considered matters such as building programs, and offered observations on school policies and practices raised by the headmistress. Much of its business was transacted by subcommittees of which the Finance Committee was the most important and acted as the executive committee of the Council. It met once a month and conducted the main administrative work of the Council. Miss Ross's relationships with the Council were cordial throughout her headmistress-ship. She would sometimes float ideas with its members for possible educational changes in the school, and she found them a useful and productive sounding board.

The School Council supported her to the best of its ability. But it is the fate of any school reformer who challenges the nostalgic orthodoxies of the past to be misinterpreted and treated with suspicion. The Council's bed of roses had its thorns. A large element of the school's parent body was very conservative, living in prosperous circumstances, working in traditional professions and businesses, educated in non-state schools, and favouring conservative politics. It was in fact remarkable that, in such an environment and within the conservative profession of education, so many reformist teachers had served on the school staff in the course of its history and that the school under successive head-mistresses had been more adventurous than many otherwise comparable schools. It was not to be wondered at, therefore, that with such a staff in such a social environment, the Council was reported to have received letters from parents complaining that the girls were learning subversive political ideas and that a number of the staff and the headmistress herself were believed to be communists.[9]

The immediate post-Second World War years in Australia were redolent of ideas for social and economic change supported by various federal and State Labor governments. Towards the end of the 1940s a reaction set in, which brought changes in government and a mild anti-communist hysteria. It produced Sir Charles Lowe's Royal Commission on Communism in Victoria (1949–50), and, at the Commonwealth level, the abortive Communist Party Dissolution Bill (1950), and a failed Communist Party Dissolution Referendum (1951). In that 'cold war' atmosphere it might be expected that teachers who encouraged their pupils to question established habits and to act in more democratic ways would be regarded as revolutionaries. Indeed, to some degree they were agents of change—in much the same sense that political leaders such as Chifly and Evatt were agents of change. Miss Ross made no secret of the fact that she voted for the Australian Labor Party. Resentment at her political preference was a minor matter while she remained headmistress and continued to run the school efficiently and humanely, with the confidence of the girls, staff and Council. After her retirement, however, conservative opinion was sufficiently strong to ensure that the side of the school's tradition which she had striven to encourage would be considerably dampened. Those events are examined by Lyndsay Gardiner in chapter 7.

In D. J. Ross's period parental interest and participation in the girls' education was carefully cultivated. In that respect she built on a tradition established by Miss Gilman Jones; the Parents' Association had been in operation since 1928 to support MCEGGS financially and to maintain personal contacts with the school. The Parents' Association elected two members to the School Council and provided many of the school's amenities. More important, however, was the effort by the school staff to discuss with parents changes in school practices and policies, and to consult them on questions of placement, selection of courses, and the general progress of the girls. A regular *Newsletter* to parents written by staff was the outcome of a parent-teacher conference in 1952. It appeared twice a term and dealt with items suggested by parents on school policy and practice. A comprehensive *Handbook for the Information of Parents* was also prepared. Many of the parents were former students and belonged to the Old Grammarians' Society which took a lively interest in the school and elected three members to the School Council. In the mid-1940s, too, about ten members of the school staff were Old Girls. They and many other members of the Old Grammarians' Society were a source of great support to the headmistress and to the school. It was the Old Grammarians' Society which requested that the building for the Junior School, acquired in 1951, be named Ross Hall. When Miss Ross announced her intention to retire in 1955 the editor of the Old Grammarians' newsletter reported that 'Everyone is desolate'. [10]

In the 1930s educational authorities began to be aware of the usefulness of psychological services in schools. The Australian Council for Educational Research (ACER), established in Melbourne in 1930, experimented with a variety of tests and promoted psychological and vocational guidance for school students. A psychology branch was set up in the Victorian Education Department in 1947. Among the independent schools MCEGGS was one of the first to employ a full-time school counsellor on its staff, appointing Alison Winfield, an Old Girl, to the position in 1944. At first she worked mainly with the primary classes, but soon moved into counselling with the lower secondary girls and the organisation of vocational guidance. Miss Winfield assessed the ability and attainment of each girl on entry, and set up a record which continued for the whole of the student's life. At fourth form level the counsellor interviewed each girl, built up individual vocational profiles and discussed them with the headmistress. The process was designed to help in the placement of the girls at fifth form level, in consultation with the parents. Miss Winfield also conducted a follow-up of the students until they entered their first job or completed their further education.

Miss Ross's first task had been to recast the Primary School curriculum into an activity pattern, and this had been done before the wartime evacuation. In subsequent years the activity curriculum was further developed and extended into the secondary level.

A pamphlet on the school written in 1953 by a group of non-matriculation sixth form girls stated that:

> Throughout the School activity methods are used whenever possible. Girls are encouraged to find out themselves and to learn by doing. This means that a great deal of work is done by means of assignments, and the Library is the centre for this. Dramatisations are used in English, Social Studies and Language work . . . In all subjects excursions by the whole form, or small groups, form an important part of the work. [11]

The school, however, did not operate to a pre-set design. Miss Ross denied that she ever had any grand idea of what the school might become. She regarded education, like politics, not as an exact science but as an exercise in the possible. The school's characteristics developed gradually through staff, student, and parent discussion, through the good sense and particular talents of teachers, and in accordance with what was then seen to be good educational practice. Yet the practice and organisation which came to characterise MCEGGS would never have emerged if staff and headmistress had not felt that a school should value individual expression and strive to become a community which shared experience and responsibility. To that extent there was a general theory lying behind the development of the school throughout the Ross era. But the actual practices which emerged were not part of a carefully thought out blueprint. They emerged slowly from many suggestions by girls and staff, and from much discussion, trial, and modification in committees. In that way, the school developed into what was later described as 'a democratic community', attending to the academic and pre-vocational development of its students and to their personal and social maturity.[12] The organisation of the curriculum throughout the secondary school exemplified that way of thinking and proceeding.

When she became headmistress Miss Ross had been intensely interested in the primary level. Yet she recalled that she became more interested in the first and second years of the secondary course because 'these are the most important years for the secondary school pupils: that is where they are made or marred, and mostly marred . . . I put the best teachers there'. Those years could 'set the stage and in point of fact I think that was where, in the Grammar School, all the good work was done'. As head of the Junior Secondary School she appointed Olive Russell, whom she described as 'a teacher after my own heart', who had joined the staff when the girls went to Marysville and remained throughout Miss Ross's era.[13]

By 1953 at the junior secondary level the girls were in a separate area of Morris Hall with a library, laboratory, and art room to themselves. Each form experienced the responsibility of running its own affairs with its own committee. The girls also gradually became accustomed to the more specialised teaching of secondary school work. They had some activities which involved them with more senior girls, while maintaining a sense of community within their own school grouping.

From the first to the fourth secondary year the school retained the parallel organisation of classes introduced by Miss Gilman Jones, with no distinction made between girls on the basis of intelligence or attainment. In the first year, English, social studies, physical education, and arithmetic were the main subjects which took five or six periods each per week, and, in addition, science, singing, art, manual work, library, mathematics, and languages occupied between one and three periods each per week. There were also two free-choice periods, and one per week for a committee meeting of each form. The form committee period was the sixth period of Thursday throughout the school and, since it appeared as a line runing from top to bottom on the master timetable, it became known as the vertical period.

In the second year of secondary level, a little more than half the program consisted of subjects taken in common—English, social studies, science, physical education, scripture, singing, library, and art and manual art. Girls were arranged in sets within the classes according to ability for mathematics or arithmetic, and French and/or Latin. They also studied home science, and extra English or arithmetic if they were weak in those subjects. The free periods were to enable students to undertake projects for which they might have a particular interest or talent. Craft, hobbies, sport, reading, art, dressmaking and cooking were among the choices.

The Middle School by name began in the third form but, educationally, the third form was part of a four-year, co-ordinated, secondary program which included forms one to four. The first two-year period, the junior secondary, was largely diagnostic, and a considerable amount of the school counsellor's time was spent with those girls. The range of subjects in the third form was similar to that of the second form but was slightly more extended. More time was allowed for science, mathematics and languages, an additional language could be taken, and craft became one of the electives. In the fourth form more time again was allotted to science, mathematics and language, and the choice of subjects was widened—geography, musical appreciation, shorthand and typing were added.

The range of subjects was such that few girls had exactly the same timetable. Much of the teaching and learning still followed activity lines but more academic procedures in language, mathematics and science were beginning. An important feature throughout the school was small group work—an exercise in planning, intellectual discussion and social co-operation.

At the end of the fourth secondary school year students could sit for the state-wide Intermediate examination controlled by the Schools Board of the University of Melbourne. In 1916, the Board had begun a scheme which enabled secondary schools to apply for permission to conduct their own examinations at the

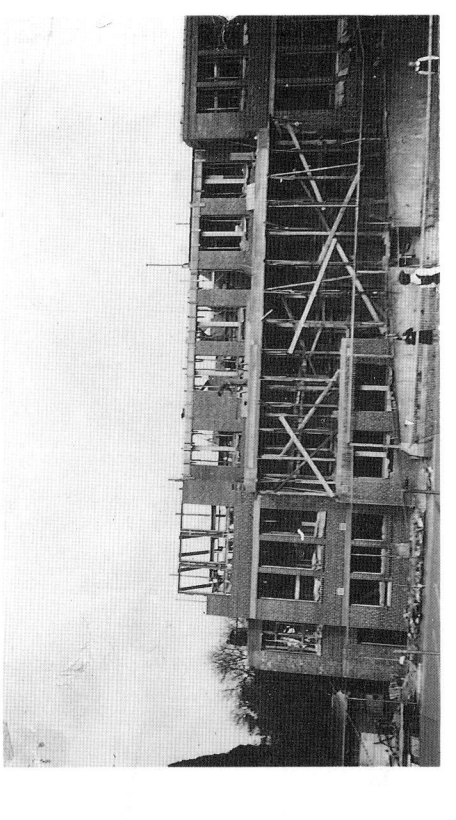

Four stages in the building of New Merton Hall in the 1930s. Later the building was renamed Gilman Jones Hall in memory of the former Headmistress.

Miss D. J. Ross, eminent educationist and Headmistress from 1939 to 1955.

(*Left*) Miss Alison Winfield and her 'family' of eight girls at Marysville, 1942. (*Right*) Outside gymnastics at Doncaster, 1942, Nancy Tait performing handstand supported by Althea Stretton (partly obscured) and Helen Webster.

Teachers and Helpers Mt Kitchener, 1942.
Standing L. to R., 'Nursie' — Nancy Price (née Lucas), Enid Miles, Margaret Mellor, Betty Sewell, Marie Donaldson, Serena McLean, Joan Mellor, Helen Price (née Evans), Alison Winfield. In front, Phyllis Knox (née Waitt), Thea Wilkinson.

Miss Edith Mountain, Michelle
Allan, and Sally Anderson, with
Bulfa, 1960.

Miss Edith Mountain and Staff, 1968.

Intermediate (fourth form) and Leaving (fifth form) Certificate levels. The schools whose applications were successful were referred to as Class-A schools, and the Schools Board certificates were awarded on the basis of the school's own internal examinations. As we have seen, Miss Gilman Jones had decided against applying to have MCEGGS made a Class-A school. During the 1940s, however, both Miss Ross and her staff were persuaded of the advantages of the freedom to design and organise their own curriculum without the restraint of external prescription by the Board's syllabuses and examinations. After considerable discussion the school applied successfully to the Board and became a Class-A school in 1944 for the Intermediate Certificate and in 1948 for the Leaving Certificate.

In the fifth and sixth forms the bifurcation in curriculum which had been slowly increasing from the second form became more distinct with the establishment of an academic and a practical stream. For many years educators had argued about the desirability of regarding secondary education as primarily a preparation for university studies. Australian secondary schools had been founded in the second half of the nineteenth century and the early twentieth century largely with that purpose in mind. By the 1920s it had become apparent that most students who entered secondary schools did not complete the full course, and that only a small proportion of secondary school students proceeded to university. The courses offered in secondary education, however, continued to be an academic preparation for public examinations with syllabuses, standards and tests largely under university control. In the 1930s and 1940s there was much discussion in educational circles about the objectives of secondary education and the need to broaden its curriculum to serve more adequately the students who were not intending to qualify for a university education.

The development of the Class-A system had made it more feasible to break away from the orthodox curriculum but very few schools attempted to do so. The principal argument against the Class-A system was that standards would deteriorate if there was any serious departure from the long-accepted academic pattern in the teaching, curriculum and examining in those schools. The girls at MCEGGS who took the matriculation examination and went to the university were among the more successful of university students, but by 1950 they represented only about one-quarter of the total number of school leavers. It was Miss Ross's view that the curriculum leading to matriculation at the university was a specialised kind of preparation which provided neither a suitable general education nor an appropriate pre-vocational education for the large proportion of girls who did not wish to go to the university or did not qualify to do so.

> the *majority* of girls [she suggested in her John Smyth Memorial Lecture] learn most easily by dealing with concrete and particular things of which they have already had day-to-day experience. For them 'activities' are more stimulating than books. They learn more directly from things and processes and from social activity than indirectly from books. It has taken us who are teachers a long time to find this out. We are bookish ourselves, and tend to think that the only criterion of education is ability in book-learning.[14]

Under earlier headmistresses special provision at various levels had been made for girls who did not intend to take the external public examinations or proceed to the university, but none of the schemes had lasted. Even in Miss Ross's time the special course in fourth and fifth forms leading to a School Certificate issued by MCEGGS lacked prestige among parents, staff and girls. The staff had to work hard to persuade a parent that they 'were not casting a slur on her daughter' when they recommended her for the internal School Certificate course. It was not until MCEGGS became a Class-A school that a reasonable degree of acceptance was gained, with the Schools Board's Leaving Certificate issued upon internal examination. Thus the practical fifth form was born.

For girls who felt that they might have been misdirected into the practical fifth there was a transition sixth in which they could spend a year and then go into the matriculation sixth form. Other girls who stayed on for an additional year after their Leaving Certificate taken in the practical fifth could continue in the post-Leaving sixth form with more advanced work of the same kind. At the end of that year the students could gain the school's post-Leaving Certificate which was recognised by the Nursing Board, the School of Occupational Therapy, and the Kindergarten Union, but not the university's Schools Board.

An ex-student of the practical fifth and transition sixth reported that she enjoyed the work in both classes, particularly history with Mrs Lloyd who introduced them to the study of original texts and library research; she also appreciated the approach of Miss Davis, their French teacher, and Miss Nugent in English who were both 'good actresses' and taught 'in a dynamic style'. Miss Ross took them for scripture which was really an intellectual exercise in comparative religion.[15]

There was nothing excitingly different about the school's

The organisation of MCEGGS in the Ross era.

School year	Age during year					
Merton Hall	13	[Extra VI]				**Senior School**
	12 or 13	17–18	Matric VI		Final VI	
	12	16–17	Transition VI			
	11	16	Year V	Year V	Year V	Year V	
	10	15	Year IV	Year IV	Year IV	Year IV	**Middle School**
	9	14	Year III	Year III	Year III	Year III	
Gilman Jones Hall	8	13	Year II	Year II	Year II	**Junior Secondary School**
	7	12	Year I	Year I	Year I	
Morris Hall	6	11	Grade VI	Grade VI	[Grade VI]	**Primary School**
	5	10	Grade V	Grade V		
	4	9	Grade IV	Grade IV		
Ross Hall	3	8	Grade III			**Sub-Primary**
	2	7	Grade II			
	1	6	Grade I and Prep. Grade			
		5	Kindergarten			

SECONDARY | PRIMARY

Note: Each rectangle represents a class of from twenty-five to thirty pupils. An Extra VI is shown to indicate that girls occasionally spent two years in a Matric VI.

curriculum. It was a fairly traditional program, carefully arranged, well taught, and modified to provide a richer experience of cultural and pre-vocational activities than were available in most comparable girls' schools in Australia. To make an inroad into the customary academic curriculum was quite an achievement but it was not a radical break with tradition. It was a change in spirit and outlook within a fairly traditional framework.

In that manner, Miss Ross was following a trend already apparent in the school's history, and proposed by many educators in the 1920s and 1930s. Miss Ross became progressive only in a modest way. She accepted the need for greater attention to individual needs and capacities, and for the cultivation of a school with a thoughtful community life. MCEGGS was not and did not ever become a progressive school in the sense that other contemporary Victorian schools such as Preshil or Koornong did. It was not driven, for example, by a particular social or psychoanalytical theory, nor was it developed according to a set plan. It remained a school with, for the most part, a traditional academic program and an organisation familiar to many teachers in other schools. What was interesting and important about the school during Miss Ross's headmistressship was its gradual development into a community of persons who were much more caring, who were more inclined to think intelligently, and who had broader general and vocational interests than were commonly found in most schools of that period.

At the heart of Dorothy Ross's educational philosophy and practice was the school as a co-operative democratic community. Introduction into democratic ways was a gradual process, which started with the staff. As physics teacher Elizabeth Pownall recalled, Miss Ross established from the outset a rapport with the teaching staff, many of whom were already friends and acquaintances, to an extent that was unprecedented in the closing years under Miss Gilman Jones.[16] Miss Ross thought of her relations with her staff as those of a conductor with an orchestra:

> I would throw out ideas at staff meetings [she said] and they would thrash them out. We'd work out how these ideas could be put into practice and they'd know much better than I would . . . the orchestra knows a lot better than the conductor how to play an oboe, but the conductor knows the sort of sounds that he wants to come out of the oboe.[17]

Staff meetings chaired by the headmistress were held once a month, and they were used to dissect school policies. The chief-of-staff produced an agenda from suggestions made by the staff and headmistress, and the items were thoroughly discussed until there was something like unanimity before they were put into operation. Some decisions needed much time — sometimes several years — and much discussion before they could be satisfactorily made. One of the teachers later wrote: 'We were, as I remember, an argumentative staff. But if we were argumentative the outcome of staff meetings was always constructive, never destructive. We were left with the strong conviction that we were building.'[18] The school thus had an enthusiastic staff with a high level of continuity. In turn, from their own experience of democratic relationships they undertook the task of teaching self-discipline and self-government to their students as 'an important part of their job'.[19]

Beginning at primary level, the girls gradually learned to make decisions individually and in groups. In secondary classes planning, discussing, and decision-making became more conscious with increasing skill. For the purposes of class management each class was a committee with office-bearers changed each half-year. The vertical period was a formal weekly meeting for each form to transact its business. The meeting was chaired by the elected form captain, its minutes were kept by the secretary, and regular reports were received from all office-bearers. In the Junior Secondary School the form teacher played an active, guiding role; from the third form on, it was expected that her role would become less prominent. In addition, there were special interest committees, such as those for social services, library and the school dance, run by fifth and sixth form girls. They were elected from the girls who shared the particular interest, included a staff member, and were run with similar care.

The most important of the committees was the School Executive Council. Before the school experienced its wartime dislocation the School Advisory Council had worked side by side with the prefects. The Advisory Council gradually developed executive powers, widened its franchise, and absorbed the prefect system. It took six patient years. By 1948 Miss Ross was able to announce on speech day that the Senior School, the prefects, and the staff had voted to establish a School Executive Council elected from the staff, senior girls, and school activity groups. The prefect system was discontinued.

The new School Executive Council consisted of five staff and twenty-five student members and was chaired by a student. Any school matter could come up for discussion but the headmistress could exercise a veto on decisions which related to religion, health, curriculum, problems of behaviour or school finance. For all other matters, the new Council had executive as well as advisory powers, and could make regulations and administer them. Explaining the Council's functions to parents, a school newsletter stated:

> In the first place the girls are given an opportunity to express through a legitimate channel their ideas for the improvement of the running of the School. In the second, girls learn the technique of running meetings, the tolerance of reasoned discussion and the unexpected difficulties in making changes however desirable. And lastly, they learn how to carry out an official job in a responsible and creative way.[20]

The establishment of the School Executive Council was at one with the total school ethos of co-operation rather than competition. Distinguished composer and musician, Helen Gifford, described the school experience from the point of view of a former student:

It was fortunate that the six years which I spent at MCEGGS were at a time when Dorothy Ross was headmistress. Especially from 1949 to 1952, the atmosphere in the senior school was one of free-thinking independence that came from girls being encouraged to form their own opinions, and to accept nothing without question . . . Miss Ross saw that intellectual maturity was possible at an earlier stage of adolescence than was normally provided for by school curricula in those days, and she encouraged it in students for some years before they were due to leave school, so that they might be better prepared to take up employment or enter university . . . The introduction of an executive council softened the standard divisions within the school hierarchy. Staff and senior students were more on a level, and the girls, collectively as well as individually, were expected to be responsible for their own behaviour. [21]

Another Old Girl wrote: 'the most important thing was that we were regarded as people—and quite responsible people at that. Our opinions were listened to and we were not prevented from making "constructive mistakes"'. [22]

Not all teachers and parents were fond of free-thinking girls. It was a 'vital and alive place', a teacher wrote, but it was 'not an easy life' for teachers—'one finished the day tired from an exacting but deeply satisfying (usually) day's work'. [23] Some teachers still thought of their work as routine academic teaching; they were not part of the 'argumentative staff'. Some found the school too unsettling and resigned, telling Miss Ross they wanted a quieter life. They looked back to the setting and academic tone of the school in Miss Gilman Jones's time, unconscious of the fact that she too was regarded as a notable reformer. To deal with replacements Miss Ross usually had a bundle of letters from teachers interested in joining the school. [24] By and large, the staff was a very stable one; the great majority enjoyed their busy life. Sylvia Martin, for many years chief-of-staff, recalled that the school under Miss Ross was 'very alive'; the staff was 'greatly interested in Miss Ross's ideas and their co-operation was at a high level'. [25]

Except for the two mid-war years when the school was evacuated to Marysville and Doncaster, the D. J. Ross era was one of continuous and rapid growth in enrolments. From a school of 540 in 1939 it rose to 600 in 1941, fell away to 480 in 1943, accelerated to 740 in 1948, continued to 890 in the Jubilee Year of 1953, and finally in 1955 topped the 900 mark. Two-thirds of the school's 900 girls were in the secondary forms. In 1939 it had been a modest-sized independent school; fifteen years later it had grown to be one of the largest girls' schools in Victoria. In consequence, it had continually enlarged its premises by purchasing neighbouring houses and by building new, and remodelling old, accommodation.

The growth was part of a general rapid increase in secondary school attendance throughout Australia, and it was also an expression of confidence in the conduct and program of the school. But Miss Ross was always uneasy about the growth in numbers. As she pointed out to the School Council in 1954 when she announced her coming retirement, the increase in numbers was accompanied by a rapid increase in expense. Because of its comprehensive program of education MCEGGS was particularly vulnerable. Much of the school's expense resulted from its philosophy and its broad curriculum — art, music, crafts, domestic arts and commercial subjects — yet they also enhanced its reputation. It would be much easier to run and less expensive, Miss Ross confessed, if it were simply an academic school like most other independent schools. She would not be happy to see such a change, but she thought that the Council should consider the situation and make up its mind before it proceeded to appoint a new headmistress. [26] In the light of later developments at MCEGGS her words were prophetic.

In the D. J. Ross era from 1939 to 1955 the emphasis at the school was on intangibles rather than measurables. Of primary importance was the quality of a girl's intellectual work, her independence of thought, her responsibility towards the school society, her ability to share, co-operate, build, and flourish in a school which was becoming a democratic community. For such matters no formal marks or prizes were possible or appropriate. The school curriculum, however, made it clear that there were facts, skills, and ideas to be learnt and that they had to be formally tested. The school did not neglect that side of its work; it was important and it was well performed, but the education of the girls was something much more than preparation for success in competitive examinations.

Education at the school was a process of growing up into a responsible, thoughtful, caring and, if possible, wise person. That was not a revolutionary doctrine, but it was more sophisticated and imaginative than the traditional program in most comparable schools at that time. Miss Ross, who set the tone and made the pace during her seventeen years as headmistress, was neither a visionary nor a radical innovator. She was a thoughtful, hard-headed reformer in tune with the democratic, educational and political spirit of the 1930s and 1940s. She and her staff saw the importance of providing an appropriate curriculum, organisation and set of experiences for girls who were growing up in a democratic society. They began the induction of their students into the kinds of intellectual, practical and social experiences which would fit them for a full and useful life in the mid-twentieth century.

After her retirement in 1955 D. J. Ross returned to her earlier work of teacher education. The ATTI had moved and changed its name to Mercer House. Miss Ross rejoined it and took over the preparation of the more mature part-time students. She enjoyed the work and her students enjoyed her wisdom. Twelve years later, in 1969, when she was seventy-eight years of age, she retired for a second time. She died in 1982 at the age of ninety-one. Her task had been, as the Reverend Dr Davis McCaughey pointed out in the memorial service, 'not that of destroying and remaking an unsympathetic tradition but one of remoulding and redirecting it. She was not a revolutionary, but she was more than a reformer.'[27]

Portrait of Miss D. J. Ross, 1979, by Diana Mogensen.

Desma P. McDonald

6 *The war years, 1939-45: an oral history*

THE OPENING OF THE SCHOOL YEAR IN 1939 USHERED IN a period of significant change in the history of MCEGGS. The school assembled on 15 February 1939 in an atmosphere of intense excitement awaiting the entrance of Archbishop F. W. Head, president of the School Council, and the school chaplain, then Reverend C. H. Murray.[1] On that occasion, the archbishop was to introduce to the girls their new head-mistress, Dorothy J. Ross. As W. F. Connell has shown, Miss Ross was to be the initiator of many innovations which significantly changed the school. Another source of cataclysmic change occurred on 3 September 1939 when the prime minister of Australia, then R. G. Menzies, announced by radio that Australia had declared war on Germany, and had thereby entered the Second World War. This decision rendered inevitable for the nation personal sacrifices, restrictions and full co-operation with the demands of wartime.

Writing of Australia's involvement in the Second World War, some authors have referred to the period from 1939 to the end of 1941, when Japan bombed Pearl Harbour, as a time of 'business as usual'. Despite a number of wartime restrictions which included the rationing of petrol, food and clothing, the formation of groups such as the Voluntary Aid Detachment (VAD) and the Air Raid Precautions (ARP), most Australians regarded the war as remote.[2] Certainly, at MCEGGS Miss Ross was planning for the future without any anticipated interruption.

Yet the encroachments of the distant war were inevitable. Judith Harley (née White) recalled that during 1939 her mother, then Mrs T. W. White (later Lady White) became Victorian

Divisional Commandant of the Red Cross Society. The school magazine reported that Mrs White was elected president of the Red Cross Emergency Service and that through the suggestion of Mrs White, other Old Grammarians and parents of girls were invited to attend first aid classes and instruction in anti-gas measures and home-nursing at the school. Mabel Merfield, the school librarian, became the superintendent in charge of these arrangements.[3]

Families and children arrived in Australia as the result of war-related events. Some had been evacuated or were escaping from Europe, England and Asia and a few of the children sought entry to MCEGGS. In 1939 Dr Shirley MacLeish (née Coombes) and her younger sister, Josephine, became students at MCEGGS after arriving from England following the appointment of their father as head of the Aeronautical Research Division in Australia. Louise Baker and her younger sister, Marigold, whose father was a commander in the Navy, arrived in Melbourne from England during July 1939 and feeling very isolated and unhappy, came under the care of Miss I. Wellings at the Junior Boarding House in Walsh Street.[4]

In 1940 further reminders of the war came when a former student, Staff Nurse Nancy Wilson, spoke to the Junior School about Anzac Day before going abroad with the nurses of the Australian Imperial Forces (AIF). At the annual luncheon for the Old Grammarians' Society a presentation was made to another nurse, Barbara Haynes, also going abroad with the AIF and the school captain, Patricia Stillman, gave a report on the school's war effort.[5] At a meeting of the School Council, Miss Ross reported that a member of the teaching staff, Miss T. Greeves, had resigned to go to air training.[6]

During 1940 the war situation worsened on the European front and by June the German armies had overrun Holland, Belgium and most of France. The French government was compelled to ask for an armistice and Italy had entered the war in support of the German leaders. To R. G. Menzies, it seemed that Britain and people of British heritage such as Australians, were being left to defend the free world. Menzies made a rousing public appeal for 'sacrifice . . . unremitting toil, [and] unflinching devotion'.[7] The Menzies government introduced an amendment to the *National Security Act* which gave enormous power to the Commonwealth government. The new section included regulations which required people to place themselves, their services and their property at the disposal of the Commonwealth.[8]

At MCEGGS during the early part of 1941, the effects of the worsening war situation continued to be felt in many small ways. It was decided to publish only two editions of the school magazine, in July and December, and owing to the paper rationing, even the size of these issues was to be reduced for the duration of the war. These magazines contained reports of various wartime projects such as the School War Purposes Fund, the Red Cross Emergency Service Company and the Red Cross Branch. These and subsequent editions of the school magazine published lists of Old Grammarians who were engaged in wartime activities. Lady Winifred MacKenzie (née Smith) was the first woman doctor to enlist in the Army Medical Corps. Fay Hollow and Margaret Mack were nurses abroad with the AIF. At Red Cross House, doing full-time voluntary work were Eileen Calvert and Jeanette Caldwell. Going overseas with the VAD were Margaret Stone and Doreen Townsend. There were three volunteers in the first training course for the Women's Australian Auxiliary Air Force (WAAAF): Margaret Blackwood, Helen Drummond and Jean Wallace Mitchell. Margaret Blackwood, Jean Wallace Mitchell, Gladys Onians, Yvonne Tuckfield (née Spry), Betty Rapke and Marjorie Wooton all became officers. Others joined the Women's Royal Australian Navy Service: Lorena Emms, Celia Wilkinson, Margaret Wood, Alison Hailes, Margaret Sanderson, Lottie McGrath, Betty Sellick and Noelie Currie. Listed also were those who joined the Australian Women's Army Service (AWAS): Margaret Snowball, Dorothy Sholl, Enid Shawe, Betty Wallace Mitchell, Cynthia Walters, Pat Fethers, Jeanette Keys, Betty Jess and Margot Thompson. Dorothy Gidison and Claire Nickson were masseurs at the Heidelberg Military Hospital.

There was an unexpected change in the teaching staff when Miss M. Monteith, who had been at the school for eleven years, was selected for training in industrial welfare work by the Commonwealth Department of Labour and National Service.[9] As the war continued each edition of the school magazine listed the names of an increasing number of former students who were now married or engaged to be married to men in the armed forces. Two former MCEGGS students who have supplied details of their war service are Elaine Markby (née Francis) who joined the Royal Australian Air Force, WAAAF branch, as a telegraph operator in 1942, becoming '105222 ACW Francis E.O.', and Margaret MacKenzie. Margaret joined the AWAS from the beginning of 1943, soon after her eighteenth birthday, and became a radar technician performing duties which enabled the release of young men for service overseas.[10]

During 1941 air-raid drill was introduced at MCEGGS and is recalled with clarity by girls who participated.[11] Since each girl was required to leave the school grounds and run across Anderson

Street to the Botanic Gardens to hide among the shrubs, it is remembered as an exciting and enjoyable diversion. At this stage the School Council was apparently not contemplating any damage to property because during 1941 planning continued for the purchase of Wildfell. The purchase of this property fulfilled a most urgent need for Junior School accommodation. There were some quick alterations and the involvement of girls from the newly formed School Certificate group. These fifth form girls painted beds and made bedspreads for the room allotted to the six youngest boarders.[12] Boarders were able to move in on the first day of third term, 17 September 1941, with Mary Davis living there in charge of the juniors. The influence of the war was evident at speech day on 17 September 1941 when instead of prizes, certificates were distributed by Sybil Irving, M.B.E., founder and controller of the AWAS.

Plans for the evacuation of Australia's schoolchildren had been formulated well before Japan's entry into the war.[13] Government representatives had evaluated the buildings of various schools to assess the possibility of moving public service departments to the suburbs. Following the Pearl Harbour attack on 9 December 1941, the long anticipated war in the Pacific Ocean became a reality. Within a week plans were being made by the state governments and private organisations for the evacuation of children from the coastal areas of Australia to the country.[14] At this stage, plans were being made by parents and authorities at MCEGGS for a private evacuation of girls from the junior and middle sections of the school to a safer area away from Anderson Street, South Yarra, as the proximity of the school to the city made it a possible target for Japanese attacks.[15] As the war intensified with the Allied defeat in the Battle of the Java Sea on 27 February 1942, MCEGGS authorities and parents decided to expedite the private evacuation of part of the school.

During late February discussions took place between Miss Ross and government officials. Miss Ross was told that more administrative offices were urgently required near Victoria Barracks in St Kilda Road, particularly to house Americans, and that no special consideration could be given to girls' schools when the time came to move. Occupation of several schools strategically placed near the barracks had already been planned. The schools selected were Melbourne Grammar School, Wesley College, Melbourne High School, MacRobertson Girls' High School, and MCEGGS, and no exceptions were to be made. Miss Ross was able to bargain with the officials for the assistance of Red Cross cars, the use of a special train, three days to complete the move, and the offer of a number of possible sites for evacuation.

Shirley MacLeish commenced writing her schoolgirl's diary in mid-February 1942 and prefaced her first entry with a brief note 'to bring things up to date': 'The Japs have bombed Darwin [and] everyone is digging air raid shelters'.[16] In Melbourne, fear of bombardment resulted in various precautionary measures. At MCEGGS girls received directions to gather their evacuation equipment and have every article marked and packed in a haversack ready for inspection by Thursday 26 February 1942. Teachers had the job of checking the contents of the haversacks and decisions concerning sufficient quantities of sanitary towels for the older girls posed a persistent problem. Parents phoned each other as speculation mounted about the date for the evacuation.[17]

After inspecting several possible sites for evacuation, Miss Ross, Miss Davis and Dr Vera Scantlebury Brown (née Scantlebury), the school doctor, consulted with other MCEGGS authorities and decided on three large guest houses in Marysville: Kooringa, Mt Kitchener House and Marylands. Healesville Golf House had been suggested but was taken by Melbourne Grammar School.[18] Evacuation circulars dated 1 and 2 March 1942 were sent to parents of girls in the Junior and Middle Schools. On Monday 2 March 1942 the school met as a whole for the last time for two and a half years. Miss Ross announced that the Junior and Middle Schools would be evacuating to Marysville by the end of the week.

The following day it was announced that Wednesday 4 March would be a holiday so that all the Morris Hall equipment could be packed and labelled. The evacuation took place over two days with assistance from some of the senior girls. On Thursday 5 March 1942 all girls in the school up to and including second form were evacuated. With them went a number of younger brothers and sisters, some as young as eighteen months, whose parents wanted their families to stay together during the anticipated catastrophes. The Red Cross Emergency Service agreed to transport all children under the age of eight and the cars lined up in Anderson Street to pick up their passengers. Alison Winfield remembers that at the last moment two young children, aged twenty months and two years, were passed through the car windows by their mothers made anxious by the drama of the departure.[19] The government made a train available for travel from Richmond station to Healesville station and the final stage of the journey was completed by bus to Kooringa and Mt Kitchener House. The following day, Friday 6 March, form three was moved to Marylands. The Middle School move was assisted by senior girls who took control of the luggage because there were no porters at Richmond station.

Although Miss Ross had not planned to move the Senior School (the fifth and sixth forms, including the School Certificate group) until a later date, notification was received on 5 March 1942 that the army was to takeover the whole school premises. There was a compulsory holiday for senior girls on Tuesday 10 March because army transports were expected at the school to transport the equipment to Marysville. Meanwhile Miss Ross had the task of choosing another location within commuting distance of Melbourne for the remaining part of the school. After 'the inspection of all the stately homes of Melbourne, South Yarra, Toorak, Armadale [and] Balwyn', where she rejected O. Gilpin's mansion on several points including the rather curious grounds that it had black marble bathrooms, Miss Ross chose the Eastern Golf Club at Doncaster and accepted the offer of three private homes in Balwyn for boarding houses.[20] At South Yarra the Senior School had settled down for a couple of days to its former routine. Then on Friday 13 March Miss Ross announced that it would have to move and a holiday of indefinite length was granted while negotiations were completed. Teachers now had the job of packing items such as chemistry laboratory equipment which could not be trusted to inexperienced packers. Elizabeth Pownall recalls taking home the precious Fortin barometer for temporary safe storage.[21]

Teachers were given the option of going either to Marysville or Doncaster. Mrs M. Smith (née Morrison), head-of-staff in 1941, chose to resign and Sylvia Martin (née Reilly) took her place and transferred to Marysville to be in charge of Marylands. Among the teachers who chose to go to Marysville were Mary Davis, Gwenda Lloyd (née Kent Hughes), Betty Sewell, Lilian Bennett (née White), Alison Winfield, Margaret Mellor and her sister Joan Mellor (not a trained teacher at that time), Trude Knight (née Cox), Enid Shann (née Wilson), Joan Webb, Pat Weir, Freda Hooper (née Mavin), Phil Knox (née Waitt), Marjorie Cromie (née Tye), Irene Webb, Mollie Bayne, Joan Waite (née Turner) and Fay Dobson (née Anderson).[22] Ruth Creer (née Chisholm) had married six months previously and chose Doncaster to remain near her husband. At the last moment, however, Freda Mavin developed acute appendicitis and Ruth Creer was obliged to replace her at Marysville. In the six weeks that it took Freda Mavin to recover, Ruth remained at Marysville often gazing at the surrounding hills, seeing no way out of 'the wretched place'. Eventually Ruth Creer joined the teaching staff at Doncaster but she then had the complication of travelling on the crowded school bus in a state of early pregnancy suffering from 'morning sickness'.[23] Ultimately all the teaching staff at

Marysville were allowed alternate weekends free and it was possible to travel back to Melbourne to maintain contact with family and friends.

The sudden orders to vacate MCEGGS and the other four schools by 16 March 1942 were caused by the arrival of high-level United States army personnel, in particular General Douglas MacArthur, Commander-in-Chief of the United States Pacific War Zone. Ironically, MacArthur made his headquarters in the Menzies Hotel, refusing offers of several 'luxurious private mansions'.[24] At MCEGGS, by Monday 16 March 1942 all school and boarding-house equipment had been moved out, either to Marysville or Doncaster. It was decided to send part of Senior School to Marysville and the departure of the School Certificate group of a further twenty-eight girls took place on Friday 20 March, bound for another guest house, Roseleigh. Gwenda Lloyd was placed in charge of Roseleigh and brought her six-year-old son Phillip to live in Marysville whilst leaving her daughter and husband in Melbourne. The decision to send the School Certificate group provided much needed assistance with the sub-primary children at Mt Kitchener House. Enid Shann recalled that these senior girls helped with the little ones by playing with them, bathing and putting them to bed, thus relieving 'the hard-pressed staff'.[25] As it turned out, the Americans did not occupy MCEGGS because, before the necessary alternations were carried out, the United States administrators moved to Queensland. The school then became the location for the RAAF Directorate of Recruiting including members of the WAAAF.[26]

The evacuation of the whole school was unexpected and came as a blow to all concerned. There was a great sense of loss but there was also a recognition that an opportunity existed for the building of new traditions that would be 'all the stronger for having been made under adverse conditions'.[27] At first glance it would seem that 'adverse conditions' was an exaggeration when describing Marysville. Before the Second World War, Marysville was already a popular holiday resort and the district was familiar to some MCEGGS girls. The family home of Betty and Roma Stephens was located at Healesville on the south side of the Black Spur en route to Marysville. Often friends of Alison, Jean and Mildred Hailes had been invited to stay for school holidays at the Hailes holiday home in Marysville. There were several guest houses where guests could enjoy a comfortable relaxing holiday in beautiful surroundings. The four guest houses occupied by MCEGGS during the evacuation were among the best and Marylands was the most notable.

During the evacuation Mt Kitchener House was occupied by

the lower part of the Junior School, the Kindergarten and the Nursery School, and included seventy-three children aged from eighteen months to nine years. Kooringa housed the upper age groups of the Junior School, ninety girls of nine, ten and eleven years of age in a guest house intended for fifty. Marylands housed 140 Middle School girls aged between eleven and fourteen years. Roseleigh took the School Certificate group. Later a small group of Junior School girls was moved from Kooringa to Roseleigh. In all there were 315 students recorded as boarders at Marysville.[28] Apart from the official teaching staff there were mothers such as the two doctors, Vera Scantlebury Brown, mother of Catherine James (née Brown), and Gladys Ferguson, mother of Alison Hunt (née Ferguson). Other mothers were nursing sisters and there were also children's nurses, one of whom, Nancy Price (née Lucas), accompanied Jacqueline Clarke (née Ward-Ambler) and was affectionately known to all as 'nursie'. Alison Winfield remembers an English woman, Marie Donaldson, and her two small children, Hamish and Patricia. Marie Donaldson made her home at Mt Kitchener House on arrival in Australia from Malaya after her husband had become a prisoner of war.[29] Mary Davis remembered Margaret Woodward, who, with her two small daughters, Joan and Ann, had recently arrived from Hong Kong. With her husband missing due to the Japanese occupation Margaret Woodward made Kooringa her home and helped the teachers.[30]

On arrival, the external appearance of the four guest houses was much the same in 1942 as before the declaration of war. Conditions inside were quite a different story. Following the mobilisation of women for the war effort, domestic staff was virtually unavailable. Austerity conditions, including rationing of petrol, had curtailed holidays in the country.[31] The guest houses had deteriorated rapidly. When the evacuation parties arrived on 5 and 6 March 1942 during a heatwave of 104°F (37°C), they were confronted with serious accommodation problems. The most pressing problem was insect infestation and general filth. On the night of 5 March 1942 Enid Shann and Trude Knight decided to move some of the girls from Kooringa, where conditions were impossibly over-crowded, to Marylands which was not due to receive the Middle School until the next day. Marylands seemed a vast and empty place and very frightening when a terrifying thunderstorm woke everyone, making some children weep in fright. Enid Shann went to the kitchen in search of equipment to tend a girl who was sick after eating too many blackberries earlier in the day. When Enid turned on the light she was 'horrorstuck' to find the kitchen a 'black moving mass' of cockroaches. Ruth Creer also has memories of the horrors of Marylands when she arrived the next day and with Marjorie Cromie (née Tye) was inspecting an area adjacent to the kitchen. There they found hanging legs of ham covered with muslin through which blowflies had found their way with the usual results. There were also concrete troughs in which milk containers had been left soaking in water which had long since evaporated, leaving a pervading stench of sour milk. Conditions were so bad that eventually the school had to engage professional cleaners from Melbourne to deal with Marylands.[32]

When the MCEGGS group arrived at Mt Kitchener House the children, exhausted by the journey and the heat, collapsed on the lounge floor until lunch was prepared by the teachers and mothers amid the filth and confusion of the guest-house kitchen. After lunch the children rested again, then explored their surroundings followed by tea, baths and bed. Mt Kitchener House was a rambling building with steep and narrow stairs characteristic of houses built on mountain slopes. There were many problems: hazardous stairs for very young children; insufficient single beds or cupboards for each child and his or her clothes; bathing children in draughty bathrooms with crude equipment; and the provision of dining-room tables and chairs of a height negotiable by small children. Anne Taylor (née Slattery) as a 'big girl' at Marysville can remember the next day helping to unload and move furniture after it had been delivered by carriers who were 'the worse for drink' and useless.[33] In the days to come, teachers had the huge task of coping with unsuitable kitchen arrangements, children who were sick at awkward moments and vast amounts of children's washing. Mary Davis recalled that 'Margaret Mellor's knuckles were red raw from all the laundry she had to do'. All milk had to be boiled in the inadequate utensils available. Candles and hurricane lamps provided the lighting for many weeks because the electricity supply depended on a water wheel which refused to function. Miss Wellings found to her horror that some of the four-year-olds newly placed under her care had been sent with supplies of 'nappies' to be used at night. However, as Mary Davis remembered, Miss Wellings 'soon got them out of that habit'.[34] The most workable plan was for each member of the teaching staff to establish a family of about seven children who were mothered and cared for entirely, except for the treatment of illnesses. Each family occupied two or three rooms near the member of staff in charge. The children became very attached to their 'families' and remained in contact for many years after the return to South Yarra, retaining fond memories of the staff and of the adventures and outings they shared.

Anne Bitcon (née Aitken) was in a 'family' at Mt Kitchener House and her older sister Janet Frecheville (née Aitken) was in another 'family' at Kooringa. Anne remembers that her sister was ten and 'seemed so old and a stranger the few times they were allowed to visit us'.[35] Reminiscing with Margaret Towl, Anne has related some of her memories which are corroborated by others.[36] Anne did not question anything and does not recollect missing her parents. On her second night at Mt Kitchener House Anne shared a room with Stephanie McGee, Eve Forgacs, Josie McCutchen and Diana Ellemor. Stephanie, Josie and Diana were very homesick, wept frequently and soon returned to Melbourne. Anne's 'family' had Miss S. McLean as the 'mother' who put the children to bed with a kiss. Anne learned to love Miss McLean although she was terrified by her at first. However, Anne 'adored' Joan Mellor who also cared for their needs.

The teaching staff were so preoccupied with organising Mt Kitchener House that it was two weeks before classes could begin. The children had to be occupied with long walks in the bush which the teachers did their best to turn into lessons. Anne remembers that the 'nature walks were a great pleasure, the beauty spots, fern dells, little rushing creeks and bright red toadstools'. The girls learned to identify different types of eucalypts, wattles and 'funny eggs on the backs of leaves', to rub bracken into bee stings and ant bites and to collect twigs to make a fire to cook sausages or chops. Surprisingly, few accidents occurred. Several girls wading in the mountain streams cut their feet, with Faye Rosefield requiring stitches after treading on broken glass. One small boy, possibly Victor Asche, disappeared. A distraught Alison Winfield organised a group of worried teachers to wade hand in hand through the guest-house swimming pools. The child was later found hiding under a bed.

Finally, when all available equipment had arrived and was sorted, Mt Kitchener House was divided to provide areas of teaching for the Junior School in the ballroom, dining room, and two verandahs, with the Nursery School and Kindergarten housed in two garages without flooring or proper doors. Later the two classes of the lower Junior School set out each morning for Kooringa, where classrooms, by some wartime miracle, were built for them. Classrooms were also planned for Mt Kitchener House and it was expected that the building would be completed when they returned from the September holidays in Melbourne. Instead, only the foundations had been laid, although the garages were demolished and the playground covered with timber, plaster and pipes. The new classrooms were completed only six weeks before the lower division of the Junior School, Nursery and Kindergarten returned to South Yarra. Under these temporary and highly unsuitable conditions there was 'no doubt that the standard of work was not maintained'. Yet the children gained so much in general knowledge, experience and understanding that this outweighed the lapse in formal studies which could easily be remedied when conditions were more favourable.

At Kooringa the first month was spent in settling down to a 'very strange . . . very different' way of life. The teaching staff were on duty virtually twenty-four hours a day, a gruelling routine which they carried out willingly as part of their war effort. They had many and varied tasks from furniture-moving to overseeing vegetable peeling, even 'getting in touch with the fairies' when children's teeth came out. Unmarked handkerchiefs for eighty children had to be boiled up and then restored to their rightful owners. Perhaps the most exciting task was putting out the fire when the fowl house caught alight. Teaching conditions at Kooringa were very bad. Music was taught in a bathroom and social studies in an old fowl house, presumably the one which burnt down.[37] Enid Shann, attired in raincoat and gumboots, pushed a mobile blackboard back and forth in the mud outside three garages which housed her class—who were learning of the beauties of the Italian climate and countryside.[38]

Janet Frecheville (née Aitken) as member of a 'family' at Kooringa was cared for by Joan Webb and Pat Weir who were friends of her mother, Bonnie Aitken (née Inge). The girls in the 'family' have remained friends for life and in 1986 at one of their regular group meetings they recalled many incidents which occurred at Marysville in 1942. Members of the group are Patricia MacKenzie (née Clark), Diana Simondson (née Cohen), Rosemary Wright (née Carmichael), Margaret Pennington (née Mitchell), Mary Baxter (née Kingsmill), Barbara Skerritt (née Schwartz), and Helen Jennings. The group could recall 'wonderful evenings' when they each took turns to brush Miss Webb's long red hair while she read from books entitled *The New Forest* and *Puck of Pook's Hill*. There are also less pleasing memories of the food available which included 'haricot beans, white and naked' on the plate because potatoes were in short supply. The girls always left the table with uneaten beans stuffed in their pockets. Also served as meals were stuffed marrow, tapioca known as 'fish eyes in glue', scalded milk which was frequently burnt, and 'pufftaloons' (fried scones) with honey for breakfast. Lilian Bennett (née White) who sat with them at the table tried very hard, but without much success, to teach the group correct table manners. During the first winter at Marysville Janet Frecheville had the worst chilblains that 'anyone had ever seen'. Her bandaged hands, cracked and split, were revealed at each daily dressing when the filthy bandages from the day before were removed. Janet can remember going to see the snow on nearby Lake Mountain and plunging her hands into the snow to relieve the itching which probably prevented them from 'going septic'.[39]

The Middle School left South Yarra at 7.30 a.m. on Friday 6 March 1942, a group of 141 girls who went by cars to Richmond station, then by electric train to Lilydale where they changed to a steam train taking them to Healesville. Finally, a bus transported the group over the Black Spur to Marysville, and their destination, Marylands guest house. Here they were met by Sylvia Martin who, faced with filthy conditions and lack of provisions, greeted them with: 'You cannot come in! We are not ready!' The girls sat on the lawn outside with the temperature at 104°F (37°C) and ate their evacuation rations covered with plenty of melted chocolate. After lunch the girls walked to Steavenson's Falls. Finally, at about 6 p.m., after the teaching staff had cleaned the neglected, cockroach-infested kitchen and eating areas and set out a hastily purchased meal of bread and butter, the girls were allowed to enter Marylands. Makeshift beds and bedding were arranged in small, crowded rooms and all thankfully went to bed. The troubles of the day were not over. The meal of melted chocolate, followed by fresh bread and butter, on top of a demanding journey, and the stress of separation from home, proved too much for digestive systems. The teachers had a sleepless night, kept busy with mops and buckets. Next day the local doctor was summoned from Marysville to examine the girls. Mrs Creer was incredulous when the doctor diagnosed 'mountain sickness' due to the sudden elevation from Melbourne to the heights of Marysville.[40] As with all the evacuation locations, teaching conditions at Marylands were appalling. The front hall, the dining room and the verandah were all used as classrooms. Ruth Creer recalls that in the 'science room' the girls had to sit on cushions on the floor and write with their books on their knees because the desks had not yet arrived. With only chalk and a mobile blackboard at her disposal Ruth Creer had to resort to an intensive study of leaves of which there was no shortage.

Roseleigh, with twenty-eight girls, was less crowded than the other three guest houses and was occupied on 20 March 1942 by the School Certificate group. As there was no domestic staff, the girls helped in the kitchen in their spare time, and swept out the house before breakfast each day. Lessons, many of which involved household duties and gardening, began at 9.30 a.m. After school the Roseleigh girls sometimes helped with the juniors at nearby Mt Kitchener House or went walking. Weekends were often spent hiking and when the destination was Keppel's Falls or Keppel's Lookout, this involved the whole day. Bush walking in this unspoiled area of fifty years ago was an exhilarating experience and the girls described the details of their climb and the splendour of the views in the school magazine.[41] In the winter term there was a measles epidemic and as there was no nursing sister at Roseleigh the girls who were still standing and 'unspotted' assisted the staff in hospital duties.

In 1942 there was a small Anglican church, Christ Church, at Marysville where the services were conducted by the Reverend E. Leaver, rector at Alexandra. The church life of the school passed into his enthusiastic care and he began preparing girls for confirmation. To cope with the increased population Christ Church was enlarged. One Sunday Mr Harold Cuzens, churchwarden and a tradesman, cut the church in two and inserted a new section. However, there was still not enough room for everyone so the Junior School alternated with the Middle School with each girl attending church once a fortnight. At first there were not enough chairs for everyone so some girls called into Crossways, the local restaurant, to collect a chair each, carrying it to the church. On the alternate Sunday there was a service conducted by Miss Davis or Miss Ross at Kooringa or Marylands. Later in the year twenty-three girls were confirmed at Marysville by the Bishop of Wangaratta.[42]

Due to clothes rationing, weather and washing difficulties, school uniform was restricted to Sundays. Girls wore informal and practical clothing more in keeping with country life and the need to keep warm when snow was falling on the surrounding mountains.[43] The relaxed clothing rules, the outside activities necessitated by lack of facilities, and classes conducted on verandahs open to changing weather conditions, contributed to the feelings of adventure which many of the evacuees recall. Betty Wood (née Adam) relates that the girls were part of a rural community far from home, together twenty-four hours of each day and they developed loyalties and initiative which would not have occurred in Melbourne.[44] At the close of the school year a nativity play was presented by the Middle School girls from Marylands at Kooringa for the MCEGGS girls, the Deaf and Dumb Institute children who were also evacuated to Marysville, and the local Marysville children. The relationship between the girls and the teachers who looked after them was so close that special church services were held to thank the teachers for all they had done. Miss Ross herself later paid tribute to the staff at Marysville: 'Pictures of the staff should be told in full (though they never will be), staff washing children's clothes, mending children's clothes, making children's beds, soothing children's fears, bearing parents' complaints, soothing parents' anxieties and reassuring parents' worries'.[45] Miss Ross herself took on the role of co-ordinator, operating from an office at Wildfell in South Yarra and visiting Marysville and Doncaster each week. Due to the scarcity of petrol Miss Ross had a gas producer fitted to her car and is remembered by Rosemary Wright arriving at Kooringa blackened by a covering of soot acquired from the frequent stoking of the gas producer as it laboured over the Black Spur. Alison Winfield can remember 'dusting down' Miss Ross on many occasions.[46]

After the decision to take over the club house of Eastern Golf Club at Doncaster, the Senior School, with the exception of the School Certificate group, assembled there on Tuesday 24 March 1942. Of the 196 girls who went to Doncaster, 57 boarded at three private homes in Balwyn: Belmore Grange, Windsor Lodge and the Annexe. As a consequence of the evacuation a number of senior girls left MCEGGS, some to begin university courses at the early age of sixteen.

The club house of the Eastern Golf Club at Doncaster was a gracious old home with an interesting history. Originally known as Tullamore, it was constructed in 1886 as a double-storey mansion with twelve rooms which was used only at weekends and holidays by Dr Thomas Fitzgerald, his wife and their family. In 1909 Tullamore was sold to William Stutt, shire councillor of Doncaster and member of parliament. Tullamore remained in the Stutt family for another forty years and was leased by the Eastern Golf Club in 1924. In 1941 Tullamore was requisitioned by the government for the evacuation of schools.[47] The house was still in its original state with the addition of a large block of locker rooms on one side. Instead of accommodating golf players relaxing after a game, it was now expected to house 196 girls and teaching staff for the full day, five days a week. Not surprisingly the existing septic tanks could not meet the increased demands placed upon them. Within a few days of arrival Miss Mona Nugent, the teacher in charge at Doncaster, was urgently called to inspect the situation. On descending the stairs Miss Nugent was aghast to find the overflow from the septic tanks 'coming to meet her'. The scene was related to Miss Davis who had encountered a similar problem at Marysville.[48] Little wonder that one golf enthusiast remarked: 'Eastern, unfortunately, had a sad time during the war, reverting to a public course and having its fine old club house requisitioned for school evacuees from inner Melbourne'.[49]

The Doncaster school included all the external examination

fifth and sixth forms, and fourth forms. It also included the 'rural school', a new group consisting of girls of various school levels who would normally be at Marysville with their forms but whose parents did not want them to leave their homes. The rural school was housed in The Cottage, a small Edwardian house which was also used for physics classes.

The Eastern Golf Club was somewhat remote from public transport and not easily accessible, with at least a thirty-minute walk from Box Hill station or Mont Albert tram terminus. Overcrowded special school buses were arranged to meet designated trains and trams, and the drivers were not required to wait for anyone who may have missed the regular trains and trams. Shirley MacLeish and June Stringer (née Swinburne) both lived within easy walking distance of the school at South Yarra. After evacuation they met on the way to South Yarra station often running the last 550 yards (500 metres) to catch the city-bound train which stopped at Richmond station in those times. At Richmond they had to sprint down the ramp from one platform and up the ramp to the next to catch another train to Box Hill where they rushed to catch the school bus to the golf house.[50] Travelling to school took up to three hours a day for some girls but this was regarded by Susan Bolton (née Hanlon) as 'but a small contribution to make to the war'.[51] For eleven students the journey was so time and energy consuming that it was necessary to open a new boarding house, also known as The Cottage. This sudden projection into boarding-school life was not very enjoyable for some who were forced to become weekly boarders. Others, such as Rosemary Jordan (née Skerritt), enjoyed the experience.[52] Belmore Grange and Windsor Lodge together housed twenty-three boarders. Belmore Grange was the home of the Minifie family, and Mrs Enid Minifie (née Oliver), a former student of MCEGGS, offered her home for the use of boarders when she heard of the move to Doncaster. Suddenly her daughter, Elizabeth, found herself sharing her bedroom with five other girls, and eventually being in charge of meal preparation when the cook left to join the AWAS and Mrs Minifie fell ill.[53]

Bicycling became a common mode of transport used by all the boarders to commute between the three boarding houses and the golf club. Others, teachers and students, whose homes were within reasonable distance of the school also rode their bicycles. Valda Harper (née Hall) found that this experience in the fresh air on roads relatively free of traffic because of petrol rationing added to the picnic atmosphere which surrounded the move to Doncaster.[54] Miss Pownall often rode her bicycle from Camberwell, sometimes accompanied by Miss Jean Harvey with her school assignments strapped to a rack for home correction. Meredith Rigby rode her horse and wore jodphurs to school. Many enjoyed travelling on the train to Box Hill; friendships made with Melbourne High and St Kevin's boys sometimes lasted into university life. Train travel also provided extra time for reading and knitting.[55] Access to Doncaster posed a problem for the musical director of the school, Dr A. E. Floyd, who was organist and choir master at St Paul's Cathedral in the city. The author remembers observing Dr Floyd descending from the front of a milk truck, the driver of which had obliged by diverting from his usual route to pass by the golf house. Dr Floyd reduced his attendance at the school to once a fortnight but he still found time to engender a love of music in Mary Franklin (née Gillespie).[56]

Unless they became members girls were not allowed to play golf but could walk and gather mushrooms from the fairways. There were no other sporting facilities such as a gymnasium, so the customary 'gym' classes, including the use of the 'horse', were held outside. As at Marysville, there was a lack of domestic help so the cleaning of the school fell to some unlucky students and the teachers. The girls travelling on the late buses and the boarders from the Lodge and the Grange were organised into squads which swept, scrubbed and dusted. There are vivid memories of Miss Margaret Davies, on her hands and knees, backing down the staircase cleaning the stairs. Every bit as vivid are memories of Miss Dorothy Irving, the chemistry teacher, conducting her class in the kitchen and at the same time stoking the wood stove and stirring soup to warm the girls at lunchtime on cold frosty days. Shirley MacLeish has memories of French lessons on the open verandah with Miss Davies, a rug wrapped around her shoulders and a hot water bottle clutched to her stomach. Some relief from crowding in the rooms of the golf house came with the building of two army huts constructed from wood and fibro-cement which provided three classrooms, a domestic science room, physics and chemistry laboratories, and a storeroom. As this construction was only completed towards the end of second term in 1942, girls preparing for external examinations, particularly in science subjects, had, for most of the year, very inadequate facilities for science practical work. Many remember performing physics experiments 'over the gardener's bath tub'. At least the new facilities ended the frantic dashes down the drive in the rain, late for the classes held in The Cottage.

Despite the difficulties encountered daily at Doncaster in 1942, many of the girls recall that they gained a great deal through the experience of closer relationships with staff and other girls. Patricia Hancock (née Plummer) and Oenone Deasey (née Gardner) were among those who gained insight into the problems of running a school. Some girls found that the adverse conditions motivated them to the extent that their academic results were better than ever before.[57]

As late as October 1942 Miss Ross had suggested to the School Council that 'another year away would do no harm, even at the expense of having a smaller enrolment in 1943'.[58] However, Allied victories in both the Pacific and North Africa in that year gave strength to suggestions that 'occupied' school premises should be returned. In this respect, Victoria was given priority and St Catherine's School, MacRobertson Girls' High School and part of Melbourne Grammar began the 1943 school year in their own premises.[59] MCEGGS was not so fortunate and 1943 found the school still scattered on nine different sites.

By 1943 the Eastern Golf Club at Doncaster and the three private homes accommodated 100 extra students. This came about through the movement from Marysville of the School Certificate group and the upper part of the Middle School. At Marysville two guest houses, Mt Kitchener House and Kooringa, were retained to accommodate most of the lower Middle School and some of the upper Junior School.

The move of MCEGGS back to South Yarra was fraught with inconvenience and frustration, as time and time again arrangements with the authorities were not fulfilled. The first girls to return from Marysville were housed at Wildfell, another rented house in Tivoli Place, South Yarra, and later Raveloe, the home of the Brooks family in Domain Road. Later in the year, on 16 June 1943, Phelia Grimwade House was returned by the authorities, and later still, New Merton Hall. On 18 March 1943 Miss Ross announced to the girls that a petition, signed by as many members of staff and parents as possible, was being sent to parliament, requesting the return of the school.[60] The Army Hirings Department did not make Phelia Grimwade House available by the opening of the school year as it had agreed, and as a result, 'junior school boarders were asked by the school to stay in their own homes'.[61] Archbishop Booth signed letters which were sent by the School Council to Air Vice-Marshall George Jones, and the politicians Arthur Drakeford, F. Forde and John Dedman. These letters protested against plans to put army huts on the hockey field, and against the fact that the Hirings Department had 'once again, broken faith' in the return of New Merton Hall. An assurance was requested that the school would be able to occupy the whole of its premises for 1944.

The return of the Junior School to South Yarra was so unsatisfactory that the School Council suggested that 'serious consideration should be given to sterner measures'. The School
Council received a letter from the Central Hirings Committee
assuring them that the school buildings would be vacated by
April 1944 unless 'unexpected difficulties as regards labour and
materials' were encountered. At that stage nothing could be done
to secure the school buildings any earlier and parents were
advised of the postponement.[62] Early the following year, 1944,
Archbishop Booth sent a letter to Senator W. Collings seeking
the return of the school buildings and warning him to anticipate
further action if this did not come about.[63]

The final denouement came only when MCEGGS drove its
transports up to the very door and moved the Marysville equipment in 'before the RAAF moved out'. There was a confrontation
between the RAAF officers and Miss Ross in which, to use her
own words, she vented 'all the rage, and fury, and frustration of
two and a half years of coping with the inefficiencies of the local
RAAF administration'.[64] This was an understandable reaction
considering the speed of the original acquisition compared with
the delay in handing back the premises. The Doncaster section of
the school returned on Sunday 15 August 1944 with the move
completed in one day. The school returned to its own premises
after 'countless irritating delays, petitions, procrastination, and
disappointments'. On 15 August 1945, VJ Day, one year after the
move back to South Yarra from Marysville and Doncaster, the
Second World War ended.

Lyndsay Gardiner

7 Back into line

O N 9 OCTOBER 1958 FIFTEEN MEMBERS OF THE SENIOR (Merton Hall) staff handed their resignations to the new headmistress, Edith Mountain.[1] On speech night of that same year there was a list of thirty-eight resignations, only five of which could reasonably be ascribed to 'natural attrition'.[2] The figure included most subject heads and twelve of the sixteen form mistresses. In terms of loss of academic quality, professional expertise and continuity, the exodus was catastrophic. The exodus, and the reasons behind it, led to a sharp fall in the numbers of pupils in senior forms, as some enrolments were cancelled and many girls were withdrawn. At the end of 1957 the total of school-leavers was 111; at the end of 1958 it was 171. In February 1958 there were 428 girls in the Senior School; in February 1959 there were 394.[3]

It is not surprising that this period in the Grammar School story has become known as 'the crisis'; so indeed it was for the school and for the individuals involved at the time. For the students it must have seemed like the destruction of a familiar, accepted environment, of an ambience loved, hated or tolerated, but always there. For a majority of the staff it meant uprooting, in some cases a parting from the workplace of ten or twenty years, from a calling in which all one's intelligence and professional skill had been unstintingly given. In their perception, the school they had served no longer existed. Many shattered lives and careers had to be rebuilt; some never completely recovered. For the headmistress, the spring of 1958 must have been pure nightmare. Edith Mountain was just entering her fourth term at the school, and the shockwave of resignations, letters, meetings, recommendations, abuse and advice had to be borne virtually alone in a strange place where, as yet, she had made few friends. In her isolation she turned to the only group of people familiar to her—the Church, under whose aegis the school existed.

The Church of England naturally carried considerable weight on the School Council; a third of the twenty-two members were clerics, and in addition four were elected by Synod and four by the Archbishop-in-Council.[4] Early in 1957 the Council had unanimously appointed Edith Mountain as headmistress;[5] most of the staff had been appointed by her predecessor, D. J. Ross, and three by Sylvia Martin, who acted as headmistress in 1956 and for two terms of 1957.[6]

Fifteen professional women, and later eighteen others, do not resign lightly. Before tracing briefly the rapid and tumultuous events of October 1958, we need to consider the fundamental causes which underlay the resignations. What convinced staff that they and their new headmistress could not survive in the same educational environment?

A reading of the essay by W. F. Connell (chapter 5) will explain the sort of school 'D. J.' had left at the end of 1955. It was a school based on democratic values, free discussion, and co-operation between headmistress, staff and girls; a school where competition was kept to a minimum, and where religion included wide-ranging discussion of moral issues and values. D. J. had met her successor, twice, in London and 'considered that Miss Mountain's application should be accepted';[7] her former staff were, therefore, confident that the newcomer understood Grammar's ethos, its educational policy and its methods of administration. Gradually it became apparent either that she did not comprehend them, or that she comprehended but wished to make fundamental changes. Perhaps no educationist from an elite English girls' high school whose pride was its academic results and its sporting prowess could be expected, in the long run, to foster and develop D. J.'s unique 'Grammar'. In October 1958 the resigning staff were accused of acting 'precipitately'; yet they waited over three terms. They waited because they assumed that any newcomer with D. J.'s recommendation was bound to share her educational philosophy; they waited because they were fair-minded enough to allow a new headmistress time to find her feet, to make mistakes, and, as was her prerogative, to make some changes; they waited because they were extremely busy with their teaching and pastoral duties.

Numerous small incidents began to rankle. They found the headmistress unapproachable; attempts to talk with her, even by senior form and subject mistresses, were usually rebuffed; the girls, too, found the previously always-open door of the head's study now shut. Attempts at social familiarisation were brushed aside or neglected; the head no longer mingled informally at morning and afternoon tea, or at lunch time in the common-room. On the rare occasions when a formal interview was granted, the new headmistress heard staff advice, made no comment, and often took a different course of action.

When girls, missing the former open discussion of matters concerning them, asked staff to explain, the staff had no satisfactory explanation to offer. While allowing the treasured School Executive Council to continue, the headmistress sometimes circumvented or ignored it. After D. J.'s religious instruction classes, the senior girls found Miss Mountain's ill-prepared and irrelevant; they were no longer permitted to conduct occasional morning assemblies. Her own assemblies they found formal and 'soulless'. Dissension and discontent spread; discipline began to suffer; tempers frayed when girls were referred to as 'hooligans' and the special 'alternative sixth' as 'dim' and 'less able'.[8]

Still the staff waited. They knew that this was Edith Mountain's first headship; they had accepted her sensible decision that she required a full year in the school before formulating and announcing her educational policy, and any changes in administration or curriculum that this might entail. By third term 1958 they were still waiting, but patience was wearing thin.

The headmistress too, had her point of view. For one thing, she was not opposed to competition; this was what spurred individuals on, so that the academic students performed to the best of their ability and those with special talent steeled themselves for greater effort. Those with less physical aptitude were required to compete because this strengthened their characters. Her educational views were, in fact, in accord with many leading English girls' high schools, where 'progressive' education, according to the gospel of the New Education Fellowship, was now regarded as outmoded. The educational philosophy propounded by D. J. Ross and accepted by most of her staff was not Edith Mountain's philosophy. Her philosophy was, however, accepted by some senior staff members at Grammar, notably Mrs Capelin and Miss Daniell who, in 1959, were to become respectively chief-of-staff and senior mistress.

Given this fundamental divergence of philosophy, it is understandable that Edith Mountain and her senior staff members found it difficult to communicate. Coming, at the age of thirty-eight, untried as a leader, to a strange country and to a school whose whole ethos was alien to her, they must have seemed — as indeed they were! — a formidable bunch of women. The most senior of them had been almost thirty years on the staff, several more over twenty; most of those appointed since the Second World War had adopted with conviction their ways and their philosophy.

To this basic problem must be added Edith Mountain's own personality. She was not by nature an outgoing person, and her fundamental reserve and shyness were exacerbated by the fact that, although a well-qualified and able teacher, she was not intellectually outstanding, nor had she any experience of head-ship. Her reaction was to withdraw into aloofness — as the traditional lady-principals of her acquaintance in England had been remote and aloof. She drew back from attempts to befriend her; dinner engagements were refused or forgotten, an invitation to spend a few days with two or three staff members in a holiday cottage was cancelled at the last moment. The customary use of Christian names at MCEGGS, the exchange of small pleasantries in passing, the development of confidence were, in the early years, difficult for her. Only two people, up to and during the time of upheaval, seemed to have her confidence. One was her secretary, Betty Murray, whom she had inherited from Sylvia Martin, and who became for her more than secretary, acting as confidante, adviser, and go-between with the staff.[9] Mrs Murray had been with Mrs Martin only one term.

Edith Mountain's other friend was the new Archbishop of Melbourne, Dr (later Sir Frank) Woods. Like Edith Mountain, Woods was a newcomer; like her, he was English; like her, he experienced a considerable cultural shock on his arrival in Australia towards the end of 1957; and like Miss Mountain, he sometimes gave the impression, unintentionally, that he was bringing enlightenment to an outpost of Empire — a belief supported by the willingness of some sections of Melbourne society to accept their religious and educational leaders from the Mother Country.[10] It was a Grammar School parent, A. A. Phillips, who had earlier coined the phrase 'cultural cringe' to describe this phenomenon. Woods was *ex officio* chairman of the School Council, but the appointment of Edith Mountain had been made before he reached Melbourne. He was presented with a *fait accompli*, but there is no evidence that he regretted the appointment — though undoubtedly he regretted the loss and turmoil of late 1958.

The 1950s was a period of conservative government in Australia. The fear of the 'Red Menace' lingered, and people of left-wing tendencies were regarded with deep suspicion by those in authority. D. J. herself, an anti-authoritarian liberal, had once experienced difficulty in obtaining a visa to the United States of America, and had been covertly accused of being left-wing or worse; and the presence on her staff of several left-wing women incurred criticism from conservative elements in the school community. The new archbishop and the new headmistress held political and social views more in common with the latter group.

In addition to staff, pupils, Council and headmistress, two other groups were also closely involved in the disturbance of 1958—the Old Grammarians and the parents. These groups were not mutually exclusive, nor was either homogeneous in its opinions. There had for some years been an undercurrent of hostility to D. J. from sections of both Old Girls and parents, based on educational, religious and socio-political grounds. While D. J. was headmistress, such opposition could only simmer in the background; her unique personality, strength of character and ability rendered her impregnable—and besides, she 'got results', shown in the production, year after year, of mature, articulate senior students with a success rate in matriculation well above average. With the departure of D. J. there was a chance—to quote Sir Frank Woods speaking to this author—'to bring the school back into line'.[11]

Such were the opposing views which divided Old Girls and parents, staff and Council.

Finally, it must be remembered that the Grammar School to which Edith Mountain came in third term 1957 was not the school which D. J. had left. Sylvia Martin had tried to keep it the same, and most of the staff had valiantly supported her. 'We are trying to carry on running the school as it has been run under Miss Ross's guidance', Sylvia Martin wrote in her first report to Council;[12] but gradually, imperceptibly, staff and, in particular, girls began to miss D. J.'s hand on the helm, her inspirational leadership, her teaching. Matriculation results were marginally weaker; discipline—seen by outsiders in the streets and on public transport—began to slacken. The interregnum was too long; the school suffered; ammunition was provided for the forces of orthodoxy.[13]

When third term 1958 began, the headmistress still had not enunciated her promised educational policy, nor had relations with her senior staff improved. The only official channel of approach for assistant mistresses to the Council was through the headmistress, but in an attempt to prevent irreparable damage to the school, senior staff members wrote privately to Bishop McKie, who was acting chairman during Woods's absence at the Lambeth

Conference, and to four other Council members, setting out the problems as they saw them and asking for advice and help. School morale, they said, 'was steadily deteriorating owing to lack of leadership and inspiration from the headmistress'. Many staff members were torn between 'their loyalty to the school . . . and their earnest desire to support the headmistress'. They asked McKie to arrange a private meeting with representatives of the staff where their anxieties could be discussed. [14]

Bishop McKie did not reply to this letter. If other Council members mentioned the letters they had received, to him, he must presumably have advised them to wait and hope that the affair might sort itself out. He has been described as 'a sleeping chairman', as a man concerned to avoid trouble, to smooth things over. In his favour it must be said that he was only acting for Woods, and may have hesitated to take any action in so sensitive a matter which might not be in line with the arch-bishop's thinking.

On the morning of Wednesday 8 October staff and girls arrived at school to find, displayed on several public notice boards, the following document:

> All members of staff are notified that a letter expressing loyalty to the school and confidence in Miss Mountain as headmistress will be sent to the archbishop and members of the school council today. The letter is available for perusal and for signatures of members of staff in the book room until 1.45 p.m. this afternoon.

This notice, when first seen before morning assembly, was not signed; by recess it bore the signature of Miss McConkey, the music mistress, a supporter of Miss Mountain who was to remain on her staff for some years. Why, and at whose instigation, Miss McConkey did this is not known. The letter 'available in the book room', was known henceforth as the 'loyalty letter'. It read:

> Your Grace,
>   We, the undersigned, being aware that within the school there is an element of personal opposition to the headmistress, hereby wish to make known to you and to members of the Council, the fact of our sincere appreciation of Miss Mountain's wise administration and our confidence in her as Headmistress of the School.
>   We feel that she is approachable at all times and is very thoughtful for the welfare of the girls and the staff, as well as being unfailingly patient in a situation of considerable difficulty.

Under the circumstances, we take this opportunity to affirm our loyalty to Miss Mountain and to the School.

We have the honour to be Your Grace's most obedient servants.[15]

Thus 'the crisis' was precipitated. The fate of the letter is unknown. On the same evening, fifteen senior staff members met, wrote individual letters of resignation to the headmistress, and drafted also a combined letter to the archbishop which he received, presumably on 9 or 10 October. The letter read:

Your Grace,

We wish to explain to the Council the letters of resignation which we have sent to the headmistress.

When the Headmistressship fell vacant in 1955, the Council expressed its appreciation of the work which had been done in applying modern educational principles in the School and in developing the School in accordance with the best traditions laid down by its founders. The School has always been regarded as a leader in educational circles and by 1955 its prestige both here and abroad was very high, and its work had been quoted in many lectures and publications both here and in other countries. The type of education given has been watched with interest by many research scholars and visiting educationists. The University results of our girls have been outstanding.

The Council assured the staff and parents that they would take care to appoint someone qualified to continue this work, and in the meantime asked the staff to carry on. For nearly two years under Mrs. Martin's leadership, we did out best to maintain the educational principles for which the school has become famous.

When Miss Mountain was appointed we welcomed her warmly and tried to help her understand the way in which the School worked, the principles underlying it, and the new environment into which she had come. At the same time we fully realised the difficulties that must inevitably face a newcomer.

After more than a year we consider that these principles are quickly disappearing and that already the School has lost a great deal. We have done our best but the only result is continual friction and tension. We know that this is very bad for the girls, and indeed for all of us, and it cannot continue.

We feel that it is our duty in loyalty to the Council and to the School, to acquaint you with our decision to resign rather than give up the educational principles in which we believe and which you asked us to maintain, but Headmistress and Staff working along widely divergent lines can cause only confusion and unhappiness for the girls.

We had hoped that Miss Mountain's promised talk on October 16th would ease the situation and give us some possible hope of working together for a common purpose; but the letter to the Council presented for Staff signatures on October 8th, with Miss Mountain's sanction, calling for an expression of confidence in her administration, has driven us to take this action.

We cannot continue to work for the School under the present conditions. It is with the deepest regret that we have come to this decision and in fairness to you we would be willing to give further details if you so desire.

Yours sincerely,

Elaine Brumley*	1951 Senior classics
Lesley Cunningham	1953 Social studies
Margaret E. Davies*	1934 Senior French
Dorothy Fitzpatrick	1949 History, social studies
Eva Gawthorne*	1953 Senior geography
Dorothy H. Irving*	1939 Senior chemistry
M. Lundie*	1953 Soc. studs, Eng., scripture
Audrey C. Margetts*	1953 Senior history, soc. studs
M. J. Nugent*	1929 Senior English
Elizabeth Pownall (COS)	1933 Senior physics, maths
Wilga M. Rivers*	1953 Senior French, Eng., and scripture
F. E. Ross*	1938 Senior German
Elisabeth Stephens*	1953 Senior English, scripture
Patricia Travers*	1956 Senior English, biology, drama
Alison Winfield	1939 School counsellor[16]

*Form mistress

A glance at the length of service and the positions held by these fifteen women reveals how great their loss would be to the school. The effects of this loss were to be felt over many years; the immediate impact was devastating. How did it happen? Clearly the match which fired the ready fuel of divergent philosophies and incompatible views was the loyalty letter. Who was responsible for it? In their letter of resignation to the archbishop the fifteen resignees used the words 'with Miss Mountain's sanction', indicating that they did not believe that the loyalty letter was the unprompted action of Miss McConkey. Mrs Murray on the other hand states that it was. Mr J. L. Daish, Council member and chairman of the Parents' Association, is reported in the *Age* on 28 October as saying that 'some members of staff—with Miss Mountain's knowledge—drew up a letter expressing loyalty to Miss Mountain and to the school'. This implied that Miss McConkey in signing acted as representative for Miss

Mountain's supporters on the staff. Betty Murray and Mr Daish thus disagree about Miss Mountain's prior knowledge of the letter; I am aware of no comment one way or the other from her. If she knew, does 'sanction' and then silence imply a desire to profit from, while refusing responsibility for, a potentially divisive action? If she did not know, why remain silent? A further interesting question arises: the closeness with which the loyalty letter reflects the earlier 'private' letters of staff to the acting chairman suggests that these letters were the immediate occasion of the loyalty letter. If so, who had 'leaked' a private letter, and who was the recipient of the 'leak'?

On the morning of 9 October 1958 when the resignations had been hand-delivered to the headmistress, one of the fifteen broke down and wept before her class. When pressed for explanation by an appalled group of senior pupils, she briefly related what had happened, though the staff had agreed to keep the matter quiet rather than cause alarm and distress before the leaving and matriculation examinations.[17] Once the story was out, the news spread quickly. One senior student recalls vividly that on that Thursday, at lunch time, practically the entire Senior School crossed Anderson Street to the Botanical Gardens (a privilege reserved for sixth formers) and sat in groups under the trees for lunch—a moving, spontaneous sign of their distress.[18] Nor was the news confined to the school community; inevitably children told their parents; one chanced to be a journalist. Within three days of the appearance of the loyalty letter, newspaper headlines read: 'Teachers Resign—Merton Hall Stir' and 'Merton Hall Storm—Parents Threat—Teachers to Quit'.[19] No official comment from headmistress, Parents' Association or Council was then available, but Council had already been called together.

It met on 10 October at the cathedral, not at the school as usual, and was given the letters written by the fifteen resignees. Next morning, Saturday, it met again and issued a statement to the press expressing its confidence in the headmistress. This was printed in the *Age* on 15 October.[20]

Meanwhile, on Monday 13 October, a message from Council to staff was received stating that Council would meet the resignees next day.[21] The resignees attended and chosen representatives stated their case. Woods later referred to the 'sympathetic hearing' they were given; the staff's version is that Council was sharply critical of their action.[22] Woods expressed the hope that after Thursday 16 October, when the headmistress was to deliver her policy speech, some staff members would reconsider their action. In the meantime, he was sending a 'letter of explanation' to all parents. Parents received this letter on Thursday 16 October.[23]

In the letter, Archbishop Woods admitted that the situation was a difficult one, and that—as a parent with two daughters at the school—he was concerned, as they must be, at the danger posed to educational standards by the resignation of so many senior staff. He assured them, however, that the headmistress was already engaging new staff 'as carefully as possible' and was 'regarding all new appointments as temporary until they had proved their quality'. He stated categorically that the Council was the constituted authority, that Council did not agree with resigning staff in their criticism of the headmistress's educational policies, and that, in any case, the educational policy of the school was the prerogative of the headmistress.

On this same Thursday, on receipt of Woods's letter, a Grammar School parent officially enters this sorry affair. He was Charles Moorhouse, Professor of Engineering at the University of Melbourne, whose wife was a Synod-elected member of the Council, and his letter to Woods expressed the views of many parents. [24] Their concern, he said, was largely an academic one; they could not believe that the past, above-average university performance and intellectual maturity of Grammar girls could continue with the loss of so many senior staff. Many parents, he wrote, had lost confidence in the headmistress, and they had not been reassured that morning by the archbishop's letter. Moorhouse concluded by suggesting that the archbishop should be careful to avoid giving the impression 'that some of those concerned are not sufficiently acquainted with the Australian scene in general, and education in particular'.

The third event of that Thursday was the delivery to the assembled staff by the headmistress of her policy speech. [25] If staff had hoped that Miss Mountain understood the differences of educational philosophy which divided them and was willing to discuss these, or that she was aware of the principles which underlay the daily conduct and administration of the school, they were disappointed. In their view, what she proposed was 'more examinations, greater uniformity of teaching, [and] more competition', and they felt that she 'revealed an ignorance of school procedures which shocked most people present'. She proposed, for example, to create heads of departments, which the school had had for more than thirty years. Her suggestion of more outside competition amounted to no more than that which already existed. Her criticism of teaching and assessment methods, they held, implied gross ignorance of the excellent results obtained at matriculation and at the university by Grammar girls under the previous system.

The policy speech, in short, reaffirmed for many Merton Hall staff what they had come to realise over the past three and a half terms, and fully justified their distrust of Edith Mountain as a suitable headmistress for the school. It did more. On Saturday 18 October a deputation of staff members from the other three sections of the school waited on the archbishop. They said that the policy speech had convinced them that 'the headmistress had no coherent policy, nor any awareness of the administrative machinery of the school'. They added that eleven of their number were also considering resignation.[26] As the original fifteen from the Senior School had now been increased by later resignations to eighteen, the archbishop faced, at this stage, a loss of twenty-nine staff members. Seriously perturbed, he suggested that an advisory panel be set up to facilitate communication between staff and headmistress.

Resignees and possible resignees discussed this proposal exhaustively on Monday 20 October and rejected it on the grounds that communication between staff and head had been tried over twelve months without success; they felt that the proposed panel was merely a device to retain staff while saving the headmistress's face. This decision was conveyed to the archbishop by chief-of-staff Elizabeth Pownall on Tuesday.[27]

At this point a group of 'concerned parents' intervened, with a suggestion to the archbishop on 21 October: the group included Charles Moorhouse; Professor of Bacteriology, Sidney Rubbo; A. A. Phillips, a senior master at Wesley and secretary of the Assistant Masters' Association; and Myra Richardson, mother of the hapless head girl for 1958.[28] Out of this meeting came the suggestion that if the resignations were withdrawn, the Council would set up an independent inquiry into the state of the school. The eighteen senior staff members agreed to this, and the eleven potential resignees agreed to suspend action. Council met twice to discuss the matter but decided against an independent inquiry. The decision was not unanimous. The archbishop wrote formally to Elizabeth Pownall on Friday 24 October assuring her that Council had not made its decision without 'long debate and a keen sense of its gravity'. All Council members, he said, had a feeling of great disappointment that the differences between headmistress and staff 'could not be resolved'. Council was aware of the 'splendid service' staff had given to the school, and wished the staff to 'give to council credit for a care for the school at least as great as your own'.[29]

At these meetings the headmistress was expressly instructed that no further resignations were to be accepted. Yet on Friday 24 October she dismissed the eleven potential resignees, an action which some on Council regarded as deliberate contravention of its instructions. Later, on 29 October, she offered to withdraw their dismissal notices.[30] None of the eleven accepted the offer, and four more staff members, upset by the dismissals, handed in their resignations also. Thus fifteen, which had grown to eighteen, then to twenty-nine, became, by the end of term, thirty-three.

By 24 October, little more than a fortnight after the appearance of the loyalty letter, there was no longer any possibility that a major loss of staff could be averted; the independent inquiry was a last desperate throw. The precipitate action of Edith Mountain that Friday merely served to make the situation even worse. Events which followed exposed the real rift which had developed within the school community, and made public—in a way which Council had striven to avoid—the magnitude of the disaster which had befallen the school.

To inform parents about the state of affairs, the 'concerned parents' had, on 24 October, sent a letter to as many of them as they could contact, although neither the school office nor the Parents' Association would supply them with a complete address list.[31] This letter presented a chronology of events between 8 and 24 October, and referred back to the attempts by some staff members earlier in the year to alert Council members. The loyalty letter they described as 'an insult' to the staff; the revelation to the students of the original fifteen resignations, so deplored by headmistress and Council, and indeed by the resignees, the 'concerned parents' regarded as revealing 'the depth of [the staff's] sincerity and the stupidity of the episode which led to their final action'.

A response to this letter, defending both headmistress and Council, appeared in the *Herald* on 28 October in an interview with J. L. Daish.[32] On the following morning in the *Age* there was an interview with Mr James Donald, one of the 'concerned parents'; in this way a skeleton of the 'concerned parents' letter was made known to some of the parents who had not received it.[33]

The letter and interviews, as well as the 'grapevine' of girls, Old Girls, parents and staff, ensured a large attendance at a meeting of parents on the evening of Wednesday 29 October. The original object of this meeting was to hear Wing-Commander A. L. Greenway speak on 'Rapid methods of reading'; alas, the poor man never opened his mouth.

The meeting overflowed into the grounds and on to the street beyond. It was addressed, first, by A. A. Phillips who attempted to give an objective account of events to date, but allegedly only confused his audience.[34] Phillips was followed by Edith Mountain who had prepared the way for her address by sending a letter to all parents outlining her position and her plans for the school. These, in both letter and speech, were a simplified version of the policy speech of the previous week. The archbishop, delayed in returning from Archbishop Mowll's funeral in Sydney, and consequently under considerable stress, also spoke. He stated the Council's position, reiterated its support for the headmistress, and urged all parents to work with the Council and headmistress to rebuild the school community. Several parents then attempted to ask questions. The archbishop said that there were to be no questions, a decision which outraged a large section of his audience. Feelings ran high, and in an allegedly responsible gathering of respectable and intelligent adults, there was much shouting, name calling and verbal abuse, culminating in minor physical violence as successful attempts were made to disconnect the tape-recorder. Appalled, the archbishop pronounced the Benediction; this produced momentary silence, but was followed immediately by renewed pandemonium. He then ordered the singing of the National Anthem and escorted Miss Mountain from the stage. The meeting dissolved noisily and in bad order.

Unhappily for authority, the journalist-parent was in the audience and the matter did not end that evening. The next day's papers carried such headlines as

SCHOOL MEETING ENDS IN CONFUSION

CLAIM OF GAGGED

and

PARENTS IN UPROAR AT MERTON HALL MEETING

and

HOOTS AT MEETING FOR DR WOODS

The *Age* carried on its front page pictures of the archbishop and Miss Mountain addressing the meeting; the *Sun* printed shots of women standing on chairs, and some of the crowd of 1000 people trying to cram into a hall designed for 450.[35] In the *Herald* the previous evening the president of the Parents' Association had expressed the hope that the meeting would be 'dignified'. His hope was not realised.[36]

Meanwhile, another section of the school community had become involved. The first Old Girl publicly to appear in the affair was Nora Stretton, who with Catherine Moorhouse resigned from the Council following Edith Mountain's dismissal of the eleven potential resignees on 24 October. Mrs Stretton made no public statement, but the views of the two women presumably coincided. Interviewed by the *Age*, Mrs Moorhouse explained that 'in the recent trying times' she had been unable 'to support the attitude and decisions of the council'. The headmistress's dismissal of the eleven 'in direct opposition to the request by Council that their services should be retained' led finally to her decision to dissociate herself from the Council. She said she had tried to see both sides of the problem, but did not think that Council had been either 'impartial or broadminded'.[37] In November Mrs Moorhouse's resignation was formally accepted by Council, while Mrs Stretton was asked to reconsider;[38] at the request of the Old Girls she rejoined Council in February 1959.* Nevertheless, writing to a friend a little earlier, she had expressed her disgust at Council's behaviour: 'I am afraid that their minds are quite impermeable. I have never been so shocked by human (or sub-human) behaviour. I keep reproaching myself that I could not do better, but sheer stupidity added to injured pride is not open to reason.'[39] Perhaps she hoped that, by returning to Council, she might help in the slow process of rebuilding.

At the University of Melbourne, nine academics who were also Old Grammarians wrote a letter to the archbishop on 31 October, protesting at the Council's actions during the upheaval.[40] Predictably, their concern, like that of the 'concerned parents', was academic. Already, they wrote, the school's academic reputation, hitherto high, was beginning to suffer in academic circles; the unsettled state of the school was bound to affect the work of senior girls planning university courses, and the virtual impossibility of providing comparable replacement staff in such numbers and in so many disciplines, would lead inevitably to lower academic standards. They recommended a small, independent inquiry into 'the crisis' — a panel of educationists acceptable to both parties, which would meet in camera and be empowered to call witnesses, and whose findings would go direct to Council.

On receipt of this letter, the archbishop arranged for members of the academics' group to meet with Mr A. M. Parker, a city actuary, elected to Council by Synod. This meeting took place on 7 November and was, apparently, a civilised exchange of views. Mr Parker suggested some weaknesses in the school's curriculum, which indicates a knowledge of and concern for educational policy, although nobody at D. J.'s Grammar supposed that the

---

* The dismissals upset also the Dean of Melbourne who, holding an *ex officio* appointment, could not resign. On 16 May 1991 he wrote to this author that Edith Mountain 'deliberately acted contrary to the explicit instructions of the Council . . . I thought that the Council showed lamentable weakness in not disciplining the headmistress after she acted in defiance of the Council's ruling'. (Stewart Barton Babbage, Australian College of Theology, Sydney.)

school was perfect, or was opposed to change introduced after discussion and on good grounds.[41]

On 14 November the academics were granted an interview with the archbishop. This was not such a restrained meeting. After a brief exchange the archbishop suggested that, if they guaranteed confidentiality, he would reveal to them a hitherto unrevealed factor in the situation. When the academics refused to regard anything as 'confidential', the archbishop left the meeting. The academics thereupon delivered to the *Age* an abridged version of their original letter; it appeared on the Saturday morning.[42]

There, publicly, the matter ended. No independent tribunal was appointed. Instead, on 3 November Council appointed from its own ranks a conciliation committee to attend the school daily for several weeks, an arrangement which meant, in practice, that the only member 'on duty' regularly was Mrs Mary Britten, as male members had professional commitments. This committee was beneficial in providing a 'safety valve'. Mary Britten provided what many staff members had lacked; a quiet, sympathetic ear for their concerns, their distress, and their reasons for resignation. She is remembered with affection and respect. Most staff members agreed that the conciliation committee tried very hard to conciliate, but 'had nothing to conciliate with!'[43] All resigning staff members were offered the opportunity to rejoin the staff, and 'closer liaison between staff and council' was promised. None of the resignees changed her mind; it was clear to them that their educational methods and philosophy would have no place in a school under Edith Mountain; they doubted that their philosophy was understood by Council; and they doubted whether 'closer liaison' could have reconciled two irreconcilables. Even before the committee had completed its task, and five days before the university academics had their interview with the archbishop, Council met, and 'after most careful consideration of all suggestions made to us, both verbally and by letter' found itself 'unable to accept any of them'. It therefore 'instructed the headmistress to proceed with the staffing of the school'.[44] The Council still hoped, Archbishop Woods wrote to Elizabeth Pownall, that 'many of the resignees would continue to serve the school'.

After speech day 1958, when they were no longer employees of the Grammar School, thirty-three former members of staff sent to all parents a letter stating their reasons for resignation.[45] The result of the exodus of teachers was that over half the staff who began the next teaching year at Grammar were newcomers. The pass rate at matriculation level that year was 56 per cent, compared with 86 per cent in 1957 and 78 per cent in 1958.[46]

The school of the 1960s, recovered from the trauma of 1958 —
for school generations, like memories, are short — was a different
school from D. J.'s Grammar and is the subject of the next
chapter. It remains here, in conclusion, to consider some of the
questions which arise from the events of October and November
1958.

In a period of increasing secondary school enrolments and a
severe shortage of academically trained and qualified teachers,
how was Miss Mountain able to staff Grammar in 1959? As early
as 28 October, even before the unruly parents' meeting, J. L.
Daish claimed that already sixteen teachers had applied for
positions at the school; and members of Council, including Sir
Frank Woods, have assured this author that this was Miss
Mountain's 'trump card' when they voiced any doubts about her
ability to fill so many vacant positions. Yet educationist Dr Ken
Cunningham, the university academics, and the 'concerned
parents' all held this to be impossible.[47] It was *not* impossible to
find teachers; the impossibility was to find teachers of comparable
experience and qualifications. Edith Mountain could not and
did not do this; many of her new appointments were recently
qualified, inexperienced young graduates who would not normally have been considered for senior positions in a school of such
academic prestige. Some vacancies were filled by former Grammarians who resigned from other positions to return to their old
school in time of need.[48]

Another question which arises is why Miss Mountain came to
be appointed in the first place? Why did Dorothy Ross recom-
mend her? D. J.'s recommendation would have carried considerable weight, yet she was well aware of her successor's background
in a direct-grant high school, and of her lack of leadership
experience. By the start of 1957 Council may have been influenced
in its decision because it was desperate to make any appointment
at all. D. J. had announced her impending resignation in mid-
1954 and the position was advertised. In 1955 there were six
applications, and all were rejected. In July 1955 the post was
re-advertised. Two more applicants were interviewed in September and rejected as 'unsuitable'. We do not know their names,
their qualifications, or the grounds for their rejection.[49] In 1956
the interregnum began with Sylvia Martin as acting head; Dr
Elwyn Morey and Dr (later Dame) Margaret Blackwood were
both offered the position; both refused it, probably because each
enjoyed the professional work on which she was engaged.
Margaret Blackwood later rejected an offer to become principal
of Janet Clarke Hall on these grounds. Meanwhile, D. J. and a
sub-committee of Lady Clarke and Lady White, both Old Gram-

marians, Sir William McKie, the organist and brother of the bishop, and Dr John Foster, registrar of the University of Melbourne, canvassed likely candidates in England. They were assisted and advised by two English headmistresses, one the president of the Headmistress's Association of Great Britain, and both heads of direct-grant high schools.[50] The upshot of this was the application of Edith Mountain. Her appointment came after two and a half years of search, effort and disappointment.

It is puzzling why such a 'plum' job should not have appealed to more Australian and English educationists. Was their reluctance simply because the salary was too low? Or was it that the job was too 'plum'? Perhaps wise women were aware of the undercurrents of political, religious and educational disagreement within the Council and the wider school community, and decided not to become involved. Edith Mountain was not aware of such undercurrents.

The most powerful undercurrent was the fear of communism, widespread in the 1950s. Among a large section of the Old Girls and parents, and among some of the clergy on Council, concern at D. J.'s liberal views and the undoubted left-wing leanings of some of her staff came gradually to be regarded as an expression of communist sympathies—even, by some, as part of a deliberate conspiracy to corrupt the minds of girls destined to be the mothers of the leaders of the community. Disgruntled mutterings became a 'smear' campaign, then overt charges; the sincere Christian beliefs of the former headmistress and most of her staff were denied; conservatives on the staff and those of no particular political persuasion were tarred with the same brush. The fact that security records, when checked in 1958, revealed *no* communists on the staff was ignored.[51] Even today phrases like 'it was an undoubted fact that' and 'it was widely known that' are used to assure the inquirer of the veracity of such charges.[52]

Mr Justice (later Sir Reginald) Sholl, who acted as adviser to Council at one stage during the furore, wrote that he 'was not prepared to deny the possibility of directional teaching even in a school like Merton Hall';[53] Mrs Jessie Clarke (née Brooks), an influential Old Girl, spoke on prime-time radio on the evening of the disastrous parents' meeting, warning of the communist influence in the school and urging the importance of parental support for the headmistress against this threat to liberty.[54] Others were concerned at the threat to liberty posed by unsubstantiated charges without a fair trial.[55]

No member of staff publicly repudiated such charges; nor did Dorothy Ross, though she wrote privately to Valentine Leeper in November that she had tried to 'keep out' fearing that she might 'add fuel to flames already fairly high'.[56] Dr Cunningham spoke for them; several parents and groups of Old Girls wrote letters to the newspapers; Valentine Leeper, daughter of one of the founders of the school, a long-time Council member, and herself an Old Girl, wrote several letters supporting them — to the school chaplain, to the Dean of Melbourne, to many of her friends and, of course, to the archbishop. She emphasised the baselessness of 'the red rumours which have been circulated', and remarked that on a large staff 'almost every kind of political view is likely to be found'. If any individual staff member could be shown to be a communist and to be abusing her position, then Council should say so specifically, its failure to do so amounting virtually to conviction by association. This failure to scotch undifferentiated rumours was, she wrote, 'doing the church incalculable harm'.[57]

The archbishop did not answer Miss Leeper's letters. Council itself at no time intimated that it had any suspicions of communism among staff members; what was discussed at Council meetings is unknown to us as the records of meetings have disappeared. Are we then to record the role of Council during the upheaval as the result of a view — not a unanimous view — of the staff as insidious purveyors of communist doctrines to innocent young females? Such a recording would account for Council's earlier failure to take pre-emptive action, and for its efforts to prevent the second wave of resignations, its object of forcing the departure of unacceptable elements having been achieved. This is so Machiavellian as to be unlikely; it implies some deep-seated plot to 'play out the rope' so that the staff would take extreme action and ultimately put themselves in an untenable position.

It is more likely that, once the storm over the loyalty letter had broken, an action for which neither resignees nor Council were responsible, only then did Council find itself compelled to take positive action. Council was led by a determined archbishop, and faced with an inexperienced headmistress, both with hierarchical views on the running of institutions and the role of authority. It was beset on the one hand by indignant academics and 'concerned parents' anxious about educational standards, and on the other by a body of orthodox parents and Old Girls warning of the 'Red Menace'. In this dilemma, Council fell back on its trump card. The whole affair resolves itself into a matter of power and authority, and ultimate authority rested with the Council. Edith Mountain was its appointment; at all costs, she had to be supported.

At the Council meetings a couple of less fundamental matters were raised which helped to stiffen wavering councillors.[58] Edith Mountain was under a five-year contract and could not be lightly dismissed. During a similar school crisis, forty-three years earlier, an English headmistress who was deemed unsatisfactory and whose staff had been resigning around her, had been asked to resign. She was younger than Edith Mountain, perhaps more pliable; perhaps she had not so thoroughly burnt her professional bridges behind her in England. The First World War had broken out since her arrival here: perhaps she was not reluctant to return to her own people. In any case, Miss Tunnicliffe bowed to pressure and resigned.[59] Edith Mountain was made of sterner stuff; she was fighting for professional survival and for educational principles which she embraced as warmly as the resignees embraced theirs. She was determined to succeed and she had powerful allies. The chances of her resignation were remote, and if Council dismissed her then it would be guilty of breach of contract. Such action might have solved one problem while raising another.

When, at one meeting, Dean Babbage moved a motion that Miss Mountain be asked to resign, Archbishop Woods refused to put the motion. He argued that if the school at the height of its prestige received so few applications, fewer still would apply when the school was in a state of disintegration. Probably this argument, as well as the stark fact of the legally binding contract, influenced all members.[60]

Ultimately, however, we return to the question of authority. The Church of England controlled the school; its Council was chaired by the archbishop; behind it was all the prestige of the hierarchy and the weight of the Anglican 'establishment'. Faced with a difficult situation it took, as was its right, the strictly constitutional approach, but in doing so showed little consideration for two of the groups for whom it was responsible — the staff and the girls. Council, at that time, seems to have forgotten that authority carries with it responsibility.

Weg's view of 'the crisis', *Herald*, 11 October 1958.

"NO, HILDEGARDE! YOU MAY NOT RESIGN!"

Rosslyn McCarthy

8 MCEGGS in a time of change: the era of Edith Mountain, 1957-74

WHEN AN ADORED HEADMISTRESS RETIRES — ONE THE SCHOOL family has come to see as the personification of the spirit of the school itself — her successor often treads a precarious path. At one time or another, a number of Melbourne's girls' schools have experienced such thorny transitions where parents, Old Girls or staff have been reluctant to accept a newcomer in their midst.[1] But none seems to have suffered a disturbance as severe as that at MCEGGS when in 1957, after a two year interregnum, the reserved Edith Mountain was appointed from England to replace the charismatic Dorothy Ross. The legacy was a painful division within the school community which even now, more than thirty years later, has not been healed. With this cloud still hanging over the Mountain era, the period sometimes tends to be dismissed as a low point in the school's history. Undoubtedly MCEGGS passed through some perilous years in the wake of the upheaval and Edith Mountain was to remain a highly controversial figure. But the school proved stronger than 'the troubles'. It recovered and moved on to new ideas and achievements in the different world of the 1960s and 1970s. Though the 'remote' style of the head and internal policies and politics no doubt gave MCEGGS the more 'traditional' stamp it acquired in the years ahead, the development of the school in the Mountain years must be set in the context of the forces which were transforming education across the country.

When Edith Mountain was appointed to MCEGGS she was thirty-eight years old, with a successful career teaching in leading English girls' schools behind her, and a long-held ambition to become a headmistress.[2] Surprisingly little detail about her background in England is known within the school community, yet her own education and earlier experience were to be fundamental factors in her approach to MCEGGS, and in the direction the school was to take for the next two decades. They therefore warrant some exploration.

On both sides her family belonged to the affluent middle classes of the English North country. She was born Edith Nickal, the daughter of George and Henrietta Nickal, on 22 July 1919. Her father died when she was very young, and her mother married Bernard Mountain, a doctor whose family were solicitors in Grimsby. His practice was in Nottingham, and the Mountains settled in Arnold House, a large Georgian building in the suburb of Arnold. Edith was close to her stepfather, who adopted her, sharing with him a love of reading and a deep interest in music and history. She was also close to her Nickal relations — her grandfather, a former professor from the Slade School of Art who had retired to the Lake Country, and two aunts, both former teachers.[3]

After commencing preparatory school in Stamford in 1924, and briefly attending the Oxford High School for Girls, in 1927 the young Edith entered Nottingham High School for Girls where she remained until the end of her secondary education.[4] Oxford and Nottingham are both schools of the Girls Public Day Schools Trust (GPDST), stemming from the same reform movement which underlay the development of the leading girls' schools in Melbourne, including MCEGGS. Founded in 1873, by 1891 the GPDST had thirty-six high schools across England whose students were winning numerous scholarships to university.[5] Yet, contrary to popular opinion, the Trust schools had never been solely interested in academic success. During the 1930s they had taken a lead in educational experiment with the appointment of a visiting psychologist who developed a curriculum and support system for non-academic students, an activity which drew considerable praise from Susan Isaacs.[6] Through the 1930s the pages of the *Girls' High School Magazine* give frequent glimpses of Edith Mountain's school days. An occasional prize winner, she held an internal Trust Scholarship from 1935 to 1937, and in her senior years she reported on the science club of which she was secretary.[7] In 1938, having passed her High School Certificate, she entered London University's Westfield College where she majored in botany, gaining an Honours Science degree in 1942 and the Cambridge Certificate of Education a year later.[8]

Teaching was in her blood. Not only were there the Nickal

Grade Three Classroom in the New Junior School.

Dean Thomas taking Communion in St Luke's Chapel.

Students of the Mountain era at assembly in the Lower Hall
after the creation of the Chapel of St Luke above.

Miss Nina Crone, Headmistress since 1975, and prominent advocate of single sex education for girls.

The Nina Crone Resource Centre opened in 1987. Members of a senior class participating in a discussion lesson.

aunts, but both parents and her mother's sister had been teachers.[9] While still a student in 1941 in the London blitz, she had taken a part-time position at St Margaret's Grammar School in Sutton Courtney, and on the completion of her studies she held a series of posts as a biology mistress: from 1943 to 1945 at Shrewsbury High School for Girls, another of the GPDST group; from 1945 to 1949 at the Kirby School in Middlesborough, a highly reputed school run by the local authority; and from 1950 onwards at Putney High School for Girls, again a GPDST school, where she was in charge of the biology department. She was a popular teacher — former students from Shrewsbury can still recall the young Miss Mountain's lessons, and she frequently took groups out on botany excursions into the unspoilt Yorkshire dales. Since her days at the Kirby School where she had been encouraged by the principal, Miss Hutt, Edith Mountain had wanted to become a headmistress.[10]

In late 1956 she was interviewed for the MCEGGS position which had been advertised throughout England, and though the Council was by then clearly anxious to make an appointment her assessment seems to have been thorough. On the London interview panel were two leading members of the English Associations of Headmistresses: its president, Miss Margaret Adams, former head of Croyden High School for Girls, (one of the leading GPDST schools) who would have had ready access to details of Edith Mountain's career, and Miss Agnes Catnach of the Putney County School who, as the guest of the Association of Heads of Independent Girls' Schools of Australia for their 1955 conference, had gained some idea of the private schools of this country which she had toured state by state.[11] Miss Dorothy Ross, who was in England at the time, had 'visited Miss Mountain's school and talked to her headmistress' and together with Miss Mary Davis she was entertained at Miss Mountain's flat, where the school film 'Learning and Living Together' was watched with interest and a copy was purchased for Putney. Edith Mountain was 'unanimously recommended' by the London committee and as she booked passage for Australia the future must have seemed rosy.[12]

But the school to which she was coming was not as untroubled as it perhaps appeared in the promotional film. Many of the forces which would affect MCEGGS in the future were already in operation before Edith Mountain's arrival, and no one had seen more clearly than the far-sighted Miss Ross how likely it was to change under her successor.

In mid-1954 Dorothy Ross gave notice of her retirement, and thereafter in her reports to the Council she looked closely at the question of the school's future. Though doubtless mindful of them, she made no mention of some of the major internal pressures for change—there had never been total support for her ideas. Rather, she placed the school in the context of the 1950s in which all the independent schools were facing an uncertain future.

By the mid-1950s the first wave of the post-war baby boom was already crowding into primary school. At the same time post-war prosperity was making secondary education possible for an ever-increasing socio-economic group, and growing technological complexity was beginning to demand increased skills in the work force. With state resources behind it, the Education Department was gearing up to provide secondary schooling on a scale never before contemplated in Victoria. 'Church schools face a challenge' ran the headline of a typical leader article in the *Age* in mid-1954.[13] Could the independent schools maintain the place they had traditionally held as student numbers rose dramatically and, without state-aid, they remained dependent on their own sources of revenue? While major independent schools such as MCEGGS, drawing students from the affluent rural, business and professional sectors, were to some extent immune, they were not unaffected. Council minutes for the period constantly reflect the pressing problems of the school. Although the figure of 920 students in the late Ross era is sometimes regarded as an indication of the strength of MCEGGS, in fact enrolments were far above capacity and sharply taxing facilities. Staff was increasingly difficult to recruit as state bursaries and allowances led trainees into state training colleges, and higher salaries for state teachers were inevitably reflected in increasing pressures from the Assistant Mistresses Association of Victoria (AMAV) for parity.[14]

Dorothy Ross was keenly aware that the system she had created for MCEGGS was a costly one and there was a limit to the amount fees could be raised. She saw that the insistent problems would very likely 'make it necessary to modify some of our present policy', but if change had to come, Miss Ross was for total revolution rather than piecemeal reform which would leave the school with open entry but weaken her comprehensive system.[15] 'Perhaps now is the time to consider whether we shall remain what the school has stood for . . . or whether we reconstitute ourselves as the equivalent of the English Grammar School for girls', she wrote in 1954, and a year later, more pointedly, 'It would be better to be completely drastic and do away with a junior school altogether, have a rigid entrance examination, and become a pure High School'. These were not changes of which she approved, nor over which she was prepared to preside. 'It would be a much easier school to run and probably much less expensive [but] I could not be satisfied', she said, advising the Council that it needed a 'younger and more vigorous woman' and to be 'clear' about the prospective nature of the school before the appointment of a new head.[16]

But the Council was far from 'clear' on the future policy for the school. As the events of 1958 were to show, there was no consensus among its members although powerful lobbies seemed to have envisaged a new headmistress who would variously tighten discipline, eradicate the 'insidious' forces of the left and cut expenses. Even so, the popular idea that the Council was seeking some 'right wing' appointment is hardly borne out by the fact that the position was offered to both Dr Elwyn Morey, a leading educational psychologist, and Dr Margaret Blackwood, a distinguished Old Grammarian and academic, neither of whom would seem to fit that label.[17] As the search for the new principal grew more and more protracted and the loyal Sylvia Martin agreed to act as head, the school went on to a holding brief. Everyone was waiting for the new headmistress who would solve all problems and fulfil all expectations.

As Edith Mountain's ship passed through Sydney Heads she was overcome by the splendour of the harbour and the bridge.[18] She was delighted by the warmth of the welcome from the Sydney Old Grammarians and on arriving at MCEGGS a few days later, she found that the House Committee had created a charming flat for her covering an entire floor of Ross Hall.[19] But the large garden party organised for her welcome in the leafy surrounds was daunting.[20] As she politely met the crowd of Old Girls, parents, friends, and dignitaries, she was amazed by the status MCEGGS held in Melbourne. It was perhaps the beginning of a realisation of the magnitude of her task and the first sign of the difficulties ahead.

The unease she felt on that first occasion remained with her in dealing with the highly qualified and experienced staff to whom the complex, decentralised system of MCEGGS was second nature. No doubt she felt insecure, even out of her depth, and she seems to have retreated into an aloofness that could only alienate. Edith Mountain had undertaken to remain as an observer for her first year in the school but she clearly intended to be its headmistress in deed as well as in name. As the months went by she began to question key aspects of the system: geography and history were poor at matriculation, she held, since social studies had replaced these disciplines in the Middle School; insufficient students were taking physics and chemistry; the timetable required some 'reorganisation'; discipline needed tightening; the constitution of the Executive Council required amendment; and the present attitude to competition needed 'some modification'. To senior staff committed to the educational ideals of Dorothy Ross, Miss Mountain seemed either ignorant of the philosophy of the school or bent on its destruction. Tension rose and the school community began to divide. In her report to Council on 8 October 1958 she indicated her time as an observer had ended.

> I should like your approval of certain measures to put right what has been considered wrong by a large number of Australians who have the welfare of the school and of their children very much at heart . . . I feel it is right that you should know that there will probably be some strong opposition.[21]

On the very same day the infamous loyalty letter appeared at the school.

Though approximately 60 girls were withdrawn from MCEGGS in the wake of the crisis of late 1958, with whatever degree of apprehension on the part of some parents, 845 remained.[22] The school had suffered a horrendous blow and its future was still in jeopardy, but Edith Mountain had fulfilled her promise to the parents at the agonising speech day in 1958—as the students arrived for the commencement of first term 1959, the school was staffed.

There was more support for Miss Mountain than is generally supposed. Not all the existing staff had resigned, and among those who would be mainstays in the difficult times ahead were Sylvia McConkey, head of music, Anne Capelin, the new chief-of-staff, Mabel Merfield, the librarian and an Old Grammarian, and Ruth Creer, who had previously been on the staff and had returned to teaching in 1957. Betty Murray, the head's secretary at the time, recalled that Edith Mountain received at least 400 letters from parents, Old Girls and friends of the school, backing the position she had taken.[23] Some of the letters still exist. Of the parents writing, many dissociated themselves from the 'vociferous minority' who had made the difficulties a press sensation. One letter, from staff of another school, offered strong support, saying: 'What has occurred has . . . borne out our worst fears . . . for anyone who accepted the position'.[24] Many felt for the school itself rather than for its head. Supporters rallied, including some from the wider community of Melbourne, dismayed that such a major institution might collapse. Other staff members were recommended by Old Girls or sympathetic headmistresses and a considerable number were recruited through the IARTV agency.

But staffing was to remain a critical issue for the next two to three years. One problem with a young staff is sheer inexperience. Another, with young married women in this era before the contraceptive pill, was pregnancy. There seemed for a time to be no surer way to start a family than to teach at MCEGGS! And in the rapidly changing society of the times, young teachers joined the crowds of Australian youth heading for England. Meanwhile the school's network of support remained in action. Jean Lawson, a former student of Lovell House, whose years in children's radio had just drawn to a close, was immediately appointed school counsellor and took on a solid teaching load as well. Ethel Colebrook had taught at MCEGGS under Miss Gilman Jones and was a friend of Dorothy Ross before becoming headmistress of Tintern and later, the New England Girls' Grammar School. Having retired in 1959 she arrived at the headmistress's office ready to 'do anything' to help. Mildred Veal, the former head of the Prep. School who left in 1939 when Dorothy Ross caused a minor furore by dismissing the Junior School staff, now returned to assist Merna Thomas, who had been on leave in 1958 and would become its new head in 1961. In 1959 Lorna Mitchell, an Old Grammarian and head of English at MLC, had recommended the appointment of Lorna Osborn as an excellent teacher of English literature, and in 1960 she herself returned to MCEGGS to head the English Department. Dora Pike (Whitelaw) left Shelford as her former school was passing 'through a very troubled time' to take over maths.[25] Other Old Grammarians who returned included Dorothy Vollugi, Florence Vasey (née Faul), Elaine Lovett (née Speed), and Mary Branigan (née Sewell). Gradually, by about 1961 the nucleus of a new staff formed which would in its turn play a vital role in the lives of a generation of students.

Nevertheless, as school resumed in 1959 many of the new staff were very inexperienced. Worse, the triennial inspection for the Class-A status of the school was due before mid-year. MCEGGS may well have been heading for changes, as Dorothy Ross had seen, but the resignation of so many senior staff at the end of 1958 was a major catalyst in the way change would occur. At one blow the core of those most committed to, and versed in, the workings of the Ross system had gone, removing that force which normally militates against changes in institutions as reforms come in with a new broom. One immediate change was inevitable. With a largely new and inexperienced staff, anxious parents seeking reassurance over their daughters' progress, and the inspectors on the doorstep, both headmistress and Council urgently needed to gauge the state of education in the school. While at special monthly meetings in February, March and

April, Edith Mountain reported fully to the Council on staff
relations and the competency of the new appointees, an examination system was rapidly introduced.[26]

The inspection took place in June, and the report, under the
auspices of the chief inspector, W. B. Russell, made some trenchant criticisms. While some syllabuses were approved, revision
was found necessary for geography and science, and university
handbooks were recommended as guides. Curiously, even the
special course for non-academic students was recommended for
revision along these lines. Record-keeping practices were questioned, and the internal assessment system was found to have
considerable weaknesses. There was strong support for examinations. 'The new method will be better for all concerned', said
the inspectors. Although the teaching they had observed 'had
varied somewhat in quality and effectiveness', it was found to be
'in accord with modern teaching principles', and the pupils and
teachers were settling down well. 'The pupils have made satisfactory progress over the first half year', they wrote. 'Improvement
must be expected as the staffing of the school becomes fully
stabilised'. The school maintained its Class-A status, though a
number of staff were approved only under the supervision of
heads of departments and certain subjects were not eligible for
internal assessment.[27] Matriculation results were weaker in 1958.
In 1959 they plummeted and it was not until 1962 that they again
began to reach the standard for which the school had been
known.[28]

The events of 1958 had deeply affected many lives, not least that
of the headmistress herself. In the opinion of many of her
friends and colleagues she never recovered from the hurt she had
experienced. Always reserved, she had withdrawn even further
from all but formal contact except with a trusted few. She had
incurred a heavy responsibility in coming to the school and,
isolated and lonely, she was inevitably drawn to the church for
support. In 1960 when the Venerable (later Dean) Tom Thomas
was appointed to the School Council, he was specifically asked
by Archbishop Woods to act as an adviser and confidant to the
head.[29] From that time on, he was a tower of strength to
MCEGGS. Nevertheless, with the combination of her innate
shyness, her English training and the open hostility she had
experienced, the administrative style that Edith Mountain adopted
was one that would be frequently criticised as 'remote', 'inaccess-
ible', and 'autocratic'.

She had many strengths. As time would show, her particular
talents lay in her administrative and organisational abilities and
after the early difficulties settled down, the school ran smoothly

even while undergoing a complete physical transformation. Her kindness to staff and students with personal problems is widely attested, as is her ability to perceive the talents of individual girls and direct them with considerable perspicacity, and though she had her finger on the pulse of the school, once she had recruited the best staff obtainable for positions of responsibility she allowed them to carry out their briefs with little interference. The feeling that they had Edith Mountain's respect 'brought out 150 per cent effort in the staff', one recalled, and many stressed her integrity. Parents, staff and students, however, are virtually unanimous in recalling the extraordinary difficulties of 'seeing' the headmistress. One former member of staff graphically described Miss Mountain's management model as that of the 'admiral on the bridge' who communicated with her staff via her 'captains' or through a series of notes. Her protective secretary, Betty Murray, was her right hand, and the various school chaplains were her supporters and advisers. The 'captains', Anne Capelin, the efficient chief-of-staff, and the heads of departments kept a firm control. Jean Lawson, the school counsellor, whose warmth and outgoing manner made her the 'front door' of the school, was the catalyst allowing the whole system to operate. In the early years, in Miss Mountain's absence, Jean Lawson acted for her, and later, Lorna Osborn was to become the assistant headmistress.[30]

In 1958 Edith Mountain's critics had condemned her for having 'no educational policy'.[31] She was not principally an educational theorist, but she certainly had a view of education, albeit a 'traditional' one, and undoubtedly it was influenced by her English background. Though her own field was the sciences, she had a deep interest in the humanities and she saw the independent schools as 'the bastion of a liberal education'. In her seventeen years at MCEGGS she played a much more limited role in educational circles than either of her predecessors, and she has left very few statements of her ideas. One of the most detailed is a paper on the role of the 'traditional' school delivered at the Headmistresses' Association of Australia conference in 1961, the theme of which was 'the place of independent schools in the educational system'.[32] Given her interest in history, it is hardly surprising that she commenced with a quotation from Pericles and traced the evolution of a 'liberal education' through the work of Thomas Arnold and Public schools of England to Miss Beale and Miss Buss, whose famous English girls' schools were the prototypes of the GPDST schools she knew so well, and of the leading independent schools of Melbourne.

Apart from . . . their direct grants from the Ministry of Education . . . [and] the fact that they are non-denominational — these

> GPDST schools are the nearest in character, I think, to a school
> such as MCEGGS . . . The girls' schools in England took their
> traditions from the boys' schools and adapted them to meet the
> needs of their girls.

Like so many before her, these traditions she summarised as the
development of responsibility, self-discipline, community spirit,
and an understanding of the Christian faith—the principles
upon which MCEGGS had been built. Yet environments within
which such ideals are pursued can vary considerably. The paper
also suggests the disciplined ethos Edith Mountain would develop
at Grammar and the extent to which her thinking had been
clarified and reinforced by her experiences in her first year at the
school. She seized the opportunity to make clear her views on the
reasons for the furore.

> The word 'discipline' in some educational circles, still acts as a 'red
> rag to a bull'. But . . . many parents today are willing to make great
> financial sacrifices to expose their children to the kind of discipline
> which emphasises good manners, a consideration for others, ability
> to take the rough with the smooth, and an attention to duties, as
> distinct from rights. These qualities cannot be practised or taught
> in a free-for-all rugger-scrum kind of atmosphere.

On the other hand, Miss Mountain emphasised the capacity of
the Public school for evolution, resulting from the freedom to
experiment and she was prepared to modernise Grammar in
accord with the latest educational requirements. While the
MCEGGS network had been activated to cope with the staffing
crisis, its public relations mechanisms had also gone into operation. Immediately after the upheaval, at a special Council
meeting in late November 1958, Miss Mountain presented a
memorandum with suggestions for future planning of the Anderson Street and Wildfell sites.[33] The building program that would
transform the school physically in the years ahead had begun. Its
fund-raising drives and continuing publicity were a powerful
means of bonding the school community and of promoting
MCEGGS as an up-to-date school, able to meet the needs of
contemporary society.

As early as 1952 Dorothy Ross had stressed that with the
unprecedented numbers of students entering the school in the
postwar years, a major building project was essential and had
outlined developments ahead to 1967 when the 'existing debt
[would] be sufficiently reduced for . . . new capital expenditure'.[34]
In the meantime, although Sylvia Martin pointed out problem

areas, the policy was one of maintenance rather than construction. As she observed, many of the staff of the day had taken part in the wartime evacuation — they were 'used to making do' and demanded little change.[35] Moves had been made only gradually. In October 1957 a building fund contribution of £2 per term had been added to fees, and in 1958 a subcommittee for long-range planning was established. Finally, in 1959 John Scarborough was appointed the school architect to draw up a master plan.

As the baby-boomers relentlessly pushed their way up through the primary grades and the birthrate gave no sign of abating, the late 1950s and early 1960s was a time of decisions for all the independent schools. Some bought new properties in areas where the suburbs were beginning to sprawl. Others, including MCEGGS, remained on existing sites, constantly watchful for vacant land or buildings in the immediate vicinity. In 1957 the school snapped up 96 Caroline Street, contiguous with the Wildfell site in Domain Road, and in 1957 a property in Walsh Street was purchased.

From the beginning, Edith Mountain had wished to expand the library which was cramped into the Merton Hall building. With her scientific background she was also critical of the existing laboratories, linking this to what she deemed to be a very small number of students taking matriculation physics and chemistry, and to the fact that no MCEGGS girls had gone into medicine in 1956 or 1957.[36] The launching of Sputnik I by the Russians in October 1957, an event which shocked the Western world into a rethinking of mathematics and science education, no doubt added grist to her mill. So did the ACER questionnaire to Australian independent schools early in 1958, aimed at gaining a picture of science teaching in the hope of attracting funding from major companies such as ICI and Shell.[37] From her days at Putney High School, Edith Mountain had first-hand experience of the British Industrial Fund for the Advancement of Scientific Education, established in 1956, which was the model for the Australian scheme. The GPDST schools had been among its initiators, and though most funding had gone to boys' schools, the Trust schools had received substantial grants for new laboratories.[38] As Miss Mountain pointed out, to gain initial funding it had been necessary not only to demonstrate genuine interest in promoting science, but to be seen to be taking some initiatives.[39] When in 1961 the Australian Industrial Fund for the Advancement of Scientific Education in Schools finally began its work, its support was extended to boys' schools only.

But MCEGGS had not waited. In September of that year F. W. G. White of the CSIRO opened a modern laboratory wing and a spacious new library linking Merton and Gilman Jones Halls to form a quadrange behind Ross Hall. In brilliant sunshine the guests sat on the hockey field and, as parents rushed to vantage points with cameras, the girls marched on to form the school badge against the green of the grass. Understandably, the school community was jubilant. 'You can't help a bit of mutual congratulation', wrote the archbishop some time later, 'when you look at the new £90,000 science and library block whose erection has been made possible only because the school's future is regarded by the "city" as a "sure bet"'.[40] Following the next Class-A inspection in 1962, though there were still problems, the headmistress could report the inspectors' comments on science with pride—MCEGGS now had 'one of the best "set ups" in Victoria', with almost every science class held in a laboratory.[41] By the end of 1961, with its staff more established and its building program well under way, MCEGGS had survived the critical years and moved on into a new era.

Many of the ideas Edith Mountain expressed in her 1961 paper can be seen reflected in the operation of the school in her time: in the curriculum, in the role of the Student Executive Council, in the attitude to competition, in the program which made her MCEGGS's 'greatest builder', and in the close links with the cathedral. Given her notion of a 'broad, liberal education', Miss Mountain valued subjects that were not purely vocational, but involved 'learning for learning's sake'.[42] She strongly encouraged the introduction of new subjects such as biblical studies and classical civilisation as they were developed through the 1960s, and her staff were encouraged to participate in subject associations and serve on syllabus committees. The excellence of the MCEGGS matriculation results, particularly in the second half of her headmistressship, are indicative of the calibre of her teachers and of the academic standards for which she aimed. Yet Edith Mountain was also concerned with providing a curriculum suited to the non-academic student. Like Miss Ross before her, she continued to remind the Council of the curricular requirements necessitated by open entry. 'Members of the council ask is it essential to keep Domestic Science in this school', she wrote in the early 1960s. 'I feel that in a non-selective school such as this it is very desirable', and the subject remained, steadily dwindling, until the end of the decade.[43] She personally worked to develop a non-academic biology course at Leaving and post-Leaving levels, and encouraged students to stay on to complete a sixth form year.[44] With changes in matriculation regulations in 1962 making it compulsory for all four subjects to be passed at one sitting, she was keen to retain a non-academic post-Leaving course, enhancing its status with approval from the Education Department.[45] The post-Leaving course, and the continuance of a second-year sixth form, inevitably lost out with the advent of the Higher School Certificate and the relentless demands of the Anderson Score from 1972 onwards, positing a second-year sixth form as indicative of 'weakness'.[46]

Her approach to the Student Executive Council is also in keeping with the ideas expressed in her 1961 conference paper. The minutes of this Council, from the first meeting of its predecessor, the Prefects' Advisory Council in 1942, through the 1950s, 1960s and 1970s sit, volume by volume, in the archives, together with the many subcommittees' minutes and reports, testifying to the very significant role it has played in the lives of generations of girls at MCEGGS. In its training for leadership, its encouragement of thoughtfulness and self-disciplined action and its representation of the student community it was perfectly in keeping with Miss Mountain's ideas, and as clouds gathered in 1958 she stressed to the girls that she was quite used to student councils in England and, contrary to rumour, she did not intend to end it; however, as she stated, she certainly wished to modify it.[47] Through 1959 the headmistress, girls and staff on the Executive Council toiled through the process of changing the constitution. Many of the changes were administrative. Edith Mountain felt that the constant round of meetings the existing system entailed was too time-consuming — the tail was beginning to wag the dog. The number of councillors was reduced, and the new position of administrator created to carry out policy. However, the main aspect of the Executive Council to which she had objected, as she pointed out in her report of October 1958, was the clause referring to self-government which stipulated 'no veto by the headmistress'. That this should be stated about any school matter she held to be misleading since it was in direct contravention of the school's constitution and, as she wrote to the School Council, 'in fact, contrary . . . to my agreement with you'.[48]

The powers of a student council will always be a vexed question. While educational progressivists stress the 'freedom' and 'rights' of students, the more traditional view stresses their 'duties'. Inevitably, even in the most 'free' of schools, it must be adults who are setting the perimeters of students' liberty, though this may be at one or two steps removed. Dorothy Ross had placed powerful limits on the Executive Council's authority, but within certain spheres her notion of the democratic school required independence. Yet the Student Executive Council minutes tell their own story. Though the girls were certainly not in awe of the staff—'brilliant' staff ideas are often torn to shreds in the spirited debates—the existing ethos clearly influences the students. In the Ross years the girls had steadily divested themselves of prizes and competition as incentives to success. Under Miss Mountain they reinstated them with just as much enthusiasm.

Moves to restore competition proceeded slowly, perhaps restrained by the memories of public outrage at the suggested demise of Dorothy Ross's 'democratic school' in 1958. Possibly the least acceptable of all Miss Ross's ideas had been her minimisation of competition in sport. To many school families competitive sport was one of the traditions expected in major Public schools like MCEGGS, and for them its advantages in developing the young and preparing them for the 'real world' outweighed any disadvantages associated with striving only for rewards.[49] Many students were also anxious for change in this area, as by 1958 athletics had dwindled to the status of a 'club', by definition with a maximum of thirty members.[50]

A major shift came when Margaret Woodlock joined the Physical Education Department in 1959. An Australian champion shot-putter, training for the Rome Olympics, she inspired the girls to enormous efforts. Athletics was rapidly reinvigorated as one of the school's major sports and in April 1960 MCEGGS took part in the combined Church of England Girls' Grammar School Athletics. Two years later they had pulled themselves up to second place and enthusiasm knew no bounds. Room for sporting activities on the Anderson Street site, already a problem, now reached crisis proportions. In a report for the Council in 1961 Miss Woodlock outlined the difficulties. The Junior School's play area was a rough vacant block in Fairlie Court. There was no room for them on the two basketball courts when fifty big girls were trying to play, nor on the hockey field where upwards of eighty were turning up to practice.[51] There has never been an easy solution to the question of sporting facilities on the inner-city campus of MCEGGS, but in the building policy of the Mountain era the need for increased playing space was a major factor. A practical approach had to overrule sentiment. The cleared site of the beautiful Wildfell mansion would be fully utilised while waiting for the building of the new Junior School, and for a number of years the site of the original Morris Hall, where generations of MCEGGS girls had played around the timbered verandahs, was to serve as tennis courts.

In 1964, the fifth year the school entered the combined athletics, MCEGGS won the Challenge Cup. The next year, as a trial for a limited period, the school was divided into five houses for internal sporting competition. The Student Executive Council supported the idea strongly, and girls enthusiastically sent in suggestions for names, finally deciding upon 'Clarke', 'Hensley', 'Mungo', 'Taylor' and 'Batman'. House activities proved very popular and in subsequent years they were extended to take in a wide range of activities, including the debating, choral and drama competitions which still continue. House captains became councillors, and vice-captains administrators. For many within the community, there was a sense not of breaking with tradition but of returning to the earlier traditions of the Gilman Jones era.[52]

The reintroduction of prizes was treated with particular caution, but given the ethos of the Mountain period it was inevitable. The major prizes which had been endowed in memory of former students, staff and benefactors of MCEGGS record a history of the school: the Madame Liet prize for French; the Dorothea Baynes prize for classics; the A. M. Mackay prize for English; the Jessie Nott prize for music; the Maude Howard and Phelia Grimwade prizes for science; the Florence Finn prize for speech work; and the highest honours of all, the Helen Patterson and Mary Michaelis prizes for all-round excellence.

The first change came in 1959 when Sir Archie Michaelis wrote requesting that the money entrusted to MCEGGS in 1920 in memory of his sister, Mary, again be used for the original purpose.[53] The Council gave permission and the Mary Michaelis prize for study, sport and service to the school was resumed in the same year. The policy in general, however, was not reversed. Then in 1962 a new prize was endowed in memory of the wife of Sir Reginald Sholl, a long-serving member of the Council and strong supporter of Edith Mountain. At the headmistress's suggestion, the Hazel Sholl memorial prize was presented for an essay on divinity. Obviously the whole question of prizes was in need of review. The Council deferred its approval, since 'a matter of principle was involved', and the feelings of other sections of the school were canvassed.[54]

The parents of the 1960s were unequivocally in favour of rewards and prizes. When the subject was raised at a Parents' Association committee meeting there was overwhelming support, and it was moved that the head put to the Council the parents' 'strong desire for the re-opening of the distribution of prizes'.[55] The staff and girls were also enthusiastic and many Old Grammarians were warmly in support of what they saw as a return to earlier traditions. The endowing families were contacted, and with the Council's permission a two-year trial period began. Mrs Mary Franks (née Patterson), an Old Grammarian and the sister of Helen Patterson, distributed the prizes at speech night at the end of 1966.[56]

As MCEGGS was slowly reshaping its internal policies, its physical form was in a constant state of transition as the master plan came rapidly into effect. With their generation all over Australia, the MCEGGS girls of the 1960s were educated to the pounding of jackhammers and the whining of saws as old buildings were altered or levelled and new ones arose. By 1967, as well as a new science and library wing, the school would have a renovated boarding house, a separate Junior School and—fulfilling its longest-held dream—a chapel of its own.

It had been quickly decided that the most efficient way of relieving the crowding at Anderson Street was to build a new Junior School on the extended Wildfell property. This meant the small groups of Wildfell boarders who had been carrying out Miss Ross's 'long cherished plan'—keeping house and living much like day girls—would have to rejoin the community on the main site.[57] This was a relief to the head in a number of ways. Wildfell had been uneconomic and very difficult to staff. Moreover, the beautiful old house had been difficult to secure. Twice intruders had terrified the girls, one managing to enter a dormitory and cut a sleeping student's pyjamas before he fled as the girls' screams gave the alarm.[58]

There were a number of steps to be taken. Gilman Jones Hall, which began life in the 1930s as the boarding house, New Merton Hall, had been used by Dorothy Ross for the Middle School. It was now completely refitted inside to revert to its original function. By early 1962 the first and second floors were completed and the girls had moved in, delighted with their up-to-date single and double study bedrooms.

Merton Hall itself was reorganised, the headmistress and Mrs Murray moving up from the old ground floor study to a new suite of offices in the former library area, with a nearby room for the counsellor, Jean Lawson, and a waiting room for parents. For the first time in many years the first and second formers were back with the main school, packed into the rooms at the very top of Merton Hall, to the excitement of the girls and the joy of the staff who had found the decentralised system somewhat hard on 'shanks' pony'.[59] The ground floor of Gilman Jones Hall remained multi-purpose, housing needlework, and shorthand and typing classes, as well as councillors' and administrators' rooms. Later a tiny chapel was created and blessed by the dean in December 1963.

As the building plan had gone into operation it was realised that a financial and public relations plan was required as well and at the end of 1962, with support from Old Grammarians and parents, the Council invited the National Fund Raising Council to organise an appeal.[60] All sections of the school community were surveyed to gauge the 'feeling of the market': the level of satisfaction with the school's record, its fee structure, its facilities and equipment, its dissemination of information, and its proposed developments. The analysis of the results provides one of the most valuable sources of information about this part of Edith Mountain's headmistressship. Many felt strongly that they were not sufficiently informed about school developments, but the overall attitude was very supportive of the planning committee's intentions. There were predictable differences between groups. Parents emphasised the need for playing space, art and craft facilities, and a swimming pool, while Old Grammarians 'welcomed a new junior school, a chapel, and modern assembly hall'. The appeal target was set at £100 000 and plans went ahead for a launching dinner at the St Kilda Palais.[61]

The school had taken giant steps to provide its own funding in the early Mountain era, but in 1963 a new factor came to bear on the issue. The Menzies government acted on the reintroduction of state aid. Explanations for this vary. Perhaps one factor was the realisation that even the prominent independent schools, with traditionally strong socio-economic links to the conservative parties, were struggling to keep their standard competitive with the burgeoning high schools. More usually, reasons are found in the party politics of the day. The economic recession which Australia experienced under the Liberal-Country Party Coalition (LCP) in the early 1960s had posed a threat to their long hold on power and, conscious of the need to win the largely Catholic Democratic Labor Party (DLP) preferences, state aid to non-government schools was an obvious move. Both major parties promised increased expenditure on education prior to the election, the LCP offering a direct grant of £5 million per annum 'for the . . . building and equipment . . . for science teaching in secondary schools . . . government or independent without discrimination'.[62] The LCP victory led in May 1964 to the passing of the *States Grants (Science Laboratories and Technical Training) Bill* and the road to federal and state funding for independent schools was finally open for the first time for almost a hundred years.

It was well timed for MCEGGS. The appeal was already fully targeted but the rapid advances in education required ever more. Increased numbers taking science, together with the new Physical Science Study Committee (PSSC) physics course which would be compulsory for science students in leaving in 1965 and matricu-

lation in 1966, necessitated even more extensive physics laboratories than those completed in 1961. At the dean's suggestion,
Miss Mountain wrote to Senator John Gorton, Minister of
Education and Science, requesting that MCEGGS be placed on
the list for financial help.[63]

Meanwhile, the school community entered into the appeal
with gusto. Teams visited potential donors and each week results
were chalked up at Monday night meetings in the hall. Old
Grammarians competed to outdo fathers and a progress chart in
the Assembly Hall proclaimed the latest figures to the girls in the
mornings. By the final night they were more than £13 000 over
the target.[64] If the school community still felt the pain of 1958
the appeal must have worked wonders in dispelling it. It had,
one writer claimed, put the Old Grammarians 'in touch with the
school and their fellows in a way surpassing anything earlier'.
Throughout country Victoria and New South Wales, committees
had been organised and while Jean Lawson held the fort in
South Yarra, Edith Mountain toured the country towns attending
functions and meeting school families. She enjoyed herself
immensely.[65]

For a short time Wildfell stood deserted and those who remembered its family atmosphere were filled with regret. But as one
correspondent to the school magazine wrote, capturing the spirit
of the times, '*some* people were still nostalgic about *Old Fairlie*'.[66]
By 1963 Wildfell was no more. The site was extended by the
purchase of a cleared block where the old prefabricated timber
house, Avoca, had stood. Despite considerable opposition from
the National Trust, it had been demolished at about the same
time. The original Morris Hall in Anderson Street fared no
better, falling to the demolition hammers at the end of 1966.

On 31 March 1966 the new Junior School was opened by the
Governor of Victoria, Sir Rohan Delacombe. In clear sunny
weather the official party sat on the open terrace with the little
Morris Hall girls on one side and the 1500 guests on the lawns.
The governor expressed satisfaction at seeing this 'large independent school not only remaining in its central position so
close to the heart of the city but also extending on such progressive lines'.[67] To maintain the link with the early history of the
school the new building was named Morris Hall and a glass
panel from the old building bearing the family crest of Clara
Morris (née French) was set into the door of the headmistress's
study. The day must have brought back many memories for Mrs
Gwynneth Colles (née Morris), who was with the official party.[68]
The somewhat harsh 1960s brick of the new Morris Hall is a far
cry from the graceful Federation original, but its light and

spacious rooms were designed with the latest educational ideas in mind and the Avoca land provided a large, tree-covered playground.

A chapel had been the dream of the school since the days of Miss Tunnicliffe, and in 1918 Miss Gilman Jones had officially opened the chapel fund, but the goal was still far off when Edith Mountain was appointed.[69] A deeply religious woman, she was convinced a chapel was essential to provide the 'focal point of the school' and she was determined to carry out the idea — discussed since the early 1930s — of using the Assembly Hall for the purpose.[70] The first design made use of the complete space with a stepped chancel floor and screens, doors, altar and reredos elaborately carved in Manchurian oak. The Council, however, preferred the design of Louis Williams, a partner with the original architects of the hall, which divided the building horizontally, creating the Chapel of St Luke, 'a beautiful modern place of worship.'[71]

In the words of Bishop Grindrod, Edith Mountain saw her work at the school as a vocation and it is remarkable that in the mid-1960s, when the young were questioning 'traditional' ideas, the new chapel became the centre of so much of the school's life.[72] Through confirmation classes and serving at the altar, students were encouraged to become further involved, and under the direction of Joan Bazeley, the Chapel Chanters (or 'Chapel Chicks') developed an outstanding repertoire of sacred music. Two of the Victorian women currently awaiting ordination — Clemence Woods and Adrienne Simondson — are girls of the Mountain era. It was with regret that the dean informed the disappointed Old Grammarians that it was the policy of the Anglican Church to 'discourage the celebration of marriage services and baptisms in places other than Parish Churches.'[73] Links with the cathedral were very strong throughout Miss Mountain's time, annual school church services commencing in 1959 and carol services in 1967.

Yet something of the controversy which accompanied Edith Mountain in her years at MCEGGS was present even in respect of the chapel. While for some she was 'too religious' in her approach, others found her way of proceeding with chapel and assembly extraordinarily difficult. All too often teachers were left to fume inwardly as first lessons ticked away and the school was still waiting in the chapel for the headmistress to appear. Was Miss Mountain indeed in prayer in her study as 'folklore' had it among the girls? Was her innate shyness a recurring problem to be faced and overcome each morning? Or was this a measure of the discipline which she imposed upon the school?[74]

Though discipline was certainly a characteristic of MCEGGS in Miss Mountain's time, the school was full of lively activity. The drawers of the archives and the pages of the magazine and the less formal student newspaper, *Brick*, are filled with the details of the co-curricular side of school life: the unending round of social service activities; Brownies and Guides; Miss Rose's ballet classes; the school's radio station, VK–3AYL; meetings of the Student Christian Movement; the annual Shakespeare celebration first instituted by Miss Gilman Jones in 1923. In 1964 the magazine relates that this 'took a different form': two sixth form girls, Christine Hooper and Christine de Wolff, gave a program of songs from the Shakespearian plays.[75]

The traumatic year of 1959 was one of the most remarkable, with Sylvia McConkey's outstanding direction of the children's opera, 'Noye's Fludde', the fifteenth-century Chester miracle play set to music by Benjamin Britten, which opened at St Paul's Cathedral in August—the first Australian performance. Except for the voice of God (the school chaplain), a handful of professional singers and musicians, and a few boys, all the parts were taken by MCEGGS students. The simple but effective sets and costumes maintained the spirit of the original play. As Mrs Noah and her 'gossips' laughed, the animals and birds trouped on to the ark, 'each pair singing a Kyrie Eleison in their own way— the doves cooing it, the mice squeaking it', while the percussionist splashed down the first raindrops. The storm and the flood, portrayed powerfully by the orchestra, climaxed with the hymn 'Eternal Father, Strong to Save', before the solo cello depicted the flight of the raven, and a solo recorder gave the song of the dove.[76] The Melbourne reviews were enthusiastic, and Benjamin Britten, to whom Miss McConkey had written, replied that the performance 'was certainly a compliment to the work'.[77] One wise old owl remains to this day in the school archives.

Jean Lawson, the school counsellor, whose wartime years as a senior administrative officer in the WAAAF had prepared her to cope with the problems of the girls, also brought her considerable theatrical experience to MCEGGS. Students seem to remember little of the counselling, but they all recall her exciting productions of attractions such as 'Salad Days'.[78] Under the editorship of Lorna Mitchell the school magazine changed in size and style over the years; a special edition in 1963 celebrated MCEGGS Diamond Jubilee with its focus on sixty years of change and memories. For leaving and matriculation girls entering Channel Seven's 'Parliament of Youth', nerves of steel were a decided advantage, along with thorough preparation under the eagle eye of Nina Crone, then a young teacher.[79]

An analysis of former students' responses to a questionnaire on the transition years of the late 1950s and early 1960s suggests that while some were permanently alienated from MCEGGS, most adjusted fairly easily to the change in ethos of the Mountain era.[80] Some found the more disciplined system supportive. Examinations quickly became part of school life. The headmistress's dogs — the huge Bulfa and her tiny mate Pug — were taken to heart by the girls, and rumours linking Bulfa's bulging waistline to missing school lunches were all too true. Nevertheless, Bulfa was the mascot of *Brick* for several years.[81]

By the later 1960s and early 1970s *Brick* was taking a more serious tone, with less schoolgirl humour and more reference to the issues of the day: civil rights, South Africa, pollution, Vietnam. The link with school matters was still there of course: 'Oh! I see you're so worried about what they are doing in Vietnam that you forgot to do your [uniform] coat up!', runs an editorial entitled 'Consideration and reformation'.[82] More students were staying on to the final school years, they were maturing earlier and demanding greater liberty of speech and action. If the young had ever been biddable they seemed to be less so in the 1960s. On one occasion boys from a leading Melbourne school entered one of the boarding houses and left an inscription that 'could only have been written by a boy', as the head informed the Council. Worse still, it seemed that some of the girls might have actually let them in![83] Freedom for the young was the catchcry of the times.

Most schools were considering ways of providing an environment which would both reflect and aid the process of social change — one in which senior students could to some extent escape from the domination of university entrance examinations and learn to handle their new-found freedom with responsibility. Many schools had already moved towards the creation of special areas and facilities for their sixth formers but it was not until 1969 that Edith Mountain found the direction she wished to take with MCEGGS. The Edith Mountain Sixth Form Centre, opened in 1973, was, she reportedly told a Council member, not just a building. It was the accomplishment of a dream which allowed her to express in tangible form an educational theory to which she was totally committed.[84] The dream stemmed from the visit of Miss Geraldine Lack, former headmistress of Rosebery County School for Girls in Epsom, England, to publicise her concept of a centre for senior girls which had made significant changes in curriculum, work and leisure patterns. At Rosebery, half the lesson schedule was comprised of academic subjects with the other half equally divided between private study and general study. Her centre was housed in a new, two-storey, open-space building, intended to provide an environment which was comfortable, and facilitated change, creative teaching methods, and ready contact between staff and students.[85]

Again the MCEGGS community swung into action with a new building appeal. The master plan was extended to incorporate a Rosebery-style wing linked to the already proposed new Assembly Hall to be ready in 1973, and a general studies program was developed by Lorna Osborn.[86] As she reported in the magazine, the course 'included lectures on subjects ranging from Greek philosophy and literature to present-day Melbourne problems such as poverty, mental health and illness, migrant assimilation . . . and family planning'. Outstanding speakers were drawn from many fields. Team teaching was introduced; and staff teaching music, science, religious instruction and languages were all involved.[87] 'Did we get an education!', exclaimed one of the students who passed through the system in its early years;[88] however, though the program was very successful and no doubt discussing the theme 'authority and the individual' helped defuse student protest of the time, the open plan building was not without its logistical and acoustic problems. After innumerable delays in meeting the deadline, the new Assembly Hall (named Ross Hall at the request of the Old Girls) and the Edith Mountain Sixth Form Centre were opened by Sir Rohan Delacombe on 30 October 1973.[89] Perhaps Edith Mountain now felt she had given to the school something that would rank with the achievements of Dorothy Ross—the Sixth Form Centre was hardly different in spirit.[90]

Early in 1973, while efforts were in progress to gain federal government assistance in the creation of a Middle School library in the old Assembly Hall, Edith Mountain announced her decision to retire at the end of the 1974.[91] 'I don't want my successor to have my experience', she told one of her closest associates, and in a final interview in the *Age*, reflecting on the changes in educational ideas, social and moral values, and the growth of bureaucracy, she pointed out how 'the responsibilities of a Headmistress . . . [had] . . . increased tremendously' since the time of her appointment.[92]

At a grand farewell luncheon given by parents and Old Grammarians on the school's birthday in October 1974, the headmistress, whose green Hillman had dashed in and out of MCEGGS for so long, was delighted by her farewell gift—a 'Matchbox' Hillman—the real thing to be collected in London.[93] Edith Mountain retired to Cartmel in the Lake District she had known so well in her childhood, to a life of involvement with the

National Trust and the local parish church. In a moment of facetiousness she pointed out that her new home gave her title to the old town gaol. 'I'm thinking of installing bunks for . . . Australians', she said.[94] Those who accepted her genuine offers of hospitality had a wonderful time. Edith Mountain died at the early age of sixty-five on 5 December 1984.

9 Melbourne Girls
Grammar School
in 1993

M ISS NINA CRONE, HEADMISTRESS OF MGGS SINCE 1975,
wrote recently in the school's *Information Exchange*
that the 'power of place' and the 'hand of history' are
powerful influences on the school community.[1] Her school
captain of 1991, Daile Kincaid, wrote in the magazine for that
year: 'It is neither reputation nor buildings nor history that
makes a school elite, but the quality of its teachers and students.
Reputation, history and buildings can inspire, to be sure, but
these must fall on fertile soil to bear fruit.'[2] Headmistress and
school captain are not in disagreement; but they are of different
generations and they are emphasising different aspects of the
same reality—that a school belongs both to the past and to the
present. Antecedents are everywhere palpable; the present has a
disconcerting tendency to double back. Old Girls who visit the
school may glimpse a younger, slimmer self vanishing round
corners obliterating, for an instant, time which has passed.

A snapshot of the school in its centenary year cannot adequately
take account of this dialogue between the past and the present,
although it may serve more humbly as a starting point for the
historian of the second hundred years. On the eve of its centenary
MGGS has an enrolment of 868 girls, comprising 23 preps, 194
juniors, and 651 seniors, among them 116 boarders.[3] In the
Senior School there is an enrolment of 79 at year seven and 125 at
year twelve. Overseas students are drawn from many parts of the
world, including Fiji, Malaysia, Hong Kong, England, and the
United States of America. The international profile which charac-
terises MGGS in the 1990s is enhanced by the participation of
many girls in 'student exchanges' schemes, where they have the

170

opportunity to immerse themselves in the culture of other lands. In 1988, for example, MGGS had a mini diplomatic corps-in-training with girls awarded exchange places under various schemes in China, the United States, Denmark, and France.[4]

The staff of Merton Hall comprises fifty-one full-time and fourteen part-time teachers, as well as a counsellor, a special education teacher and a careers adviser. Morris Hall has sixteen full-time and four part-time teachers. There are also four full-time and three part-time library staff, five boarding-house staff, two part-time sick bay nurses, and four ancillary staff such as laboratory technicians.

This community of students and staff goes about its daily life on two inner-city campuses which are part of the historic landscape of South Yarra. In the minds of generations of girls, the boundaries of the school are permeable: to the west, across Anderson Street, the Royal Botanic Gardens; to the north, the Yarra River; to the south and east the beautiful tree-lined streets of South Yarra. The junior campus, Morris Hall, is still in Caroline Street on the old Wildfell site, not far from the original Merton Hall in Domain Road. In November 1987 Morris Hall girls, staff, and parents held a party to mark their twenty-first birthday on the site. The Preparatory School is in Walsh Street adjacent to Merton Hall, the Senior School campus in Anderson Street. Within walking distance are the Victorian Arts Centre, the Sidney Myer Music Bowl, the State Swimming Centre, the Olympic Park Athletics Stadium, and the National Tennis Centre. In the late twentieth century, when MGGS sends most of its girls on to tertiary education, many country and overseas parents choose to send their daughters as boarders because the location allows them to experience the bustling inner city before university life brings its added pressures.

It was a sign of the times that the annual School Council Seminar for 1991 took as its theme 'School Development— Marketing'. Guest speakers emphasised the vital importance for a girls' school like MGGS of the changing patterns of women's lives: their patterns of work; the decrease in family size and the postponement of child-bearing; and the changing basis of decisions about the education of female children. The consequences for MGGS of the 1990s' economic recession and the formation of state senior secondary campuses were also discussed. One positive outcome of the seminar was the formulation of a mission statement, setting out both the school's traditions and aspirations for the future. As the school enters its second century MGGS articulates its aims in this way: to maintain and enhance an Anglican school for girls which values excellence and which reflects in its enrolment the community it serves; to provide for day girls and boarders from Melbourne, rural Australia, and abroad an education which offers a world view in the humane and scientific disciplines; to impart the fundamental knowledge inherent in a scholastic tradition and to develop the critical and creative skills required to apply that knowledge towards a purposeful future; to develop young women who are articulate, confident, responsible for their personal well-being and willing to serve their community; to be a responsible employer mindful of staff career development and with concern for the surrounding community and environment; and to manage a sound independent enterprise with sufficient capital and income to carry out its mission.

Ultimately responsible for the fulfilment of this mission is the School Council, the governing body representing the diocese, the parents and the Old Grammarians. In 1989 the MGGS community was greatly saddened by the death of its *ex-officio* president of the School Council, Archbishop David Penman. In his memory, an icon of Christ Pantocrator has been placed in the Chapel of St Luke. With his election as Archbishop of Melbourne in July 1990, the Most Reverend Keith Raynor became president of the MGGS Council. Early in 1991 Archbishop Raynor paid his first visit to MGGS, meeting for the first time the heads of Anglican schools and attending a School Council meeting. MGGS girls sang during the special Eucharist service which preceded the meetings. The deputy chair of the School Council is the Dean of Melbourne, the Right Reverend James Grant, and it is he who has the day-to-day responsibility for the functioning of the Council.

Since the appointment of the first interim School Council by Bishop Goe in 1901, women have been represented. On the eve of the school's centenary there are six Old Grammarians on the Council. Dr Margaret Clark (née Sanders) has had a long association with MGGS. She was enrolled in 1940 and consequently was evacuated to Marysville and Doncaster. Her mother, Old Grammarian Mrs Joan Sanders (née Brett), also served on the School Council. Margaret Clark graduated in medicine from the University of Melbourne in 1953, and went on to an interesting and varied medical career. Her daughter Meriel attended MGGS from 1972–78. The mother of her husband, Charles, was Alice Bage, and his three sisters were also Old Grammarians.

Mrs Caroline Dowling (née Purbrick) attended MGGS from 1946–58. She attended Invergowrie and then the Royal Melbourne Institute of Technology where she studied fashion. Her daughters Sarah and Sophie are Old Grammarians. Ms Susan McCarthy, who attended MGGS from 1958–64, also has a long association with the school. Her mother Margaret McCarthy (née Coulter) and her sister Meg McPherson (née McCarthy) are Old Grammarians, and Meg taught Latin at MGGS for two years. Sue is a banker who joined the ANZ Bank as an economic research officer and now holds a senior position doing strategic planning work. Mrs Margaret Spring (née Colclough) attended MGGS from 1933–38. Margaret became a nurse, and while raising her five children worked with her husband, Dr Ted Spring, in his practice. Her daughter Amanda is also an Old Grammarian. As president of the Parents' Association Margaret became a member of the School Council in 1979.

Mrs Barbara Tolson (née Selleck) entered MGGS in 1939. She was first elected to Council in 1966 as a representative of the Old Grammarians who have made her a life member. Ms Sally Walker attended MGGS from 1969–72 as a boarder. She studied law at the University of Melbourne where she was placed first in her final year. Sally practised as a solicitor and then returned to the Law School at the University of Melbourne where she is now a Reader.

Immediate responsibility for the well-being of MGGS is in the hands of Miss Nina Crone, who has been headmistress since the retirement of Edith Mountain in 1974. Born in 1934 at Grays, Essex, England, she is the daughter of Grace (née Hall) and James Crone, a Commonwealth public servant. The family, which included two brothers, came to Australia when she was a child, and she received her secondary education at PLC when it was in Albert Street, East Melbourne. There she was greatly influenced by the first female head of the school, Scotswoman Mary Neilson, who had been appointed in 1938 after sixty-three years of male heads. Nina Crone graduated B.A. from the University of Melbourne in 1956, and B.Ed. in 1962. In the years 1957 to 1964 she gained wide teaching experience in Australia (at Clarendon College, Ballarat, at PLC and at MGGS), in England (at Spring Grove Grammar School, Essex) and in Switzerland (at the Institut Bénédict, Montreux). She then made a conscious decision to 'test myself away from teaching . . . as I'd only known the academic milieu, school, university, [and] school again'. For the next decade she worked for the Australian Broadcasting Commission as a radio and TV producer in the Schools Broadcasts Division. 'I left teaching [she added] to test myself on adults, learn more of people under pressure of family and the wide world. But I never had any doubt my interest was in education.'[5]

Like most of her predecessors at MGGS, Nina Crone has taken

a leading role in the educational world. Her commitments over the years have included the presidency of the Association of Independent Girls' Schools of Victoria, the Ministerial Review of Post Compulsory Education (Blackburn Committee), the Council of University College (formerly Women's College), the Independent Schools Conciliation and Arbitration Board, and the committee of the Association of Independent Schools of Victoria. These onerous commitments, together with the many commitments of the MGGS staff on professional bodies, provide a vital link between the school and the wider educational world.

Under Miss Crone's headmistressship the transformation of the school's physical environment has gone on relentlessly. Property acquisitions include 280 Walsh Street in 1976, 290 Walsh Street in 1978, and 233 Walsh Street in 1988. Jessie Bage House for senior boarders, named after Old Grammarian and Council member, Jessie Bage, was opened in 1979. The new physical education complex was opened and dedicated by Archbishop Penman in March 1985. It was named the Tom Thomas Building after the former Dean of Melbourne who retired after twenty-two years as chairman of the Finance Committee of Council in 1984. Dean Thomas's two daughters, Angela and Jane, are Old Grammarians. The Tom Thomas Building provided MGGS with an impressive stadium designed to accommodate gymnastics, as well as a variety of field and court sports. Facilities include a studio, a bio-mechanics lecture room, an electronic scoreboard, equipment storage space, and fully equipped changing rooms.

With the opening of the Nina Crone Centre in 1987 the libraries and the audio-visual facilities were housed under the one roof for the first time. The Centre, which won a citation for architectural excellence, is an innovative and elegant solution to the perennial problems of space at MGGS. It is situated at the centre of the campus, built into the sloping site, with a magnificent roof garden and theatre to replace the lost garden space of the old quadrangle. The top entrance descends by a spiralling staircase around an amphitheatre with a view into the library through curved panels. The interior has room for quiet study and browsing, yet allows several classes to be accommodated at any one time. Individual retreats and computer bays have been created by portable screens.

The new laboratory complex on the top floor of the Science Block was completed in 1988. It comprises two new science laboratories and a preparation room in what was previously the old library, leaving the block wholly devoted to science. The new physics laboratory has a variety of built-in demonstration equipment. At MGGS the numbers of year twelve students taking physics is about two and a half times the state average. The new general science laboratory has island benches for practical work and a central desk area. Each work station is self-contained, including wash-up facilities. The Garnsworthy Centre for Computer Studies, opened in 1992, was named after long-serving School Council member, Mr Lance Garnsworthy, whose wife Marcia (née Graham) and daughters Sally, Jane, Prudence, and Elizabeth were all educated at MGGS. As the school is working to integrate computers into all areas of the curriculum the Garnsworthy Centre is used in a wide range of subject areas. The Junior School Music Centre opened in 1990.

For many years, indeed since the last great fund-raising effort in Miss Mountain's time, MGGS had managed its recurrent and capital budgets without a major fund-raising appeal. This had been possible for three reasons: the fees had been increased to keep pace with inflation; governments both state and federal had underwritten parents' right to choose the education they wished for their children by partial subsidy of recurrent costs; and the school family, particularly the Parents' Association and the Old Grammarians' Society, had been generous with time and effort in raising funds. In the early 1980s, however, the election of Labor governments at both state and federal levels appeared to throw into doubt the future of state funding to church schools. In 1983 the Federal Minister of Education, Senator Susan Ryan, wrote advising that MGGS fell within the category of schools 'which have the capacity from cash income from private sources alone to operate at 95% of average government school standard costs [and that consequently] Commonwealth per capita grants for 1984 will be reduced by 24%'.[6] While the bi-partisan policy of the main political parties on state aid remained intact in principle, the MGGS Council became convinced that the school should seek 'other means of guaranteeing the school's financial independence in keeping with its desire to offer educational opportunities to as many girls from as wide a cross section of the community as possible'.[7] The *Information Exchange* for March 1982 politely drew the attention of parents to the fact that 'a building fund set up at the time when the Sixth Form Centre was planned' was still operative, and that donations would be tax deductible.

In 1985 the Council established the Merton Hall Foundation with the dual aims of providing capital to maintain the building program and establishing an endowment fund sufficient to secure the independent future of the school.[8] In many ways the second aim is the more difficult to achieve. The income of the endowment fund is to be applied to several purposes: to make good any future reduction in government support, enabling fees to be maintained at the same relative level; to offer terms and conditions of employment to attract the best teachers; to provide a wide range of subjects whilst maintaining the existing enrolment; and to provide scholarships, bursaries and prizes. As the foundation's president, Douglas Meagher, reported in 1988, the capital required in the endowment fund to achieve these ends is difficult to calculate, but it is in the order of $15 to $20 million. The Merton Hall Foundation provides a structure for marshalling the financial, managerial, and executive resources of the school. It consists of parents, Old Grammarians and friends who are prepared to use their influence and talents to support MGGS. In 1990 Dean Tom Thomas agreed to become heritage officer for the foundation. To anyone familiar with the history of MGGS, it is apparent that the Merton Hall Foundation is the crystallisation of longstanding traditions and commitments rather than a radical new departure in the life of the school.

The Merton Hall Foundation has been moderately successful in its short existence. In 1988 the foundation gained an independent income through the introduction of a registration fee of $500 for each new pupil, replacing the previous $300 loan repayable when the child left school. In common with other independent girls' schools, however, the Merton Hall Foundation has encountered some problems. Firstly, support has tended to come from present parents rather than past students. Present parents are often transitory, and indeed, as relatively young people with dependent families and mortgages, not always in a position to give as generously as they might like. Secondly, it has become apparent that many of those who command considerable wealth see more kudos in giving money to boys' schools than to girls' schools. In his report for 1989 Douglas Meagher confronted the issue:

> Our community cannot afford to treat this school as inferior to a boys' school, or to treat the education of its students as of lesser consequence. The truth is, it is of far greater consequence. Those who accept these views are invited to attend to the financial needs of this school with the same conviction, and liberalism, as they do or would do in a boys' school.[9]

In 1993 MGGS is still first and foremost an Anglican school, which aims to foster tolerance and understanding of all religions consistent with Anglican faith and practice. The inclusion of religious studies in the formal curriculum not only expresses the school's religious foundations but also offers the means to a deeper understanding of the meaning and purpose of life. Symbolic of the school's religious commitment is the Chapel of St Luke. In the words of the Reverend Dr Stuart Blackler: 'There is never a need to explain why a school should have a chapel; rather a school which professes to be concerned with an holistic education should be asked to explain why it does not have one'.[10] There is regular worship in the program of the school, including the celebration of the Eucharist during the week. Sunday services are held for boarders in the chapel, and marriages are now celebrated there. There are traditional inauguration services for girls elected to hold special offices within the school such as the boarding-house councillors and the Executive Council. Special occasions of worship are the annual carol service in the cathedral church, and combined services with boarders from Melbourne Grammar School. Girls are prepared for baptism and confirmation by the school chaplains. In 1987, following the adoption in Australia of the term Anglican to replace Church of England, the Anglican Diocesan Synod approved the new name 'Melbourne Girls Grammar School — an Anglican School', after a ballot held in the school's constituency.

All members of staff share with the chaplains a responsibility for pastoral care, and subject teachers, form teachers, level coordinators and specialist staff work closely with individual students. The school counsellor assists students in a range of areas — peer relationships, family problems, study habits — and welcomes referrals from parents and staff. The special education teacher assists girls with specific difficulties in the basic skills and organisation of their work. Nevertheless, it is ultimately the quality of the relationships among the girls themselves which determines the well-being of any school.

The careers adviser has developed a well-resourced careers room where girls may use computerised career exploration systems. In year ten, before they select their subjects for the VCE, the girls go through a comprehensive assessment program with 'Consultants for Change' who assist with career advice in the school. The girls are offered a work experience program in years ten to twelve, and are encouraged to participate at least once. The annual careers night, held in the second week of May, is very popular with the girls and parents. At the reunion for the class of '77 held in 1988, as well as the usual complement of doctors, lawyers, teachers and social workers there was a book editor, a trade union official, a provender, a psychiatrist, a personnel officer, an administrator with the Australian Opera, a commercial artist, a computer consultant, and a television producer.[11]

The continuing achievements of Old Girls in the public sphere are a reminder that for decades MGGS has encouraged girls to achieve in areas traditionally reserved for men. Scientist Nancy Millis was only the third woman to be appointed professor at the University of Melbourne when she was awarded a personal chair in microbiology in 1981. She attended MGGS from 1934 to 1937 in Miss Gilman Jones's era. Now Emeritus Professor, Nancy has been involved in the development and implementation of guidelines for genetic engineering. She chaired the founding government advisory body on recombinant DNA, and in 1989 was appointed to head the Genetic Manipulation Advisory Committee. In 1992 she was appointed Chancellor of La Trobe University. Another of Australia's most distinguished scientists, Dame Margaret Blackwood, attended MGGS from 1916 to 1927, also under Miss Gilman Jones, and was a prefect and captain of the school. She later served as the Old Grammarians' representative on the MGGS Council. Dame Margaret's field was plant cytology and genetics, and she gained her Doctorate of Philosophy from Cambridge University. During the war she served in the WAAAF and afterwards was appointed a lecturer at the University of Melbourne, becoming Dean of Women at the short-lived Mildura Branch campus. In 1981 she became Deputy Chancellor of the University of Melbourne—the first woman to hold the position. She died in June 1986 and is greatly missed by the school community.

A third Old Grammarian to achieve distinction in university governance is barrister and solicitor, Mrs Elsbeth Hallows (née Haydon). She was appointed Deputy Chancellor of Deakin University in 1984. In 1989 Old Grammarian Cheryl Saunders, mother of Susan and Jennifer Wells, was appointed to a personal chair in the Law Faculty of the University of Melbourne. It is also fitting for a school with a dazzling record in competitive swimming in recent years to remember Old Grammarian Mrs Frances Vorrath (née Bult) who left school in 1931 and swam for Australia in the 1932 Los Angeles Olympics. In 1985 she competed in the Aussie Swimmers' Contest in Canberra, winning the medal for the best performance in the 70-74 age group. Mrs Vorrath won seven races and broke six Australian records.

At Morris Hall, under the headship of Miss Pamela Ayers, the staff have developed an integrated academic curriculum based on language skills, numeracy, problem-solving, and research. The 'whole language' approach is used throughout. Like most girls' schools MGGS is especially aware of the need to initiate girls into the so-called 'non-traditional' areas of study for women: mathematics, science and technology. At Morris Hall the computer literacy program begins at year four. Staff believe that the enjoyment of mathematics in the primary years encourages a positive attitude to the subject at the senior levels. They have developed a program which offers every child the opportunity to understand concept as well as process and to think laterally and creatively. Years three to six girls may work at two levels with the 'Challenge' program for the academically more able. The primary science curriculum is skill-based, with an over-arching theme of the environment.

The Morris Hall social education program is also based on the holistic approach, developing in the girls an understanding of Australian society and the world in which they live. The program extends beyond the classroom to include excursions, drama, music, art and craft. Italian and Chinese are taught in the Junior School. The special education teacher works in small groups with children experiencing difficulty in languages or mathematics, as well as with groups of academically gifted children who require extra stimulation.

Many co-curricular activities—debating, team sports, and music—are woven into the house system at Morris Hall, where the three houses are named for pioneer Australian women whose contribution has been underplayed in the writing of Australian history: Chisholm, named after Caroline Chisholm who sponsored and assisted female immigrants in the early settlement of Australia; Franklin, named after Lady Jane Franklin, wife of the Governor of Tasmania, who had a special interest in the education of women; and Gould, named after Elizabeth Gould who sketched the bird specimens gathered by her husband, John.

At the Senior School the academic program consists of core and elective subjects at each level. At years seven and eight all girls take art, computer work, English, general science, geography, history, mathematics, music, physical education and religious studies. At year seven, girls choose either Chinese or Italian. The following year they continue these languages, and in addition, choose either Latin or power English. At year nine, all girls take computer work, creative arts (units of music, craft and drama), English, general science, mathematics, physical education, religious studies and the study of society, which is an integrated two-unit subject of Australian history and geography. Girls may continue their Chinese, Italian or Latin, with art and civilisation as alternatives to languages other than English (LOTE). French is introduced as an elective at this level. At year ten, all girls take English, mathematics, science, physical education and religious studies. Elective studies continue in LOTE, and to these are added art (ceramics, flatwork or textiles), drama, geography, history, musicianship and physical recreation studies.

In 1992 years eleven and twelve students and teachers at

MGGS, with their counterparts all over Victoria, were in the first year of the complete implementation of the VCE program. It is salutary to realise that Victorian schools have been coping with major changes in curriculum and assessment procedures for at least a decade and a half. In 1981 the Victorian Institute of Secondary Education (VISE) introduced a system of Group 1 subjects which were partly internally and partly externally assessed. Another group of subjects (Group 2) were assessed entirely by the school. In that year MGGS offered twenty-six Group 1 subjects and two subjects (media studies, and values and human ecology) from Group 2. In 1982 a report in the *Information Exchange* summed up the experience in language eerily predictive of the VCE implementation ten years later:

> The system provided little flexibility and students, teachers and the school generally faced a most demanding year. The application of rigid deadlines for work made it extremely difficult for Year 12 girls to participate in all areas of extra curricular activities and staff were constantly concerned that teaching time was maintained. The way in which girls and members of staff met the challenge of a new system was very gratifying.[12]

Nevertheless, MGGS girls for both Group 1 and Group 2 subjects attained a pass rate of 90 per cent and their highest percentage of honours for eight years.

In 1983 VISE again foreshadowed major changes by establishing a working party to review the structure of the Higher School Certificate (HSC). VISE and its working party were eventually engulfed by the Blackburn Report which was released in 1985. Its recommendations involved sweeping changes in the final two years of school. VISE was replaced by the Victorian Curriculum and Assessment Board (VCAB) with responsibility for the development and accreditation of curricula, for modes of assessment, and for certification at the senior secondary level. The hotch potch of credentialling arrangements in existence at year twelve were to be replaced by a single certificate, the VCE, to mark the completion of the final two years of secondary school in Victoria.

In the same year MGGS initiated its own in-service program to cope with the rapid and dramatic changes which were inevitable. This began with a full-day conference in September 1985 entitled 'Change—and responding creatively', which produced an in-service interim report as a basis for future planning. From that time onwards, staff at MGGS were fully engaged in preparation for the new VCE: Fields of Study Committees, VCAB and other seminars, out-of-hours network meetings with other inde-

Girls in the Garnsworthy Centre for Computer Studies opened
in 1992.

Sport continues to play a major role in school life. The 1990
Swimming Team scooped the pool in the Inter-School
competitions.

Rehearsing for 'Noye's Fludde' in 1959 and for 'Professor Taranne',
one of the four French plays produced in 1990.

pendent schools, and a gruelling round of internal staff meetings. In 1988 MGGS took part in the trials of the physics common assessment tasks (CATS).

To this was added the onerous task of keeping anxious parents informed through information evenings and the *Information Exchange*. Media coverage of the VCE implementation was unprecedented, often ill-informed, and largely unfavourable. Predictably, concern centred round tertiary selection procedures in relation to the VCE. Verification procedures, that is, external moderating of school-based assessment, came under close scrutiny. With a large increase in work done outside the direct oversight by the teacher, authentication of students' work became a major issue. Student and staff workloads came in for extreme criticism.[13] In December 1989 Nina Crone, who had always supported the positive aspects of the VCE, appealed for calm:

> Much has been written in recent weeks regarding the new VCE to be fully implemented in 1992. Far more has been quietly going on in preparation for an orderly transition to this new form of assessment. Of course, there are aspects of it which remain to be resolved and the question of the university selection mode is of utmost importance. Nonetheless the fact that some details have yet to be finalised is no reason for abandoning what has been achieved or for delaying the introduction of those aspects which are generally accepted.[14]

Writing 'history on the run' can be a perilous undertaking but it can capture the rough edges of experience which may be smoothed with the passage of time. It would be a serious disservice to the pioneer group of VCE students and teachers in 1992 to ignore the fact that they are under enormous pressure. They are determined to continue the MGGS tradition of academic excellence: of the VCE class of 1991, 98 per cent gained tertiary places, 88 per cent in degree courses: thirty-six at the University of Melbourne, twenty-six at La Trobe University, nineteen at Monash University, and one at Deakin University. But the VCE has been politicised to a degree which few could have anticipated. Even as the girls work they know that universities are unhappy with aspects of VCE content and assessment; they also know that the centenary year at MGGS may see a new state government in office which has as part of its platform the revamping of the VCE. Most staff and students at MGGS would agree that the VCE has many admirable features, but they would want to record that its implementation has not been an entirely happy experience. The first results under the complete VCE system are not yet to hand.

To Old Girls who have not visited MGGS over the last few decades the present curriculum will suggest both continuities and discontinuities. To those at the school in Miss Ross's era, electives will be no novelty. Yet the holy grail of the 'alternative fifth', sought by every headmistress from the Morris sisters to Miss Mountain, has disappeared, not from any lack of concern for the less academic girls, but subsumed within the philosophy and practice of the VCE. The domestic arts, too, have lost their traditionally precarious toehold at MGGS, a victim f scarce resources and the changing role of women at the en. of the twentieth century. European languages are not as central as they once were, and the Asian languages offered are more in keeping with Australia's economic and geographical realities. Science has continued its rise to prominence, and has been joined by information technology and computer studies.

A unique course offered in the Middle School is 'civilisation'. Begun in 1978 as an extra English subject for some students, and, with its classic background, a subject which students could enter at year nine instead of Latin, 'civ.' has become a very popular option. Part of the history curriculum, it is based on an approach to understanding various eras and cultures through the art and literature they produced. Each year the girls work as a group to produce a major art assignment: the shields of Achilles in studying Ancient Greece, *Wayang Kulit* puppets in examining pre-colonial Indonesia, 'Little Hours of MCEGGS' in looking at the medieval period. Younger Old Girls returning to school enjoy seeing their particular project, each of which is permanently preserved in the Nina Crone Resource Centre.

Despite the pressures for academic success MGGS remains committed to a broad general education with a program of co-curricular activities to appeal to all students. The program of camping is continued in the Senior School, especially at year nine, when the girls spend ten days at the Outward Bound Camp in the Grampians. Year eleven students have the excursion to 'The Centre', 'surviving with cold showers, living without a hair dryer and drying our own dishes without a dishwasher . . . to become "Central Buddies" forever'.[15] More ambitious excursions in recent years have been to China, to France and to Italy. The production of the school magazine (totally transformed since Gwynneth Morris began her *School Notes* in 1906) still attracts a dedicated band of girls—the 'magcom' for 1991 listed twenty-two names. In 1990 MGGS girls won the School of the Year Award at Victoria's Science Talent Search. One hundred and forty-six girls from years seven to ten entered a variety of research projects spanning topics from the effectiveness of solar hot water services to the effectiveness of mouth-washes and toothpaste. In 1989 two teams of MGGS girls competed for the first time in the Tournament of Minds at Monash University and the team which designed a water-tower suitable for an earthquake zone was awarded third prize.

The houses at Merton Hall remain unchanged since they were re-established in Edith Mountain's time and continue to provide a focus for debating, drama, music and sport. The school play remains a highlight of the year's program: the ambitious and varied productions in recent years include The House of Bernarda Alba, The Fall of the House of Usher, and Dags. As the drama captain for 1991 commented: 'The wider school community sees the performance, but not the most important aspect: the process. House Drama . . . can be the culmination of anywhere from a month to six months' work'.[16] Combined productions with Melbourne Grammar School offer further opportunities for girls with a special interest in theatre. The famous 'Quad Play' at the boys' school has in recent years included Antony and Cleopatra, Romeo and Juliet, and Hamlet.

As with Morris Hall, Merton Hall has a rich musical life: the senior orchestra; the years seven and eight orchestra; the concert band; the jazz ensemble; the woodwind ensemble; the chamber music group; and the Chapel Chanters. There are choirs, both auditioned and open, for all girls. As with the drama productions, the long hours of rehearsal which staff and students are willing to put in come to those exhilarating conclusions, so familiar to Old Girls, which give the school year its shape and are recalled long after the everyday humdrum of school life has faded. These include the Junior School concert, the years seven and eight concert, the school concert at the Robert Blackwood Hall, the carol service at St Paul's Cathedral, the outside music festivals, and the ANZAC Day service at the Shrine of Remembrance.

In 1992 MGGS commissioned a major piece of research to 'help us keep in touch with our parents' and prospective parents' attitudes and expectations'. As the survey was conducted among parents of all girls in Prep. through to year seven, and those who have daughters enrolled to enter up to the year 2000, it was to be expected that there would be a reasonable degree of confidence in the basic mission of the school. But it is reassuring indeed to find that MGGS is held in very high esteem among this, its future constituency. Perceived advantages to emerge from the survey were the school's academic excellence, its good boarding facilities, its pastoral care and standard of discipline, and its highly competent staff. Parents were asked to indicate the priority they attached to various elements of the formal curriculum. Of prime importance were English expression, with a traditional approach to writing and grammar, and English literature. Mathematics and science were assigned high priority, as was computer technology, and there was considerable emphasis on career development. Extension studies for both the gifted and those with learning difficulties were considered important. The study of the humanities and the performing arts remained important, though languages, with the exception of Japanese and Chinese, have declined in importance with this generation of parents. Clearly, parents looked to MGGS for the development of personal and moral qualities in students (manners, moral values, inter-personal skills, life skills, and health education were seen as interconnected) with formal religious studies rating below the development of moral values. Nina Crone commented:

> The future curriculum appears to require a school which produces students competent in traditional, academic core skills, e.g. English, mathematics and science. They should be computer literate; well versed in the arts, e.g. music, theatre; capable of coping with the physical environment; and intellectually aware of the total world environment, i.e. politics, history, geography. The school would be expected to prepare students to live in a 'difficult' world and also to help students at either end of the intellectual scale. [17]

As it goes into the twenty-first century MGGS can take heart that its policies and programs, developed in the rapidly changing world of female education in the last two decades, are in accord with the wishes of its future clientele.

There is a pleasing historical symmetry in the circumstance that on the eve of its centenary MGGS was obliged to examine one of its most fundamental traditions—its mission as a school for girls. In late 1991 its brother school, Melbourne Grammar School, announced that it intended to implement immediately a thoroughgoing transformation to co-education. This was in many ways a courageous and an honourable decision, made on grounds other than economic necessity and against considerable opposition from sections of its constituency. In making the decision Melbourne Grammar was also following a trend towards co-education among independent boys' schools which began in the 1970s. [18]

Yet this move to claim the high moral ground for co-education has coincided with mounting concern by educationists and feminist thinkers, both in Australia and overseas, that co-education has been less than satisfactory for girls. The usual claim for co-education is that it is more 'natural'; since men and women must live together in the world outside school they should go to school together. Another permutation of this argument is that girls exert a civilising influence over boys. The difficulty with this argument is that it glosses over the unequal power relationships between men and women which still exist even at the end of the twentieth century. There is persuasive evidence that girls in co-educational schools act as a negative reference group for boys who are learning to identify with a dominant male culture still powerfully validated in Western society—by the media, by men's monopoly of power in the public sphere of politics, business, the church, and the professions, and indeed by relationships within the home. Treatment of girls as the less powerful 'other' may range from chivalrous goodwill to ugly sexual harassment; but the result is often to persuade girls that the traditional male domains of physical prowess, leadership, and the cognate areas of science and technology are forbidden territory. When men and women are not equally powerful in our society it is naive to assume that a school can create an oasis 'where members of both sexes are equally valued and where nothing, anywhere in the school, suggests otherwise'—especially when that school has been a boys' school for well over a century. In April 1992 Nina Crone announced the school's decision to remain for girls only. She reminded her readers that:

> It is important that change is regularly contemplated but the manner in which change can most effectively be realised is a critical component in the decision. A rapid and revolutionary process can be contemplated if a new site is a possibility . . . [but] . . . where the change involves maintaining long-established sites, an evolutionary process involving interchange, exchange and joint activities is likely to be the most effective manner of implementing change. The 'power of place' and the 'hand of history' should not be under-estimated.[19]

There have been few dissenting voices from the MGGS community—indeed single-sex education was strongly endorsed by the 1992 survey of parental expectations—but there can be no doubt that the courageous decision to stand alone as a girls' school in the twenty-first century will, of necessity, call upon all the resources which that community can muster.

When in the early 1980s MGGS was among the independent schools to have its Commonwealth government subsidy severely pruned, the School Council commissioned Mr Philip Roff to examine every aspect of the school and its future prospects in an era of diminishing government assistance. His outsider's view of the school's greatest assets is timely in the present context: the school's location close to the city centre and its amenities; the good mix of students from geographically, culturally and socio-economically varied backgrounds; the school's ability to give a broad education; its ingenuity in adapting to a confined and crowded site; the beautiful environment with its blend of old and new buildings enhanced by trees and lawns; its consistently high academic results achieved without selective enrolment procedures; the survival of the boarding house and the excellent approach to boarding life in the school; close church involvement and genuine concern for moral values as part of school life; a dedicated and well-qualified teaching staff; a strong Old Grammarians' Society which is very supportive of the school; and a population of girls who are open, interested and happy, and who get on well together across the age groups. These are qualities hard won over a century of education at MGGS, and they are qualities which will endure.

Notes

Chapter 1 Beginnings: 1893–1912

The author wishes to acknowledge the research assistance of Desma McDonald,
Georgina McDonnell, Lorna Mitchell and Sally Roberts.

[1] Letter, Alice (Taylor) Craig to Jessie Bage, 13 April 1928, MGGS Archives.
[2] School Roll, MGGS Archives.
[3] This account of the Trinity Hostel affair is taken from Lyndsay Gardiner, *Janet Clarke Hall, 1886–1986*, Hyland House, Melbourne, 1986, chs 1 and 2 unless otherwise stated.
[4] For biographical details, see letter, Elizabeth Spurrell to Lyndsay Gardiner, 11 April 1989; for the history of Newnham College, see Alice Gardner, *A Short History of Newnham College Cambridge*, Bowes & Bowes, Cambridge, 1921, Emily Hensley is on the far right of the photograph facing p. 2; for her qualifications see *Argus*, 4 January 1893, Gardiner, *Janet Clarke Hall*, p. 18 and *Newnham College Register 1871–1971*, vol. 1, p. 55.
[5] Letter, Alice (Taylor) Craig to Jessie Bage, 23 April 1928.
[6] *C. of E. Mess.*, 1 December 1896.
[7] *SN*, no. 38, December 1916, pp. 3–4.
[8] Gwenda Kent Hughes, *Melbourne Church of England Girls' Grammar School: History of the school 1893–1928*, MCEGGS, Melbourne, 1928, Foreword.
[9] Matriculation entries and results, University of Melbourne Archives (hereafter, Matric. entries).
[10] Letter, Alice (Taylor) Craig to Jessie Bage, 13 April 1928.
[11] Unless otherwise cited, all biographical details on the Morris family are from Betty G. Forster, *The Family and Descendants of Commander George Brooks Forster, R. N. 1792–1874*, no publishing details, and W. P. F. Morris, *Sons of Magnus: First steps of a Queensland school*, William Brooks, Brisbane, 1948.
[12] Morris, *Magnus*, p. 15.
[13] Matric. entries, 1892, 1893.
[14] VPRS 10061, item 3466, registration of Adele Ingram.
[15] *SN*, no. 38, December 1916, pp. 3–4, obituary to Emily Hensley written by Ada Lambert (à Beckett).

16 VPRS 10063, item 4647, registration of Mary Morris.
17 *SN*, no. 4, 1906, p. 28.
18 For evidence of the Morris sisters' feminism see Farley Kelly, *Degrees of Liberation: A short history of women in the University of Melbourne*, Women's Graduate Centenary Committee, University of Melbourne, Melbourne, 1985, p. 35; Edith Morris, 'Men and women', *SN*, no. 5, 1907, pp. 39–40; Edith Morris, 'The present trend of the education of women', paper read before the National Council of Women, May 1912, *SN*, no. 24, 1912, pp. 266–8.
19 HM Rep., 1901, pp. 4–5.
20 Results at public exams and university from HM Reps and *SN*, 1901–10.
21 Kelly, p. 39.
22 HM Rep., 1902, p. 13; 1904, pp. 3–4; 1905, p. 2.
23 Information on the alternative senior course from HM Reps, 1901–10.
24 HM Rep., 1905, pp. 65–6; IARTV papers, University of Melbourne Archives.
25 For the effect on the girls' schools of the *Registration Act*, see Ailsa G. Thomson Zainu'ddin, '"The poor widow, the ignoramus and the humbug": an examination of rhetoric and reality in Victoria's 1905 act for the registration of teachers and schools', *History of Education Review*, vol. 13, no. 2, 1984.
26 VPRS 10063, item 4639, registration of Edith Morris.
27 Georgina McDonnell and Sally Roberts, 'The MCEGGS staff and the Registration Act of 1905', Bachelor of Education essay, University of Melbourne, 1991.
28 Gardiner, *Janet Clarke Hall*, chs 1–3; *Newnham College Register*, p. 144; *SN*, 1906–12.
29 C. Mins, 23 November 1910, pp. 55–6.
30 *ADB*, vol. 10, p. 590.
31 VPRS 10063, item 6729, registration of Georgina Sweet.
32 Kelly, pp. 43–4.
33 Marjorie R. Theobald, *Ruyton Remembers 1878–1978*, Hawthorn Press, Melbourne, 1978, p. 49.
34 VPRS 10063, items 2928 (Hardie) and 3115 (Henderson).
35 HM Rep. 1904, pp. 37–8; *SN*, 1906–12.
36 HM Rep., 1904, pp. 1–2.
37 HM Rep., 1902, p. 1.
38 HM Rep. 1904, p. 2.
39 C. Mins, undated, but late in 1904, p. 13.
40 C. Mins, 21 August 1905.
41 Lyndsay Gardiner, *Tintern School and Anglican Girls' Education 1877–1977*, Tintern CEGGS, Melbourne, 1977, ch. 1.
42 C. Mins, 5 September 1905, p. 19.
43 *SN*, no. 26, p. 291.
44 *SN*, no. 16, p. 144.
45 *SN*, no. 19, pp. 180–1.
46 *SN*, no. 2, p. 11; no. 16, p. 145; no. 20, pp. 196–7.
47 HM Rep., 1904, p. 41.
48 *SN*, no. 11, 1908, p. 102.
49 *SN*, no. 10, p. 92.
50 *SN*, no. 7, p. 58.
51 *MCEGGS Magazine*, 1963, p. 20.

Chapter 2 A very Anglican arrangement

1   HM Rep., 1903, pp. 1–2.
2   HM Rep., 1904, p. 1.
3   C. R. Badger, 'James Moorhouse' in D. Pike (ed.), *ADB*, Melbourne University Press, Melbourne, 1974, vol. 5, pp. 281–3.
4   *Church Assembly 1884, Abstract of Proceedings and Address of the President* (hereafter *Church Assembly*), p. 39.
5   *Church Assembly 1884*, p. 12.
6   *Church Assembly 1884*, p. 37.
7   All references to the 1885 debate are to *Church Assembly 1885*, pp. 14–38 unless otherwise noted.
8   *Sacre Coeur, Burke Road, 1888–1988*, Sacre Coeur, Melbourne, 1988, p. 5; for a history of Catholic education in Australia see R. Fogarty, *Catholic Education in Australia 1806–1950*, Melbourne University Press, Melbourne, 1959.
9   All references to the 1887 debate are from the *Church Assembly 1887*, pp. 37–40 unless otherwise given.
10 References from *Church Assembly 1888*, pp. 19–20 unless otherwise noted.
11 For a discussion of this issue, see Ray Elliott, 'In quest for integrity in Protestant church-related schools', *Religious Education Journal of Australia*, vol. 4, no. 1, 1988.
12 *Nisi Dominus Frustra: MCEGGS jubilee history*, MCEGGS, Melbourne, 1953, p. 19.
13 G. O. Vance, *Church of England Girls' Grammar School: Memorandum for the information of the members of the Church Assembly*, Melbourne, undated, *circa* 1903, p. 1.
14 *C. of E. Mess.*, 2 November 1903, p. 130.
15 Vance, p. 1.
16 *Church Assembly 1887*, p. 37.
17 Vance, p. 1.
18 *C. of E. Mess.*, 2 November 1903, p. 8.
19 *Church Assembly 1887*, p. 41.
20 Minutes of the Council of the Diocese, 31 January 1900.
21 All references to the business of the Provisional Council are from the minutes of that body, on loose sheets of paper in varying condition, in the MGGS Archives.
22 *SN*, October 1907, p. 39.
23 E. C. Rickards, *Bishop Moorhouse of Melbourne and Manchester*, Murray, London, 1920, p. 165.
24 *C. of E. Mess.*, 2 March 1903.
25 *C. of E. Mess.*, 7 October 1926; J. Grant, 'Henry Lowther Clarke' in B. Nairn and G. Serle (eds), *ADB*, Melbourne University Press, Melbourne, 1981, vol. 8, pp. 14–15.
26 *C. of E. Mess.*, 15 December 1905.
27 H. L. Clarke, *Address to Synod*, 1906, p. 63.
28 *C. of E. Mess.*, 11 December 1908.
29 *C. of E. Mess.*, 1 November 1918.
30 H. L. Clarke, *Address to Synod*, 1906, p. 64.
31 H. L. Clarke, *Address to Synod*, 1905, pp. 63–4.
32 H. L. Clarke, *Address to Synod*, 1918, pp. 15–16.

[33] For a history of the sisters see *A Valiant Victorian: The life and times of Mother Emily Ayckbowm, 1836–1900, of the Community of the Sisters of the Church*, Community of the Sisters of the Church, London, 1964; and Geoffrey Stephens, *History of St Michael's Collegiate School Hobart*, St Michael's Collegiate School, Hobart, 1991.

[34] H. L. Clarke, *Address to Synod*, 1918, p. 16.

[35] A. Inch, *Honour the Work: A history of Melbourne High School*, Lloyd O'Neill, Melbourne, 1977, esp. ch. 1.

[36] *C. of E. Mess.*, 29 October 1909.

[37] Reports of the Minister for Public Instruction, 1906–21, *Victorian Parliamentary Papers*.

[38] *C. of E. Mess.*, 1 November 1918.

[39] H. L. Clarke, *Address to Synod*, 1909, p. 148.

[40] H. A. Brooksbank, 'Church Schools', typescript held in the Mollison Library, Trinity College, University of Melbourne.

[41] Constance Tisdall, *Forerunners: The saga of a family of teachers*, Graham Publications, Walhalla, 1979, p. 207.

[42] A. D. Pyke, *The Gold and the Blue: A history of Lowther Hall*, Lowther Hall, Melbourne, 1983.

[43] *C. of E. Mess.*, 8 January 1908 and subsequent issues.

[44] *C. of E. Mess.*, 31 May 1918 and subsequent issues; Lyndsay Gardiner, *Tintern School and Anglican Girls' Education 1877–1977*, Tintern CEGGS, Melbourne, 1977.

[45] Marjorie R. Theobald, *Ruyton Remembers 1878–1978*, Hawthorn Press, Melbourne, 1978, p. 78.

[46] N. Brennan, *Village School: Ivanhoe Girls' Grammar School*, Hawthorn Press, Melbourne, 1973, esp. ch. 1.

[47] P. Burren, *Mentone: The place for a school*, Hyland House, Melbourne, 1984, pp. 52–3.

[48] P. Chessell, *And, As We Journey: A history of Korowa Anglican Girls' School 1890–1990*, Coghill Publishing, Melbourne, 1990.

[49] See Bishop's Letter Books, H. L. Clarke, held in Diocesan Archives.

[50] Brooksbank; H. L. Clarke, *The Church and Her Schools*, speech to Synod, 1918.

[51] G. Goodman, *The Church of Victoria during the Episcopate of Charles Perry*, Melville Mullen & Slade, Melbourne, 1892, p. 301.

[52] H. C. Lees, *Addresses to Synod*, Melbourne, n.d., *circa* 1924, the quotation is from the 1924 address, p. 13.

Chapter 3 The Gilman Jones era: 1916–38

[1] Geoffrey Sherington, R. C. Petersen and Ian Brice, *Learning To Lead: a history of girls' and boys' corporate secondary schools in Australia*, Allen and Unwin, Sydney, 1987; K. S. Cunningham and Dorothy J. Ross, *An Australian School At Work*, ACER, Melbourne, 1967; W. F. Connell, 'Innovative headmistress—D. J. Ross' in C. Turney (ed.), *Pioneers of Australian Education 1900–1950*, Sydney University Press, Sydney, 1983, vol. 3, pp. 200–30.

[2] HM Rep., 1914, p. 5; interview with Valentine Leeper, 27 July 1972.

[3] HM Rep., 1930, p. 9; Alice Zimmern, *The Renaissance of Girls' Education in England: a record of fifty years' progress*, A. D. Innes, London, 1898, pp. 154–6.

[4] *SN*, 27 August 1928, p. 41.

5 Letter, Reverend Keith Hallett to Lorna Mitchell, 11 June 1982.

6 *Newnham College Register 1871–1971*, vol. 1, p. 158; letter, Keith Hallett to Lorna Mitchell, 11 June 1982.

7 Great Britain, *Parliamentary Papers*, Irish Collection, Bryce Secondary Education Commission, 1895, VI, County of Warwick (2), Girls' Schools, pp. 331–2; Janet Whitcut, *Edgbaston High School 1876–1976*, Edgbaston High School, Birmingham, 1976, pp. 9, 80–4.

8 VPRS 10061, box 29, item 9376; testimonial from George Stone, MGGS Archives.

9 Herbert Wilkinson, *The G.H.S. Queenstown (Queenstown Girls' High School)*, Daily Representative, Queenstown, 1950, pp. 47, 54. My thanks to R. S. Edkins, the present headmaster, for a copy of this book.

10 Margaret Bailey, H. J. Carter, Caroline Fairfax Simpson *et al.* (eds), *Ascham Remembered 1886–1986*, Ure Smith, Sydney, 1986, p. 21.

11 K. A. Gilman Jones to Council, letter of application, MGGS Archives.

12 *SN*, no. 36, May 1916, p. 1.

13 *SN*, no. 36, May 1916, p. 3.

14 *SN*, no. 41, December 1917, p. 26.

15 HM Rep., no. 37, August 1917, pp. 8, 4.

16 *SN*, no. 37, August 1917, p. 7, and no. 38, December 1916, p. 8.

17 *SN*, no. 41, December 1917, p. 10.

18 *SN*, no. 43, August 1918, p. 8.

19 *SN*, no. 44, December 1918, pp. 4, 22.

20 *SN*, no. 45, May 1919, p. 7; no. 47, December 1919, p. 2; no. 45, May 1919, p. 22, 2.

21 *SN*, no. 50, December 1920, pp. 2, 4.

22 HM Rep., 1920, p. 5.

23 C. Mins, 5 December 1923, p. 120; 13 December 1923, p. 121.

24 HM Mins, vol. 2, 1911–16, n.p.

25 VPRS 802, unit 118, SC 1299, F. Tate to Minister; C. P. Ed. Mins, 8 June 1920.

26 IASTV Council Minutes, June 1919.

27 IASTV Council Minutes, 13 July 1922; 8 April 1938.

28 C. P. Ed. Mins, 19 June, 2 October, 4 December 1923.

29 M. Harris, *Towards Freedom: the Howard plan of individual timetables*, University of London Press, London, 1923, p. 32.

30 *AEQ*, vol. 1, no. 1, September 1924, pp. 1–2, 35–6.

31 HM Rep., 1924.

32 The reorganisation of the Middle School, May 1925, MGGS Archives.

33 *SN*, no. 63, May 1925, p. 3.

34 HM Rep., 1925, p. 10.

35 *SN*, no. 71, December 1927, pp. 25–8; no. 82, August 1931, pp. 13–14, 24.

36 *SN*, no. 63, May 1925, pp. 20–1.

37 VPRS 10061, items 2445, 9066.

38 *SN*, no. 40, August 1917, p. 2.

39 Letters from K. A. Gilman Jones to Council, 12 and 18 August 1925, loose in MCEGGS minute book, vol. 1915–32.

40 Acting HM Rep., 1926, p. 5.

41 *AEQ*, vol. 3, no. 1, 1927, pp. 1–2.

42 *Who's Who in the World of Women: activities and interests social, philanthropic, historic, scholastic, sport and travel*, vol. 1, Reference Press Association, Melbourne, 1930, n.p.; *SN*, no. 81, May 1931, p. 4.

43 C. Mins, 23 February and 4 March 1927, pp. 165–7; HM Rep., 1928, p. 6.

44 HM Rep., 1927, pp. 7, 9; D. Avery, 'The Parents' National Education Union', *AEQ*, vol. 1, no. 1, 1924, pp. 18–25.

45 C. Mins, 2 May 1928; 29 September 1929.
46 *SN*, no. 73, August 1928, pp. 28–47; Gwenda Kent Hughes, *Melbourne Church of England Girls' Grammar School: history of the school, 1893–1928*, MCEGGS, Melbourne, 1928.
47 HM Rep., 1928, pp. 7–8.
48 HM Rep., 1930, p. 8.
49 C. Mins, 26 November 1930, p. 251.
50 Quoted in P. Gronn, 'Sister of an educated man: Margaret Robertson Darling at Corio, 1931–3', *History of Education Review*, no. 20, vol. 1, 1991, p. 14.
51 HM Rep., 1930, p. 5.
52 HM Rep., 1931, pp. 3,4.
53 HM Rep., 1927, p. 6; Jukes/Hoggart letter to Lorna Mitchell.
54 HM Rep., 1932, p. 4.
55 HM Rep., 1931, p. 5.
56 *Who's Who in the World of Women*, n.p.
57 HM Rep., 1933, pp. 4–6.
58 'The Church and the New Age', *Official Report of the Sixtieth Annual Church Congress*, Melbourne, 3–13 May 1925, pp. 217–18.
59 HM Rep., 1933, pp. 5–6.
60 C. Mins, 12 and 28 July 1933, p. 280; 25 October 1933, p. 283; vol. 1934–60, 21 March 1934, p. 3; 3 April 1935, p. 12.
61 C. Mins, 26 April 1933, p. 275; 17 July 1935, p. 13.
62 C. Mins, 28 October 1936, p. 28, 18 November 1936, p. 30; HM Rep., 1937, pp. 4–5.
63 Letter, Kathleen Gilman Jones, 18 August 1938, MGGS Archives.
64 HM Rep., 1939, p. 4.
65 *SN*, no. 100, August 1937, pp. 3, 10; C. Mins, 28 July 1937, p. 50.
66 HM Rep., 1937, pp. 5,10.
67 Letter, Kathleen Gilman Jones, 18 August 1938, MGGS Archives.
68 HM Rep., 1938, p. 4.
69 HM Rep., 1938, p. 3.
70 Letters from Kathleen Gilman Jones, MGGS Archives.
71 *SN*, no. 114, December 1942, p. 39.
72 Muriel Maxwell, 'In appreciation', *SN*, no. 114, December 1942, pp. 37–9.
73 *SN*, no. 104, December 1938, p. 6.
74 Letter, M. Eltringham to I. Day, 7 March 1982.
75 Jan Milburn, 'The secondary schoolmistress. A study of her professional views and their significance in the developments of the period 1895–1914', Ph.D. thesis, University of London, 1969, p. 295.
76 *SN*, no. 104, December 1938, p. 7.
77 *SN*, no. 104, December 1938, p. 1.
78 *SN*, no. 104, December 1938, p. 2.
79 *SN*, no. 103, August 1938, p. 45; no. 114, December 1942, p. 39.
80 Lyndsay Gardiner, *Janet Clarke Hall 1886–1986*, Hyland House, Melbourne, 1986, pp. 83, 109; HM Rep., 1927, p. 9; P. Maddern, *St Hilda's College: forerunners and foundations*, St Hilda's College, Melbourne, 1989, p. 13.
81 Martha Vicinus, *Independent Women: work and community for single women 1850–1920*, Virago, London, 1985, pp. 209–10.
82 Geraldine Clifford, 'Women's liberation and women's professions: reconsidering the past, present and future' in J. M. Faragher and E. Howe (eds), *Women and Higher Education in American History*, W. W. Naughton, New York, 1988, p. 182.
83 *SN*, no. 104, December 1938, p. 5.

[84] C. M. H. Clark, *A History of Australia, Volume 6: 'The Old Dead Tree and the Young Tree Green', 1916–1935 with an epilogue*, Melbourne University Press, Melbourne, 1989, vol. 6, pp. 280, 461.

[85] *SN*, no. 104, December 1938, p. 5.

[86] Betty Wilmot, *SN*, no. 104, December 1938, pp. 50–1.

Chapter 4 Merton Hall women and professional life: 1917–38

Biographical information for this article was obtained from interviews by the author with Dr Betty Wilmot, Miss Lorna Mitchell, Miss Mary Cameron, Dr Jean Laby, and Dr Gwyneth Dow. Additional information was obtained from the *MCEGGS Prospectus*, 1927; *School Notes*, nos 36–102, 1919–38; and the *Melbourne University Calendar*, 1918–39.

[1] Farley Kelly, *Degrees of Liberation: A short history of women in the University of Melbourne*, Women's Graduate Centenary Committee of the University of Melbourne, Melbourne, 1985, p. 97.

[2] *SN*, nos 36–102, 1919–38; University of Melbourne Alumni Association Records, 1919–37.

[3] Mimi Colligan, 'Alice Anderson: garage proprietor' in Marilyn Lake and Farley Kelly (eds), *Double Time: Women in Victoria—150 years*, Penguin, Melbourne, 1985, pp. 305–11.

[4] Glen Tomasetti, 'Reflections on six years (1941–46) at MLC Hawthorn', quoted in Ailsa G. Thomson Zainu'ddin, *They Dreamt of a School: A centenary history of Methodist Ladies' College, Kew 1882–1982*, Hyland House, Melbourne, 1982, p. 333.

[5] Gwyneth Dow, *Samuel Terry: The Botany Rothschild*, Sydney University Press, Sydney, 1974.

[6] Gwyneth Dow, *Uncommon Common Sense*, Cheshire, Melbourne, 1962.

[7] Gwyneth Dow, *Learning to Teach: Teaching to learn*, Routledge and Kegan Paul, London, 1979.

[8] Gwyneth Dow, *George Higinbotham: Church and state*, Pitman, Melbourne, 1964.

[9] Gwyneth Dow and June Factor (eds), *Australian Childhood: An anthology*, McPhee Gribble, Melbourne, 1991.

[10] Jean Blackburn, 'Schooling and injustice for girls' in Dorothy Broom (ed.), *Unfinished Business: Social justice for women in Australia*, Allen and Unwin, Sydney, 1984, p. 16.

Chapter 5 The school as a democratic community

The author would like to acknowledge the immense help given by Sally Gray who, as research assistant, interviewed a number of people and commented perceptively on many of the documents used in this chapter.

[1] D. J. Ross, interview by W. F. Connell, 25 February 1971.

[2] June Epstein, *A Golden String: The story of Dorothy J. Ross*, Greenhouse, Melbourne, 1981, Foreword.

[3] D. J. Ross, interview by W. F. Connell, 25 February 1971.

[4] HM Rep., Speech Day 1953, p. 4.

[5] HM Rep. to Council, 5 April and 19 July 1939; HM Rep., 1940, Senior School 1940, p. 3.

[6] HM Rep., 1940, Senior School, p. 7.

[7] *MCEGGS Magazine*, no. 146, December 1963, p. 6.

8   HM Rep., Speech Day 1948, pp. 2–4; 1949, pp. 1–2.
9   D. J. Ross, interview by W. F. Connell, 22 June 1981; Mrs Sylvia Martin, interview by Sally Gray, 27 October 1975.
10 *Old Grammarians' Society Branch News*, 30 June 1951; 6 November 1954.
11 *The School in 1953*, compiled by VI F, MGGS Archives.
12 K. S. Cunningham and D. J. Ross, *An Austraian School at Work*, ACER, Melbourne, 1967, p. 83.
13 D. J. Ross, interview by W. F. Connell, 25 February 1971.
14 D. J. Ross, 'The trend towards the comprehensive school', *John Smyth Memorial Lecture*, 17 August 1954, reprint from *Circular to Schools*, no. 85, p. 4.
15 Jill Everist (Holman), interview by W. F. Connell, 6 May 1991.
16 Elizabeth Pownall, interview by Desma McDonald, 16 October 1985.
17 D. J. Ross, interview by W. F. Connell, 25 February 1971.
18 Anonymous typescript from a former member of staff during the 1940s, p. 3, MGGS Archives.
19 Memorandum by a group of staff members, MCEGGS; . . . notable features of its past development, mimeo, *circa* 1958, p. 3, University of Melbourne Archives.
20 *Newsletter*, 28 October 1953.
21 Helen Gifford, 'Raison d'etre' in Patricia Grimshaw and Lynne Strahan (eds), *The Half-Open Door: sixteen modern Australian women look at professional life and achievement*, Hale and Iremonger, Sydney, 1982, pp. 182–3.
22 Remarks sent to Miss Ross by an Old Girl, manuscript in possession of the author.
23 Anonymous unpublished manuscript by a member of staff, 1942–52, in the possession of the author.
24 D. J. Ross, interview by W. F. Connell, 25 February 1971.
25 Sylvia Martin, interview by Sally Gray, 27 October 1975.
26 HM Rep. to Council, 14 July 1954, p. 2; 12 October 1955, pp. 1–2.
27 *MCEGGS Magazine*, 1982, p. 11.

Chapter 6 The war years, 1939–45: an oral history

The following former students, teachers and others supplied information to the author for this chapter: Louise Baker, Ruth Barton (née Posner), Anne Bitcon (née Aitken), Susan Bolton (née Hanlon), Jennifer Bourke (née Sanders), Elizabeth Brett (née Minifie), Anne Browne (née Nevett), Wendye Camier (née Johnston), Margaret Clark (née Sanders), Ruth Creer (née Chisholm), Barbara Crompton (née Wilson), Geraldine Currie (née Dexter), Colin Dance, Mary Davis, Elizabeth Davis (née Crockett), Oenone Deasey (née Gardner), Merylin Duncan (née Johnson), George Edwards (Reverend), Constance Ewald (née Emery), Helen Farmer (née London), Mary Franklin (née Gillespie), Janet Frecheville (née Aitken), Valerie Freed (née Bailhache), Gaynor Genders (née Stidson), Estelle Gillespie (née Gillespie), Barbara Hamer (née McPherson), Patricia Hancock (née Plummer), Judith Harley (née White), Valda Harper (née Hall), June Harrison, Susan Harvey (née Hunt), Joan Hiller (née Warnock), Judy Jarman (née Daniell), Rosemary Jordan (née Skerritt), Lois Latimer (née Naunton), Mary Legge (née Duffield), Beverley Lewis (née Borland), Molly Longfield (née Herring), Margaret Mackenzie, Shirley MacLeish (née Coombes), Elaine Markby (née Francis), Judith Moore (née Price), Janet Muirhead (née Finlayson), Barbara Nixon (née Scales), Patricia Permezel (née

Sholl), Elizabeth Pownall, Helen Rowan (née McArthur), Marian Sargood (née Evans), Nancy Stephens (née Tait), Anne Taylor (née Slattery), Margaret Towl, Audrey Wain (née Maclure), Alison Winfield, Betty Wood (née Adam).

1   The author and her contemporary, Wendye Camier (née Johnston), were students at MCEGGS from February 1938 until December 1942, which included one year of evacuation to Doncaster. Their friendship has been maintained to the present time and both recall many of the events described in this chapter.

2   M. McKernan, *All In!: Australia during the Second World War*, Nelson, Melbourne, 1983, p. 208; letter, Merylin Duncan (née Johnson) to the author, 11 May 1991.

3   Interview with J. Harley (née White), 30 July 1991; *MCEGGS Magazine*, no. 105, May 1939, p. 48, and no. 106, August 1939, p. 57.

4   Interview with S. MacLeish (née Coombes), 19 March 1991; interview with L. Baker, 14 March 1991.

5   *MCEGGS Magazine*, no. 109, August 1940, p. 66.

6   C. Mins, 30 October 1940.

7   R. Lewis, *A Nation at War: The Australian home front in the Second World War*, Longman Cheshire, Melbourne, 1982, p. 40.

8   Lewis, p. 47.

9   *MCEGGS Magazine*, no. 111, July 1941, pp. 41–5; no. 112, December 1941, pp. 5, 41, 35; no. 115, July 1943, p. 43; HM Rep., 29 October 1941.

10 Letter, E. Markby (née Francis) to the author, 19 March 1991.

11 Gaynor Genders, 'Letters to Pat' in Barbara Page (ed.), *Keep Me Posted: P. S. How's the war over there?*, Kensington Park Writers, Adelaide, 1988, p. 35; interview with Margaret Clark (née Sanders) and Anne Taylor (née Slattery), 17 April 1991.

12 *MCEGGS Magazine*, no. 112, December 1941, p. 34.

13 A. Spaull, *Australian Education in the Second World War*, University of Queensland Press, Brisbane, 1982, p. 10.

14 Copies of evacuation notices in the possession of Estelle Gillespie.

15 HM Rep., 15 April 1942; interview with M. Davis, 2 December 1985; Margaret Clark papers, reminiscences of Marysville (hereafter Clark papers).

16 Diary of S. MacLeish, MCEGGS student evacuated to Doncaster (hereafter MacLeish diary).

17 MacLeish diary, 21 February to 2 March 1942; interview with Elizabeth Pownall, 16 October 1985.

18 Interview with M. Davis, 2 December 1985.

19 Interview with A. Winfield, 16 January 1986.

20 D. J. Ross, 'An untold tale', typescript, MGGS Archives, p. 6; interview with M. Davis, 2 December 1985.

21 *MCEGGS Magazine*, no. 113, July 1942, p. 5; interview with E. Pownall, 16 October 1985.

22 Clark papers.

23 Interview with R. Creer (née Chisholm), 17 October 1985.

24 E. D. Potts and A. Potts, *Yanks Down Under 1941–1945*, Oxford University Press, Melbourne, 1985, pp. 9–10.

25 Clark papers.

26 C. Stevenson and H. Darling (eds), *The WAAAF Book*, Hale and Iremonger, Sydney, 1984, p. 113.

27 *MCEGGS Magazine*, no. 113, July 1942, p. 9.

28 *Nisi Dominus Frustra: MCEGGS jubilee history*, MCEGGS, Melbourne, 1953, p. 120.

29 Interview with A. Winfield, 16 January 1986.

30 Interview with M. Davis, 2 December 1985.
31 *Victorian Year Book 1984*, AGPS, Melbourne, 1984, p. 39.
32 Clark papers; interview with R. Creer, 17 October 1985.
33 Interview with A. Taylor, 17 April 1991.
34 A. Winfield, unpublished report on evacuation to Marysville, copy in MGGS Archives; interview with M. Davis, 2 December 1985.
35 Letter, A. Bitcom (née Aitken) to the author, 29 May 1991.
36 Letters to the author from Mary Legge (née Duffield), 5 April 1986, Elizabeth Davis (née Crockett), 2 May 1991; Winfield report; Clark papers.
37 Clark papers.
38 Letter, Lilian White to Dorothy Ross, undated, in MGGS Archives.
39 Letter, Janet Frecheville (née Aitken) to the author, 12 April 1986.
40 Interview with Ruth Creer, 17 October 1985.
41 *MCEGGS Magazine*, no. 113, July 1942, p. 6.
42 Information from Reverend G. Edwards, Christ Church, Marysville, 30 January 1992; Clark papers.
43 Letters to the author from A. Bitcom, 29 May 1991 and Elizabeth Davis, 2 May 1991.
44 Letter, B. Wood (née Adam) to the author, 14 April 1986.
45 Ross, 'An untold tale', pp. 7–8.
46 Interviews with R. Wright, 4 February 1992, A. Winfield, 16 January 1986, and A. Taylor, 17 April 1991.
47 'Tullamore 1887', *Doncaster-Templestowe Historical Society Newsletter*, vol. 8, no. 2, 1974, p. 4; 'Tullamore 1887–1987: One hundred years of history', *Eastern Golf Club Magazine*, August 1987, vol. 26, no. 4, p. 1.
48 Interview with M. Davis, 2 December 1985.
49 Ian MacRobertson Craig, 'Four decades of Huntingdale', *Golf in Victoria*, April 1981, p. 16.
50 Interview with E. Pownall, 16 October 1985; interview with S. MacLeish (née Coomes), 19 March 1991.
51 Letter, S. Bolton (née Hanlon) to the author, 3 July 1991.
52 Letter, R. Jordan (née Skerritt) to the author, 23 April 1991.
53 Interview with Elizabeth Brett (née Minifie), 5 October 1985.
54 Letter, V. Harper (née Hall) to the author, 23 April 1991.
55 Letters to the author from Patricia Hancock (née Plummer), 10 June 1991, Mary Franklin (née Gillespie), 3 May 1991, Molly Longfield (née Herring), 3 March 1991.
56 Letter, Mary Franklin to the author, 3 May 1991.
57 Letters to the author from P. Hancock (née Plummer), 10 June 1991, O. Deasey (née Gardner), 5 April 1986; responses to questionnaire from Estelle Gillespie (née Gillespie) and Nancy Stephens (née Tait), responses to questionnaire in the possession of the author.
58 C. Mins, 28 October 1942.
59 Spaull, p. 18.
60 *MCEGGS Magazine*, no. 115, July 1943, p. 4.
61 C. Mins, 14 July 1943.
62 C. Mins, 27 October 1943.
63 C. Mins, 22 March 1944.
64 Ross, 'An untold tale', pp. 11–12.

Chapter 7 Back into line

1 Letter from fifteen staff members to archbishop, 8 Otober 1958, MGGS Archives, F35 POW25. Many documents which would have clarified the

story of how Grammar was brought 'back into line' are missing. We have no official minutes of the meetings of Council between 10 October and 26 November 1958. When this chapter was researched there were no speech day reports for either 1958 or 1959, though those for preceding and succeeding years are on file. There is no trace of the 'policy speech'. There are no documents covering this period in the 'Mountain' file in the school archives. The only document originating with the headmistress is her Letter to Parents of 24 October 1958. There are no copies of individual letters of resignation.

2 *MCEGGS Magazine*, December 1958, p. 13.
3 C. Mins, HM Rep., 26 February 1959.
4 Pamphlet, *Information for Applicants for the Position of Headmistress*, prepared by Council, enclosed in C. Mins, 23 August 1954.
5 C. Mins, special meeting, 22 January 1957.
6 Signatures from letter to archbishop, 8 October 1958; length of service from the *Herald*, 28 October 1958. Where I have been able to check this it appears to be accurate.
7 C. Mins, special meeting, 22 January 1957.
8 Interviews with staff members and girls who were sixth formers in 1958; documents written by the staff at the time to explain their action to the archbishop and Council, and later to parents, MGGS Archives, F35 POW23, 7, 25; papers held by Lesley Cunningham (hereafter Cunningham papers) which include longer, more detailed drafts of these letters.
9 Interview with Mrs Betty Murray, 14 February 1991.
10 Interview with Sir James Darling, 3 June 1991.
11 Telephone conversation with Sir Frank Woods, 6 March 1991.
12 C. Mins, Acting HM Rep., 11 April 1956.
13 Interviews with former staff members, with women who were then senior pupils, and with their mothers.
14 Two drafts of the letters to go to the acting chairman of Council and 'two or three members' before October 1958, MGGS Archives, F35 POW18; letter from twelve 'concerned parents' to parents delivered 24 October 1958, MGGS Archives, F35 POW24—this letter says that five Council members were contacted over a period of six months.
15 Copies of the public notice and the 'loyalty letter', MGGS Archives, F35 POW15 and 29.
16 MGGS Archives, F35 POW25, asterisk not in original; *Herald*, 28 October 1958; *MCEGGS Magazine*, 1958, p. 9.
17 Interviews, Elizabeth Pownall, chief-of-staff, 20 January 1991; Wilga Rivers, French mistress, 2 May 1991.
18 Interview, Penelope Buckley (née Curtis), 26 March 1991.
19 *Herald*, 10 October 1958; *Sun*, 11 October 1958.
20 Evidence of some of the special meetings is in press releases: *Age*, 15 and 28 October 1958; letters sent as a result of meetings, notably to the chief-of-staff, MGGS Archives, F35 POW16 and 24; interviews with Mrs Mary Britten (née Herring), former School Council member, 10 April 1991; letter from Dr S. Barton Babbage to the author, 16 May 1991; diary kept by staff member at the time, Cunningham papers; letter from 'concerned parents'; archbishop's letter to parents, MGGS Archives, F35 Lee(s) 19.
21 Archbishop to Pownall, 10 October 1958; diary for 13 October 1958, Cunningham papers.
22 Archbishop, reported in *Age*, 15 October 1958.
23 Archbishop's letter to parents, undated copy, MGGS Archives, F35 (s) 19; there is also a copy in the Cunningham papers, dated 18 October 1958, but

this is evidently retyped, possibly for distribution to staff, as it is on school letterhead. Charles Moorhouse undoubtedly had a copy on 16 October 1958.

24 Charles Moorhouse to Archbishop Woods, 16 October 1958, copy held by Gwyneth Dow.

25 There appears to be no extant copy of the policy speech. It has been reported to me as a lengthier version of Miss Mountain's letter to parents, 24 October 1958, MGGS Archives, F35 POW19, and her speech at the parents' meeting, 29 October 1958, which received wide press coverage on 30 October 1958.

26 'Concerned parents', especially points 4 and 7; circular from former staff members to parents, written after speech day 1958, p. 4, MGGS Archives, F35 POW23.

27 Pownall to archbishop by telephone, 21 October 1958; diary, Cunningham papers; also MGGS Archives, F35 POW23 and 24.

28 'Concerned parents', especially point 6.

29 Archbishop to Pownall, 24 October 1958, MGGS Archives, F35 POW16.

30 'Concerned parents', especially point 8; diary, 30 October 1958, Cunningham papers; reports in *Herald*, 12 November 1958; *Age*, 13 November 1958. (These later reports do not entirely tally with the first-mentioned sources).

31 'Concerned parents', 24 October 1958.

32 J. L. Daish, interview reported in the *Herald*, 28 October 1958.

33 James Donald, interview reported in *Age*, 29 October 1958.

34 A. A. Phillips to parents' meeting, 29 October 1958, comments by Valentine Leeper to Bertha [Hitchcock], 1 December 1958, MGGS Archives, F35 Lee(s) 3.

35 *Age* and *Sun*, 30 October 1958.

36 *Herald*, 29 October 1958.

37 *Age*, 28 October 1958.

38 C. Mins, 26 November 1958.

39 Norah Stretton to Lesley Cunningham, 11 January 1959, Cunningham papers.

40 Nine Old Grammarians on staff of University of Melbourne to archbishop, 31 October 1958, copy held by Gwyneth Dow.

41 Interview with Gwyneth Dow, 9 January 1991.

42 *Age*, 15 November 1958; interview with Gwyneth Dow, 9 January 1991.

43 Interview with Mary Britten, 10 April 1991; former staff to parents, December 1958, p. 4; *Sun*, 4 November 1958.

44 Archbishop to Pownall, 10 November 1958; *Herald*, 10 November 1958; *Age* 13 November 1958.

45 'Reasons for staff resignations at MCEGGS', letter from resignees to parents, MGGS Archives, n.d.

46 C. Mins, HM. Rep., 26 February 1959.

47 Daish reported in *Sun*, 28 October 1958; academics' letter; K. Cunningham, letter to *Age*, 29 October 1958.

48 Information from Lorna Mitchell, Old Grammarian who returned to take charge of English in 1960 after seventeen years on the staff at MLC.

49 C. Mins, 14 July 1954, 29 June 1955, 12 October 1955.

50 C. Mins, 12 October 1955, 27 October 1955, 11 April 1956, 11 July 1956; interview with the late Mary Davis.

51 Valentine Leeper to Bertha [Hitchcock], 1 December 1958, MGGS Archives, F35 Lee(s)3.

52 Several people interviewed by the author used such phrases with evident conviction.

53 R. Sholl to K. Cunningham, 24 November 1958, Cunningham papers.

54 Jessie Clarke (née Brooks), talk on 3DB at 6.45 p.m., 30 October 1958. The

relevant number of the *Listener-In-TV* does not itemise talks or speakers, but this was the slot for a regular news/current affairs program called 'On the spot'. Notes by Audrey Margetts, former staff member, Cunningham papers; Valentine Leeper to Bertha [Hitchcock], 1 December 1958, MGGS Archives, F35 Lee(s)3; information Pownall and Cunningham.

55 K. Cunningham to R. Sholl, 10 November 1958, Cunningham papers.
56 Dorothy Ross to Valentine Leeper, 13 November 1958, F58 Lee(s)6.
57 Valentine Leeper to the Reverend Sidney Ball, 2 November 1958, to the Dean of Melbourne, 2 November 1958, to the archbishop, 9 and 19 November 1958, and to Bertha [Hitchcock] 1, 7 and 10 December 1958, MGGS Archives, F35 Lee(s) 5, 10, 16, 20.
58 Information from Woods; Britten; Babbage. Canon R. M. Hudson, interview 17 June 1991.
59 C. Mins, 12 May, 11 November, 28 December 1914; 26 July, 11 August, 25 August 1915.
60 Interview with Mary Britten, 10 April 1991.

Chapter 8 MCEGGS in a time of change

1   Marjorie R. Theobald, *Ruyton Remembers 1878–1978*, Hawthorn Press, Melbourne, 1978, ch. 10.
2   Letter, Ursula Gottschalk to the author, 16 January 1992 (hereafter Gottschalk letter).
3   Family details from Gottschalk letter, interviews with Betty Murray and Stuart Blackler.
4   Registry records, Oxford High School for Girls, Nottingham High School for Girls, Queen Mary and Westfield Colleges, University of London.
5   J. Kamm, *Indicative Past: a hundred years of the Girls' Public Day School Trust*, Allen and Unwin, London, 1971.
6   Kamm, p. 134 ff.
7   *Girls' High School Magazine*, 1930, p. 35; 1932–33, p. 33; 1932–33, p. 33; 1936–37, pp. 22–3; registry records, Nottingham.
8   Registry records, Westfield.
9   Gottschalk letter; interview with Stuart Blackler, 17 May 1991.
10 Gottschalk letter; registry records, Westfield.
11 N. Glenday and M. Price, *Reluctant Revolutionaries: a century of headmistresses, 1874–1974*, Pitman, London, 1974, pp. 98–9; D. Hansen and I. Hansen, *Feminine Singular: a history of the Association of Heads of Independent Girls' Schools Australia*, Hyland House, Melbourne, 1989, pp. 46–50.
12 Gottschalk letter; C. Mins, 22 January 1957.
13 *Age*, 9 July 1954, p. 11.
14 C. Mins, 1954–57; HM Rep. and Acting HM Rep., 1954–57.
15 HM Rep., 12 October 1955.
16 HM Rep., 14 July 1954, 12 October 1955.
17 C. Mins, 12 October 1955, 22 January 1957.
18 *MCEGGS Magazine*, no. 140, December 1957, p. 11.
19 HM Rep., 9 October 1957.
20 Interview with Betty Murray, 17 January 1992.
21 HM Rep., 16 April, 8 October 1958.
22 HM Rep., 26 February 1959; headmistress's Valedictory Speech Day Report, 1958, p. 9.
23 Interviews with Betty Murray, 16 May 1991, 17 January 1992.

24 Letters to Edith Mountain, 1958, private collection.
25 Interviews with Lorna Osborn (6 May 1991), Lorna Mitchell (May 1991), Elizabeth Murray (16 May 1991); *Shelford Magazine*, 1991, p. 71; C. Mins and HM Reps, 1959–61.
26 C. Mins, 23 April 1959.
27 HM Rep., 25 June 1959.
28 Reports of the Headmistress to the Diocesan Council . . . on the State of Education, 1958–61.
29 Interview with Dean Tom Thomas, 16 May 1991.
30 Interviews with Merna Thomas (18 May 1991), Lorna Osborn (6 May 1991), Betty Murray (16 May 1991), and former parents and students.
31 'Reasons for staff resignations at MCEGGS', letter from resignees to parents, MGGS Archives, n.d.
32 E. F. M. Mountain, 'The place of the independent school as an educating body of the traditional type' in *The Report of the Seventh Interstate Conference of the Headmistresses' Association of Australia*, 1961, pp. 36–41.
33 C. Mins, 26 November 1958.
34 D. J. Ross, 'Progressive development scheme for MCEGGS', MGGS Archives.
35 Acting HM Rep., 10 April 1957.
36 HM Rep., 16 April 1958.
37 ACER, *Report on Provision for Science Teaching in the Non-Government Schools of Australia*, ACER, Melbourne, 1958.
38 Kamm, pp. 191–2.
39 ACER, *Report*; HM Rep., 16 April 1958.
40 MCEGGS, *The Jubilee Story*, no. 1, MCEGGS, Melbourne, 1963, p. 2.
41 HM Rep., 10 October 1962.
42 Mountain, 'The place of the independent school', p. 41.
43 HM Rep., 10 October 1962.
44 Interview with Betty Murray, 17 January 1992.
45 HM Rep., 10 October 1962.
46 Interview with Lorna Osborn, 6 May 1991.
47 'Headmistress's talk . . . at inauguration of the Executive Council, 24th July, 1958', p. 1, Daish papers.
48 HM Rep., 8 October 1958.
49 *MCEGGS Newsletter*, no. 9, 14 July 1954.
50 Student Executive Council Minutes (SEC Mins), 10 February 1959.
51 M. Woodlock, 'Physical education report', 11 October 1961.
52 HM Reps, 28 April and 7 July 1965; SEC Mins, April–June 1965.
53 HM Rep., 23 July 1959.
54 C. Mins, 28 April 1965.
55 C. Mins, 11 May 1966.
56 HM Rep., 11 May 1966.
57 Acting HM Rep., 11 April 1956.
58 HM Reps, 16 April 1958; 23 July 1959.
59 Interviews with former staff and students.
60 C. Mins, 21 February 1963.
61 HM Rep., 14 November 1963.
62 *Age*, 13 November 1963; P. Gill, 'The federal science grants scheme . . . 1963–64' in E. L. French (ed.), *Melbourne Studies in Education 1964*, Melbourne University Press, Melbourne, 1964, pp. 270–354.
63 C. Mins, 11 March 1964.
64 MCEGGS, *The Jubilee Story*, no. 3, May 1964, pp. 1–3.
65 *MCEGGS Magazine*, no. 147, December 1964.
66 *MCEGGS Magazine*, no. 146, December 1963, p. 76.

67 MCEGGS, *The Jubilee Story*, no. 6, May 1966, p. 2.
68 MCEGGS, *The Jubilee Story*, no. 6, May 1966, p. 2.
69 *Nisi Dominus Frustra: MCEGGS jubilee history*, MCEGGS, Melbourne, 1953, pp. 37–8.
70 HM Rep., 15 March 1961.
71 *MCEGGS Magazine*, no. 150, December 1967, p. 5.
72 Service of thanksgiving for the life of Edith Florence Mary Mountain, 25 February 1985, p. 1.
73 Old Grammarians Executive Committee Minutes, 20 June 1967.
74 Interviews with former staff and students.
75 *MCEGGS Magazine*, no. 147, December 1964, p. 17.
76 Sylvia McConkey's scrapbook, MGGS Archives; *Herald*, 18 August 1959.
77 Letter, Benjamin Britten to Sylvia McConkey, 19 November 1959, MGGS Archives.
78 Interviews with former students.
79 *MCEGGS Magazine*, no. 146, December 1963, p. 38.
80 The author wishes to thank Desma McDonald for access to her research into the attitudes and opinions of past students of MCEGGS. The responses to questionnaires are in the possession of Desma McDonald.
81 Interview with Joan Bazeley, 18 May 1991.
82 *Brick*, vol. 16, no. 3, September 1970, p. 1.
83 HM Rep., 19 October 1966.
84 Interview with Lorna Osborn, 6 May 1991.
85 *MCEGGS Magazine*, no. 152, December 1969, p. 28; *Sixth Form Centre*, Building Bulletin no. 41, HMSO, London, 1969.
86 Interviews with Lorna Osborn (6 May 1991), Lorna Mitchell (11 May 1991) and J. Bazeley (18 May 1991).
87 *MCEGGS Magazine*, no. 153, December 1970, pp. 18–19.
88 Interviews with former students.
89 C. Mins, 18 July 1973.
90 Interview with Lorna Osborn, 6 May 1991.
91 HM Rep, 4 April 1973.
92 Interview with Betty Murray, 17 January 1992; *Age*, undated clipping, MGGS Archives.
93 *MCEGGS Magazine*, no. 157, December 1974, p. 47.
94 *Age*, undated clipping, MGGS Archives.

Chapter 9 Melbourne Girls Grammar School in 1993

1 *IE*, April 1992, p. 3. Information for this chapter was obtained from *IE*, *MGGS Magazine*, *MGGS Prospectus*, and interviews with Miss Nina Crone and other members of the academic and administrative staff.
2 *MGGS Magazine*, 1991, p. 7.
3 MGGS preliminary census returns, 4 February 1992.
4 *IE*, June 1988, p. 2.
5 Caroline Ross, 'The new head', reprinted in *A Pictorial History of Melbourne Church of England Girls' Grammar School*, MGGS, Melbourne, 1984, p. 106.
6 *IE*, August 1983, p. 4.
7 *IE*, December 1985, p. 1.
8 Details on the Merton Hall Foundation are from its newsletter, *Foundation Update*, from its inception in December 1985.
9 *Foundation Update*, December 1989.

[10]   *MGGS Magazine*, 1991, p. 10.
[11]   *IE*, March 1988, p. 1.
[12]   *IE*, March 1982, p. 3.
[13]   'The Victorian Certificate of Education', *IE*, June 1990.
[14]   *IE*, December 1989, p. 1.
[15]   *MGGS Magazine*, 1991, p. 22.
[16]   *MGGS Magazine*, 1991, p. 32.
[17]   *IE*, June 1992. The research was commissioned from Quantum Market Research.
[18]   The decision by Melbourne Grammar School to go co-educational was reversed in September 1992.
[19]   *IE*, April 1992, p. 4.

Index

à Beckett, Mrs Ada (née Lambert), 22
à Beckett, Mrs, 13
Adams, Professor John, 55, 89
Adams, Miss Margaret, 149
Adamson, L. A., 57
administrator, 159
aims, 94–5, 171–2
air-raid drill, 112–13
Aitken, Mrs Bonnie (née Inge), 120
Akehurst, Miss Ethel, 47
'alternative fifth', 182
Anderson, Miss Alice, 69
Anderson, Miss Sarah, 31
the Annexe, Balwyn, 123
anniversaries
    Silver Jubilee (1928), 4–5, 29, 58–9
    Jubilee (1953), 5
    Diamond Jubilee (1963), 5, 166
    Centenary (1993), 4
anthem, 52
Armstrong, Rev. T. H., 35
Army Medical Corps, 112
assembly hall, 2, 27, 50, 52, 53
    see also Ross Hall (new Assembly Hall)
Assistant Mistresses' Association of
    Victoria (AMAV), 150
Associated Teachers' Training Institute
    (ATTI), 2, 7, 55, 90, 108
Australian Council for Educational
    Research (ACER), 98, 157
Australian Educational Quarterly, 55
Australian Imperial Forces (AIF), 112
Australian Women's Army Service (AWAS),
    112
authors, notes on, 5–8
Avoca (Caroline St), 164
Ayers, Miss Pamela, 178

Babbage, Stewart Barton (Dean of
    Melbourne), 141, 146
Bage, Alice, 172
Bage, Jessie, 12, 174
Baker, Miss Louise, 111
Baker, Miss Marigold, 111
Ball, Hilda, 46
baptisms discouraged in chapel, 165
Baxter, Mrs Mary (née Kingsmill), 120
Bayne, Mollie, 115
Bazeley, Miss Joan, 165
Behan, Sir John and Lady, 76
Belmore Grange, Balwyn, 123, 124
Bennett, Mrs Lilian (née White), 115, 120
Bill for 'The Establishment and
    Constitution of a Church of England
    Girls' High School', 32, 34, 35
Bitcon, Mrs Anne (née Aitken), 119
Blackburn Report, 180
Blackburn, Jean, 86

Blackler, Rev. Dr Stuart, 6, 177
Blackwood, Miss (later Dame) Margaret.
    60, 89, 112, 143, 151, 178
Blanch, George Ernest, 39
Blanch, Mrs Margaret, 39
boarders, 14, 16, 24, 27, 53, 65, 70, 124, 126,
    170, 171, 172, 173, 183
    fees, 60
    scholarships, 6, 70
    worship at Christ Church, 38
boarding houses, 8, 62, 162
    in Balwyn, 115
    The Cottage, Balwyn, 124
    Gilman Jones Hall, 4, 162
    Jessie Bage House, 174
    Merton Hall, 24, 58
    Morris Hall, 26
    Old Fairlie, 25
    Phelia Grimwade House, 59
    staff of, 171
    in Walsh St, 111
    Wildfell, 92, 113, 162
    see also buildings and properties;
    evacuation during World War II
Bolton, Mrs Susan (née Hanlon), 124
Booth, Archbishop, 126–7
Booth, Mrs Beryl (née Bradshaw), 38
boys, 44, 86, 167, 184–5
    see also co-education
Branigan, Mrs Mary (née Sewell), 75, 153
Brick, 166, 167
Britten, Benjamin, 166
Britten, Mrs Mary, 142
Brookes, Mrs Herbert (née Ivy Deakin), 57
Brooks family, 126
Brooksbank, H. A., 45
Brown, Mrs Margaret (née McMahon), 29
Brumley, Elaine, 135
buildings and properties, 24–7
    appeals, 59, 60, 156–7, 163, 168, 175
    assembly hall, 2, 27, 52, 53
    Avoca (Caroline St), 164
    see also Morris Hall (Caroline St)
    Caroline St, 8, 157
    chapel, 4, 8, 52, 59, 61, 62–3, 65, 162, 165,
    177
    Clarendon St, 35–6
    extensions, 2, 4, 24–5, 54, 59, 62–3, 156–7,
    162–3
    funding, 162–4, 168, 175–6
    see also Merton Hall Foundation
    Garnsworthy Centre for Computer Studies,
    175
    Gilman Jones Hall, 4, 96, 162
    see also New Merton Hall
    gymnasium, 54, 174
    Jessie Bage House, 174
    Junior School Music Centre, 175

library, 157, 158, 168, 174
Lovell House, 47, 54
Merton Hall (249 Domain Rd), 1, 5, 11, 13–14
Merton Hall (82 Anderson St), 1, 2, 8, 16, 24, 162, 171
Merton Hall Foundation, 175–6
Morris Hall (80 Anderson St), 2, 26, 91–2, 96, 98, 160, 164
Morris Hall (Caroline St), 162, 164–5, 171
New Merton Hall, 63, 126
　　see also Gilman Jones Hall
Nina Crone Centre (library/audio-visual), 174
Old Fairlie (80 Anderson St), 2, 8, 25–6
Phelia Grimwade House (86 Anderson St), 2, 8, 59, 126
renovations, 54
Ross Hall (new Assembly Hall) (84 Anderson St), 4, 168
Ross Hall (old) (84 Anderson St), 8, 96, 151
science laboratories, 4, 157–8, 174–5
Tom Thomas Building (physical education), 174
in Walsh St, 8, 157
233 Walsh St, 174
280 Walsh St, 174
290 Walsh St, 174
Wildfell (Domain Rd), 4, 8, 92, 113, 123, 126, 156, 160, 162, 164
　　see also boarding houses
'Bulfa', 167
Buntine, W. M., 57

Cain, William, 16, 39
Cain, Mrs William, 16, 39
Caldwell, Jeanette, 112
Calvert, Eileen, 112
Cameron, Miss Mary, 75–8, 86
　articled clerk, 77
　boarder at The Hermitage, 75
　debating, 75
　at Janet Clarke Hall, 76, 77
　at Kiddle, Briggs and Willox, 77
　law studies, 76
　at Merton Hall, 75
　parents, 76
　Stedman Cameron legal practice, 77
　tutorials at Trinity College, 76
　at University of Melbourne, 76
camping, 182
Capelin, Mrs Anne, 130, 152, 155
career advice, 177
Carr, Archbishop, 45
Catnach, Miss Agnes, 149
chapel
　baptisms discouraged, 165
　Chapel Chanters, 165, 183
　Chapel of St Luke, 4, 8, 165, 172, 177
　fund, 52, 62–3, 165
　in Gilman Jones Hall, 162
　marriage services discouraged, 165
　need for, 50, 52, 59, 60, 61, 65, 162, 165
Christ Church, South Yarra, 38
Church of England, 31–49 passim, 129
　association with school, 1, 6, 13
　Community of the Holy Name, 43
　Community of the Sisters of the Church, 43

ethos in schools, 35
　funding proposals for schools, 43–4
　purchase of ladies' schools, 5
　purchase of Merton Hall, 31
　Religious teaching order proposed, 43
　　see also Diocese of Melbourne
Church of England Trusts Corporation of the Diocese of Melbourne, 40
civic values, 85
Cizek, Franz, 90
Clarke, Mrs, 38
Clarke family, 1, 30
Clarke, Bishop (later Archbishop) of Melbourne, Henry Lowther, 5, 26, 41, 51
Clarke, Mrs Jacqueline (née Ward-Ambler), 117
Clarke, Janet, Lady, 12, 13, 38–9, 143
Clarke, Mrs Jessie (née Brooks), 144
Clark, Dr Margaret (née Sanders), 172
Clark, Miss Meriel, 172
Class-A schools, 53, 101
　registration as, 65
　triennial inspection, 153–4, 158
co-curricular activities, 84, 166, 182–3
co-education, 44
　Melbourne Grammar School proposal, 184
　rejected by MGGS, 184
　value for girls, 184
co-operation v. competition, 94, 160
Colebrook, Ethel, 153
Colles, Mrs Gwynneth (née Morris), 164
　　see also Morris, Miss Gwynneth
committees, 105
Commonwealth per capita grants, 175, 186
communism, 97, 131–2, 144–5
Connell, W. F., 7
Coombes, Miss Josephine, 111
Council of Public Education, 54, 55
councillors, 91, 105, 130, 159–60
　　see also Student Executive Council
Craig, Mrs Alice (née Taylor), 5
Creer, Mrs Ruth (née Chisholm), 115, 118, 121, 152
crisis of 1958, 128–46
　concern over academic standards, 137, 141
　conciliation committee appointed, 142
　inquiry, 141–2
　'loyalty letter', 135, 152
　newspaper coverage, 140
　Old Girls' and Old Grammarians' involvement, 132, 140–2
　parents' role, 132, 138–40
　School Council meeting, 136
　support for Edith Mountain, 152
　teaching staff concern about morale, 132–3
　teaching staff replaced, 143
　teaching staff resignations, 128–9, 134–5
Cromie, Mrs Marjorie (née Tye), 115, 118
Crone, Miss Nina, 4, 166, 170
　at ABC, 173
　comments on VCE, 181
　committee involvements, 174
　education, 173
　parents, 173
　teaching experience, 173
　at University of Melbourne, 173
Cross, Miss Agnes, 46

Cullen, Mrs Stephanie (née Mitchell), 73
Cunningham, Dr K. S., 145
Cunningham, Miss Lesley, 135
curriculum
  academic v. non-academic, 18–20
  criticisms of, 154
  in Edwardian era, 17
  effect of Class-A system, 101–2
  of Gilman Jones' era, 58, 62
  Group 1, Group 2 subjects, 180
  Howard Plan, 55–6, 60, 89
  Montessori influenced, 55, 90
  at Morris Hall, 178–9
  of Mountain era, 151–2, 154
  new subjects offered, 182
  non-academic subjects included, 101–3,
    158
  'non-traditional' areas, 178
  in open-entry school, 8
  parents' priorities, 184
  in Ross era, 98–104
  in Senior School, 17, 18–20, 55–6, 58, 60,
    101–2, 151–2, 154, 179–82
  subject choices, 100, 179
  subjects discontinued, 182
Currie, Noelie, 112
Cuzens, Harold, 122

Daish, J. L., 135–6, 139
Daniell, Miss, 130
Davidson, Miss Eliza, 57–8
Davies, Miss Margaret E., 80, 125, 135
Davis, Miss Mary, 91–2, 102, 113, 114, 115,
  117, 118, 122, 149
Deakin, Miss Stella, 18
Deasey, Mrs Oenone (née Gardner), 126
debating, 53, 73, 75, 183
Delacombe, Sir Rohan, 164, 168
democratic evolution, 99
depression (1930s), 9, 59–60
depression (early 1890s), 9, 35–6
Diocese of Melbourne, 36
  Board of Education, 42–3, 47, 65
  establishment of girls schools, 32–7
  purchase of Merton Hall, 47–8
  secondary schools, 45–9
Dixson, Miss Irene, 19
Dobson, Mrs Fay (née Anderson), 115
Donald, James, 139
Donaldson, Hamish, 117
Donaldson, Mrs Marie, 117
Donaldson, Miss Patricia, 117
Dow, Mrs (later Dr) Gwyneth (née Terry,
    later Rivett), 82
  B.Ed., 82
  doctorate, 82
  Freda Cohen prize, 82
  Fulbright scholarship, 82
  involvement in teacher education, 82
  M.Ed., 82
  marriage to Rohan Rivett, 81
  marriage to Hume Dow, 82
  memories of teachers, 84, 86, 87
  at Merton Hall, 80
  parents, 81
  personnel management, 81
  studies in industrial welfare, 81
  teaching, 82

  teaching at MacRobertson Girls' High
    School, 82
  teaching at University High School, 82
  at University of Melbourne, 81
  Victorian Curriculum Advisory Board, 82
  Australian Childhood: An Anthology,
    80–3
  George Higinbotham: Church and State,
    82
  Learning to Teach: Teaching to Learn, 82
  Samuel Terry: The Botany Rothschild, 81
  Uncommon Common Sense, 82
Dow, Hume, 82, 87
Dowling, Mrs Caroline (née Purbrick), 172
Dowling, Miss Sarah, 172
Dowling, Miss Sophie, 172
drama productions, 73, 84, 166, 183
Drummond, Helen, 112

Eastern Golf Club, Doncaster, 3, 115,
    123–6
  construction of army huts, 125
  rural school group, 124
  transport, 124
Edith Mountain Sixth Form Centre, 4,
    167–8
Education Act 1872, 33, 34
education of girls, 68–87 passim
  in Edwardian era, 16–17
Ellemor, Diana, 119
Eltringham, Miss Mary, 64
Emms, Lorena, 112
enrolment statistics, 2, 11, 15–16, 24, 27–8,
    107, 128, 152, 169
evacuation during World War II, 93–4,
    113–17
  end of, 126–7
  'families' of staff and children, 118–19
  to Marysville, 114–16
  role of D. J. Ross, 94
  of School Certificate Group to Marysville,
    116
  of Senior School to Eastern Golf Club,
    Doncaster, 3, 123–6
  of Senior School to Marysville, 116
examinations, 154, 158
Executive Council, 159
  see also Prefects' Executive Committee;
    School Advisory Council; School
    Executive Council (SEC); Student
    Executive Council
extra-curricular activities see co-curricular
    activities

Farrell, Miss Jane, 57
fees, 62, 150, 157, 175
feminist movement, 66
  see also women's movements
Ferguson, Dr Gladys, 117
Ferguson, Miss Joan, 70
Fethers, Pat, 112
Finance Committee, 96
Firbank CEGGS, 5, 45–6
Fison, Miss Mary, 73
Fitzgerald, Dr Thomas, 123
Fitzpatrick, Dorothy, 135
Floyd, Dr A. E., 52, 58, 125
Ford, Rev. W. C., 35

Forerunners, Constance Tisdall, 45–6
Forgacs, Eve, 119
form committee period *see* vertical period
Foster, Dr John, 144
Franklin, Mrs Mary (née Gillespie), 125
Franks, Mrs Mary (née Patterson), 161–2
Frecheville, Mrs Janet (née Aitken), 119,
    120–1
Free Kindergarten Union, 28
Friend, Miss Marjorie, 57
funding
    state and federal, 163–4, 168, 175, 186
    see also Commonwealth per capita grants
fundraising, 59, 60, 162–3, 164, 168, 175
    see also Merton Hall Foundation

Gardiner, Lyndsay, 7–8
Garlick, Rev. T., 32
Garnsworthy Centre for Computer Studies,
    175
Garnsworthy, Miss Elizabeth, 175
Garnsworthy, Miss Jane, 175
Garnsworthy, Lance, 175
Garnsworthy, Mrs Marcia (née Graham),
    175
Garnsworthy, Miss Prudence, 175
Garnsworthy, Miss Sally, 175
Gawler, Dorothy, 79
Gawthorne, Eva, 135
Gellatly, Miss Adele, 29
Gellatly, Miss Hilda, 29
general studies program, 168
Gidison, Dorothy, 112
Gifford, Helen, 106
Gilbert, Miss Noela, 19
Gilman Jones Hall, 4, 96, 162
    see also New Merton Hall
Gilman Jones Scholarship, 65
Gilman Jones, Miss Kathleen Annie,
    50–67 *passim*
    arrives at school, 52
    attitude to marriage, 69
    at Cambridge University, 2
    characteristics, 64
    church links, 65
    committee memberships, 61
    compares Australian and English schools,
        58
    entry in *Who's Who in the World of
        Women*, 60–1
    feminism, 2, 66
    health, 63
    membership of educational organisations,
        54–5
    opened chapel fund, 165
    remembered by students, 73, 83, 84, 106
    retirement, 62–3
    succeeded by D. J. Ross, 88
    women's network, 66
    workload, 65
Girls Public Day Schools Trust (GPDST)
    (UK), 148, 155–6, 157
Goe, Mrs Elizabeth, 38
Goe, Bishop, (later Archbishop) Field
    Flowers, 34, 37
Grant, Rt Rev. James, 172
Greeves, Miss T., 111

Greyholm (84 Anderson St), 16, 96
    see also Ross Hall (old)
Grimwade family, 1, 30
Grimwade, E. Norton, 59
Grimade, F. S., 25, 37, 38, 41
Grimwade, Mrs, 13
Grimwade, Mrs Phelia (wife of E. Norton),
    59
Grindrod, Bishop John, 165

Hailes, Miss Alison, 112, 116
Hailes, Miss Jean, 116
Hailes, Miss Mildred, 116
Hallows, Mrs Elsbeth (née Haydon), 178
Hancock, Mrs Patricia (née Plummer), 126
Handbook for the Information of Parents,
    97
Hardie, Elsie, 23
Harley, Mrs Judith (née White), 110
Harper, Mrs Valda (née Hall), 124
Harris, Dr M. O'Brien, 55
    *Towards Freedom: the Howard plan of
        individual timetables*, 55
Harvey, Miss Jean, 124–5
Haynes, Barbara, 111
Head Mistresses' Association of Great
    Britain, 55
Head, Mrs Edith (wife of Archbishop), 38,
    65
Head, Archbishop F. W., 110
headmistresses, 1–5, 14, 40
    search for replacement for Dorothy Ross,
        143–4
    see also Crone, Miss Nina; Gilman Jones,
        Miss Kathleen Annie; Hensley, Miss
        Emily Marianne; Morris, Miss Edith
        Nina; Morris, Miss Mary Elizabeth;
        Mountain, Miss Edith; Ross, Miss
        Dorothy J.; Taylor, Miss Alice;
        Tunnicliffe, Miss A.
Headmistresses' Association, 54
Heidelberg Military Hospital, 112
Henderson, Ethel, 23
Henderson, Miss Isobel, 54
Hensley, Miss Emily Marianne, 1, 4, 11–14
    passim, 30
Hensley, Miss Florence, 14
The Hermitage (Geelong CEGGS), 45
Herring, Miss Margery, 19, 29, 65
high schools, 20
Higher School Certificate (HSC), 159, 180
    see also Matriculation; Victorian
        Certificate of Education (VCE)
Hindley, Mrs Sarah, 39
Hindley, Rev. William George, 39
histories of the school
    MCEGGS: History of the School, (Gwenda
        Kent Hughes), 4
    Nisi Dominus Frustra, (Gwenda Lloyd), 5
hockey field, 26
Hollow, Fay, 112
Hooper, Mrs Freda (née Mavin), 115
houses, 183
    badges, 56–7
    Clarke, Hensley, Mungo, Taylor, Batman,
        161
    house mistresses, 57

Howard Plan, 55–6
in Morris Hall, 179
St Cecilia, St Hilda, St Joan, 56–7
Howard Plan, 55–6, 60, 89
Hughes, Gwenda Kent, wrote history of school, 59
Hunt, Mrs Alison (née Ferguson), 117

Independent Association of Registered Teachers of Victoria (IARTV), 55, 152
Independent Association of Secondary Teachers of Victoria (IASTV), 20, 54–5
independent schools
challenges of 1950s, 150–1
expansion of, 157
Information Exchange, 175
Ingram, Adele, 28
Intermediate (4th form) examination, 100–1
Irving, Miss Dorothy, 125, 135
Isaacs, Susan, 90, 148
Ivanhoe Girls' Grammar School, 5
Ivanhoe Grammar School, 46

James, Mrs Catherine (née Brown), 117
Janet Clarke Hall, 65, 70–1
see also Trinity College Hostel
Jennings, Helen, 120
Jess, Betty, 112
Jessie Bage House, 174
Jessie Grimwade Scholarship, 25
Jordan, Mrs Rosemary (née Skerritt), 124
Joske, Miss Enid, 19, 29, 65
Junior Red Cross, 65
Junior School see Morris Hall
Junior School Music Centre, 175
Junior Secondary School, 96, 99

Kelsey, Miss (later Dr) Helen Frances, 19, 29
Keys, Jeanette, 112
Kincaid, Miss Daile, 169
kindergarten, 96
see also nursery school
Knight, Mrs Trude (née Cox), 115, 117
Knox, Mrs Phil (née Waitt), 115
Kooringa guest house, Marysville, 114, 120, 126
classrooms built, 119
food, 120
upper Junior School at, 117
Koornong School, 104
Korowa Anglican Girls' School, 5, 47

Laby, Miss Betty, 78
Laby, Miss Jean, 78–80, 85, 86
childhood at University of Melbourne, 78
at Merton Hall, 78
'Old Grammarian' Baseball Team, 79
parents, 79
PhD in physics, 79
physics department, University of Melbourne, 79
research work, 79–80
science studies, 78–9
teaching at RAAF Point Cook, 80

at University of Melbourne, 78
work on Climatic Impact Assessment Program, 80
Laby, Thomas, 79
Lack, Miss Geraldine, 167–8
Lawson, Miss Jean, 8, 153, 155, 164, 166
League of Nations, 65
Leaver, Rev. E., 122
Leaving (5th form) examination, 101
Leeper, Mrs, 57
Leeper, Dr Alexander, 12–13, 19, 38, 57, 61
Leeper, Miss Molly, 12
Leeper, Miss Valentine, 12, 79, 144–5
Lees, Archbishop Harrington Clare, 48–9
library, 4, 157, 158
committee, 105
Middle School, 168
Nina Crone Centre, 174
Liet, Madame Augustine, 22–3
Lloyd, Mrs Gwenda (née Kent Hughes), 73, 80, 83, 84, 85, 102, 115, 116
Lothian, Elisabeth, 73
Lovell House, 47, 54
Lovett, Mrs Elaine (née Speed), 75, 153
Lowther Hall Anglican Grammar School, 46
Lundie, M., 135
Lyceum Club, 28

MacArthur, General Douglas, 116
Macartney, Miss Charlotte, 13
Macartney, Hussey Burgh, 32
McCarthy, Mrs Margaret (née Coulter), 173
McCarthy, Mrs Rosslyn, 7–8
McCarthy, Ms Susan, 172–3
McCaughey, Rev. Dr Davis, 108
McConachie, Miss Madeline, 18, 29
McConkey, Miss Sylvia, 133, 135, 152, 166
McCutchen, Josie, 119
McDonald, Mrs Desma (née Stephenson), 7
McGee, Stephanie, 119
McGrath, Lorrie, 112
Mackay, Ada, 73, 83, 84
MacKenzie, Miss Margaret, 112
MacKenzie, Mrs Patricia (née Clark), 120
MacKenzie, Lady Winifred (née Smith), 112
McKie, Bishop, 132–3
McKie, Sir William, 144
Mack, Margaret, 112
McLean, Miss S., 119
MacLeish, Mrs (later Dr) Shirley (née Coombes), 111, 113–14, 124, 125
McPherson, Mrs Meg (née McCarthy), 173
Madame Osterberg's Physical Training College (Kent, England), 23
Mannix, Archbishop Daniel, 45
Margetts, Audrey C., 135
Markby, Mrs Elaine (née Francis), 112
marriage services discouraged in chapel, 165
married women, employment of, 85–6
Martin, Mrs Sylvia (née Reilly), 3, 94, 106, 115, 121, 129, 132, 143, 151, 156
Marylands guest house, Marysville, 114, 116
arrival, 121

illness, 121, 122
Middle School, 117
teaching conditions, 121
Marysville
    Christ Church, 122
    clothing, 122
    guest houses, 3, 117–23
Matriculation
    results, 154, 158
    statistics, 18
    see also Higher School Certificate (HSC);
        Victorian Certificate of Education (VCE)
Maxwell, Mrs Muriel (née Berry), 64
MCEGGS: History of the School (1928),
    (Gwenda Lloyd), 4
MCEGGS Magazine, 5, 73, 112, 166, 182
Meagher, Douglas, 176
Melbourne Church of England Girls'
        Grammar School (MCEGGS)
    Diamond Jubilee (1963), 5, 166
    Jubilee (1953), 5
    name decided, 58
    origins, 1–2, 11, 29–41
    Silver Jubilee (1928), 4–5, 29, 58–9
    see also Church of England; Melbourne
        Girls Grammar School (MGGS); Merton
        Hall; school
Melbourne Continuation School (later
        Melbourne High School), 44
Melbourne Girls Grammar School
        (MGGS)
    Centenary (1993), 4
    name, 9, 177
    origins, 1–2, 4–5, 11, 16, 29–41
    see also Melbourne Church of England
        Girls' Grammar School (MCEGGS);
        Merton Hall; school
Melbourne Grammar School, 1, 39
Mellor, Miss Joan, 115, 119
Mellor, Miss Margaret, 115, 118
Mentone Girls' Grammar School, 5, 46–7
Menzies, R. G., 111
Mercer House see Associated Teachers
    Training Institute (ATTI)
Merfield, Mabel, 111, 152
Merton Hall (249 Domain Rd), 11, 13–14
    origins, 1, 4–5, 11–30 passim
Merton Hall (82 Anderson St), 8, 16, 24, 37,
    96, 162, 171
    extensions to, 2
    origins, 1, 16
    see also Melbourne Church of England
        Girls' Grammar School (MCEGGS);
        Melbourne Girls Grammar School
        (MGGS)
Merton Hall Foundation, 175–6
Methodist Ladies' College (MLC), 17
Michaelis, Sir Archie, 161
Middle School, 96, 100–1
    reorganisation of, 55–6
Millis, Emeritus Prof. Nancy, 178
Minifie, Miss Elizabeth, 124
Minifie, Mrs Enid (née Oliver), 124
mission statement, 171–2
Mitchell, Dr Leonard, 59, 73
Mitchell, Miss Lorna, 69, 72–5, 84, 85–6,
    87, 153, 166
    at MLC, 74
    at Oxford University, 73–4
    at St Margaret's, Toorak, 74
    schooling at Merton Hall, 73
    teaching at Merton Hall, 74
    at University of Melbourne, 73
    at Women's Christian College, Madras, 74
Molesworth, Judge Hickman, 32–5
Monteith, Miss M., 112
Montessori, Dr Maria, 55, 90
Moorhouse, Catherine, 140–1
Moorhouse, Charles, 137, 138
Moorhouse, Bishop James, 31–4, 40, 48
moral values, 84–5
Morey, Dr Elwyn, 143, 151
Morres, Miss Elsie, 22, 31, 45
Morris, Mrs, 13
Morris Hall (80 Anderson St), 26, 96, 160,
    164
    activity pattern, 98
    curriculum review by Ross, 92
    demolition, 164
    origins, 2, 26–7
    reorganisation of, 91–2
    see also Old Fairlie
Morris Hall (Caroline St), 162, 164–5
    21st birthday, 171
    co-curricular activities, 179
    curriculum, 178–9
    house system, 179
    opened, 164
    social education program, 179
    special education, 179
    see also Wildfell (Domain Rd)
Morris, Mrs Clara Elizabeth (née French),
    1, 5, 15, 27, 41, 164
Morris, Miss Edith Nina, 1–2, 5, 14–15,
    23–4, 28, 30, 41
Morris, Miss Gwynneth, 1, 14, 23–4
    see also Colles, Mrs Gwynneth (née
        Morris)
Morris, Miss Katie, 14
Morris, Miss Marcia, 14
Morris, Miss Mary Elizabeth, 1–2, 5,
    14–15, 21, 23–4, 28, 30, 41
Morris, Rev. W. P. F., 22
Morris, William E., 1, 15, 32, 41, 48
    financial support of school, 5, 24, 25, 30
    sold school, 37
Morris, William (son of William E.), 15
Moule, F. G., 32, 35
Mountain, Miss Edith, 3–4, 147–69
    appointment, 143, 147–8, 149
    arrival at school, 151
    assemblies, 165
    biology teaching, 149
    building program, 4, 156–8, 160, 162–5
    childhood, 148
    crisis of 1958, 3–4, 7, 128–46, 147, 152
    curriculum policy, 154, 158–9
    death, 169
    dismissed staff, 138–9
    educational policy speech, 137–8
    educational views, 129, 130, 155–6
    introduction of new subjects, 158
    at London University, 148
    manner 'unapproachable', 129–30, 131,
        154–5
    paper on role of 'traditional' school, 155–6

proposed changes to school organisation, 151–2
religious views, 165
retirement, 168–9
secondary education, 148
staff join, 74–5
strengths, 154–5
see also Edith Mountain Sixth Form Centre
Mt Kitchener House (guest house), Marysville, 114, 118–19, 126
junior girls at, 116–17
lessons at, 119
sub-primary group at, 116
Muntz, Miss Edith, 22
Murray, Mrs Betty, 131, 135–6, 152, 155
Murray, Rev. C. H., 110
music, 58, 165, 166, 183

National Council of Women, 28, 54, 72
National Fund Raising Council, 163
National Security Act, 111
New Education Movement, 55, 89, 90, 92, 130
New Merton Hall, 126
see also Gilman Jones Hall
Newnham College, 66
Newsletter to parents, 97
Nicholson, Pip, 6
Nickson, Claire, 112
Nisi Dominus Frustra, (Gwenda Lloyd), 5
'Noye's Fludde', 166
Nugent, Miss Mona J., 73, 76, 80, 84, 102, 129, 135
nursery school, 92
see also kindergarten

Ogilvy, Miss Adele, 66
Old Fairlie (80 Anderson St), 2, 8, 25–6
Old Girls, 10
careers, 68–87 passim, 177–8
on teaching staff, 98
at University of Melbourne, 18–19, 69–87 passim, 178
Old Grammarians, 10, 29
return as teachers, 153
in wartime roles, 112
Old Grammarians' Society, 64, 98, 111, 165
establishment of Gilman Jones Scholarship, 65
formation, 28
fund-raising, 175
London meeting, 28
presidents, 28, 29
register of members, 29
Oliver, Miss Freda, 29
Oliver, Miss Kathleen, 28–9
Onians, Gladys, 112
Ormiston Ladies' College, 15
Osborne, Dr Ethel, 78
Osborne, Miss Yrsa, 78
Osborn, Mrs Lorna, 153, 155, 168
overseas students, 170–1
overseas visits, 182

parents
curriculum priorities, 184
role in crisis of 1958, 132, 138–40

support prize-giving, 161–2
survey of attitudes, 163, 167, 183–4
Parents' Association, 59, 64, 73, 97, 173
fundraising, 175
Parker, A. M., 141
'Parliament of Youth', 166
pastoral care, 177
Patterson, Miss Helen, 162
Penman, Archbishop David, 172
Pennington, Mrs Margaret (née Mitchell), 120
Perry, Bishop, 48
Phelia Grimwade House (86 Anderson St), 2, 8, 59, 126
Phillips, A. A., 138, 139
physical education, 23, 92–3
see also sport
Pike, Mrs Dora (née Whitelaw), 74–5, 153
post-Leaving course, 158–9
Pownall, Miss Elizabeth, 104, 115, 124, 135, 138
practical fifth form, 102
Prefects' Advisory Council, 159
Prefects' Executive Committee, 91
see also Executive Council; School Advisory Council; School Executive Council (SEC); Student Executive Council (SEC)
Preparatory School, 171
Presbyterian Ladies' College (PLC), 17
Preshil—The Margaret Lyttle Memorial School, 104
Price, Mrs Nancy (née Lucas), 117
Primary School, 96
see also Morris Hall
prizes, 161, 176
A. M. Mackay prize for English, 161
Dorothea Baynes prize for classics, 161
Florence Finn prize for speech work, 161
Hazel Sholl memorial prize for an essay on divinity, 161
Helen Patterson prize for all-round excellence, 161
Jessie Nott prize for music, 161
Madame Liet prize for French, 161
Mary Michaelis prize for study, sport and service to the school, 161
Maude Howard prize for science, 161
not awarded, 93–4
parents in favour, 161–2
Phelia Grimwade prize for science, 161
properties, see also buildings
Provisional Council, 37–9
chairmen, 37–8
'Pug', 167

RAAF Directorate of Recruiting
delays in vacating school, 126–7
occupation of school, 116
Rapke, Betty, 112
Raveloe (Domain Rd), 126
Raw, J. J., Dr, 61
Raynor, Archbishop Keith, 172
Red Cross Emergency Service, 111, 114
Red Cross Society, 111, 112
registration
of secondary schools, 20–1
of teachers, 21

see also Teachers and Schools
        Registration Act (1905)
religious education, 40, 61, 83, 102, 130,
        158, 176–7
    see also chapel
religious foundations, 176–7
Remfrey, Miss Ethel (later Morris), 22
Remington, Miss Catherine, 54
reunions of Old Girls, 177
Richardson, Mrs Myra, 138
Rigby, Meredith, 125
Rivers, Wilga, M., 135
Roff, Philip, 186
Roman Catholic convents
    Anglican girls attend, 33–4, 43
    staffed by Religious, 34, 43
Rosebery County School for Girls (UK),
        167–8
Rosefield, Faye, 119
Roseleigh guest house, Marysville, School
        Certificate group at, 116, 117, 121–2
Ross Hall (new Assembly Hall) (84
        Anderson St) 4, 168
Ross Hall (old) (84 Anderson St), 8, 96, 151
    see also Greyholm
Ross, Miss Dorothy J., 2–4, 14, 55, 57,
        88–109 *passim*, 122–3
    at Associated Teachers Training Institute
        (ATTI), 90
    attitude of Old Girls and parents to, 132
    biography, 7
    car and gas producer, 123
    child development studies, 90
    childhood, 88
    co-ordinating role in evacuation, 123
    curriculum reform, 91–3
    educational views, 3, 89–91, 107–8, 129
    evacuation during World War II, 113–15
    interview with Edith Mountain, 149
    introduced to school, 110
    at Mercer House, 108
    organisation of forms under, 95–6
    organised return to school from RAAF,
        126–7
    parents, 88
    political and social view, 3, 97, 131–2, 144
    progressive educational views, 97, 103–4
    proposed building project, 156
    recommendation of Edith Mountain, 143
    relations with staff, 104
    resignation, 143
    retirement, 98, 108, 149
    scripture classes, 102
    search for replacement, 143–4
    staff appointed by, 129
    studies in Europe, 90
    teaching at MCEGGS, 89
    teaching positions, 89
    at University of London, 90
    at University of Melbourne, 88–9
    views school as co-operative democracy,
        104
Ross, F. E., 135
Rubbo, Sidney, 138
Russell, Olive, 99
Russell, W. B., 154
Ruyton Girls' School, 46
Ryan, Senator Susan, 175

St Michael's Grammar School, 43–4
Sanders, Mrs Joan (née Brett), 172
Sanderson, Margaret, 112
Saunders, Cheryl, 178
Scantlebury Brown, Dr Vera (née
        Scantlebury), 114, 117
school
    aims of, 94–5, 171–2
    assets, 186
    captains, 6, 29, 60, 70, 170, 178
    constitution, 39
    crest, 38
    magazine, 5, 73, 112, 166, 182
    motto, 38
    name, 9, 39, 58, 177
    organisation of forms, 95–6, 99–100, 103
    rules, 39
School Advisory Council, 91, 105
    see also Executive Council; Prefects'
        Executive Committee; School Executive
        Council (SEC); Student Executive
        Council (SEC)
School Certificate, 93, 102
School Council, 96, 172
    conservative political & social views, 97
    constituted, 39
    membership, 40, 57, 61, 172–3
    1991 seminar, 171
    Old Grammarian members, 172
    powers, 40
    role in crisis of 1958, 129, 132–42, 145–6
    unclear of vision for school, 151
    women members, 172
school councils, role, 49
school dance committee, 105
School Executive Council (SEC), 91, 105,
        130
    executive & advisory powers, 105
    role, 105
    veto by headmistress, 105
    see also Executive Council; Prefects'
        Executive Committee; School Advisory
        Council; Student Executive Council
        (SEC)
School Notes, 19, 23, 27, 28, 29, 52
science
    at Eastern Golf Club, Doncaster, 125
    education, 69, 78–80, 121, 157, 163–4
    laboratories, 4, 157–8, 174–5
    more students taking, 175
    teaching of, 68–9
Science Talent Search, 182–3
sectarianism, 45
Sellick, Betty, 112
Senior School
    academic v. practical streams, 101–3
    curriculum, 179–81
Sewell, Betty, 115
Shann, Mrs Enid (née Wilson), 115, 116,
        117, 120
Sharp, Miss Cecily, 29
Shawe, Enid, 112
Sholl, Dorothy, 112
Sholl, Mr Justice (later Sir) Reginald, 144
Simondson, Miss Adrienne, 165
Simondson, Mrs Diana (née Cohen), 120
Simpson, Mrs Honor (née Mitchell), 73
Skerritt, Mrs Barbara (née Schwartz), 120

Smith, Mrs M. (née Morrison), 115
Snodgrass, Miss Agnes, 14
Snowball, Margaret, 112
social changes, 167
social services committee, 105
sport, 23–4, 73, 183
    athletics, 160
    at Eastern Golf Club, 125
    facilities, 160
    see also physical education
Spowers, Miss Ethel Louisa, 29
Spring, Miss Amanda, 173
Spring, Mrs Margaret (née Colclough), 173
Sproule, Miss Theodora, 19
state government
    aid to non-government schools, 4, 33,
        163–4
    educational policies, 9
    involvement in education, 20–1, 44
    secondary schools, 4, 44, 150
States Grants (Science Laboratories and
    Technical Training) Bill, 163
Staughton, Miss Dorothy, 14
Stephens, Miss Betty, 116
Stephens, Elisabeth, 135
Stephens, Miss Roma, 116
Stillman, Miss Patricia, 111
Stone, Margaret, 112
Stott, Miss Muriel Millicent, 29
Stretton, Mrs Nora, 140
Stringer, Mrs June (née Swinburne), 124
Student Christian Movement, 65
Student Executive Council (SEC), 152, 159
    powers, 159–60
    see also Executive Council; Prefects'
        Executive Committee; School Advisory
        Council; School Executive Council
        (SEC)
students
    exchange schemes, 170–1
    self-government see School Executive
        Council (SEC); vertical period
    type of development valued, 107–8
Stutt, William, 123
sub-primary group, 96
surveys, 163, 167, 183–4
Suttie, I. D., 90
Swedish gymnastics, 23
Sweet, Dr Georgina, 22
swimming, 178
Syme, Mrs, 28
Syme, Miss Constance, 29
Syme, Miss Eveline, 18, 29
Syme, Miss Marjorie, 28–9
Syme, Miss Mildred, 29

Taylor, Miss Alice, 1, 4, 11–14 passim, 30
Taylor, Mrs Anne (née Slattery), 118
teachers, qualifications, 21
Teachers and Schools Registration Act
    (1905), 20–1
    see also registration of teachers
teaching staff, 171
    appointment of, 40–1
    closeness to girls at Marysville, 122–3
    'communist' accusations, 144–5
    concern with school morale, 132–3
    demands on, 106

deputation to archbishop, 138
dismissals, 138–9
duties, 41
duties at Marysville, 120
evacuation during World War II, 115–16
inexperienced, 153
married women, 85
meetings, 104–5
Old Girls' memories of, 83–4
Old Girls/Grammarians, 98, 153
pastoral care role, 177
psychological counsellor, 98
relations with D. J. Ross, 104
replaced after crisis of 1958, 143
resignations, 128–9, 134–5, 138, 142
salaries, 54–5, 60, 62, 150
scholarship of, 83–4
superannuation scheme, 62
support for Edith Mountain, 152
team teaching, 168
Terry, Miss Mollie, 81
Theobald, Marjorie, 6
Thomas, Miss Angela, 174
Thomas, Miss Jane, 174
Thomas, Miss Merna, 153
Thomas, Venerable (later Dean) Tom, 154,
    174, 176
Thompson, Margot, 112
timetable, 100
Tintern CEGGS, 5, 46
Tolson, Mrs Barbara (née Selleck), 173
Tom Thomas Building (physical
    education), 174
Topp, Miss Ruth, 18, 19
Tournament of the Minds, 183
Towl, Margaret, 119
Townsend, Doreen, 112
Travers, Patricia, 135
Trinity College Hostel, 11–13, 19
Tucker, Rev. Horace Finn, 32, 38
Tucker, Prof. T. G., 26–7
Tuckfield, Mrs Yvonne (née Spry), 112
Tunnicliffe, Miss A., 2, 22, 50–1, 165
    resignation, 146

University of Melbourne
    Liet Prize for French, 23
    Old Girls at, 18–19, 69–87 passim, 178
    reaction of Old Girls to crisis of 1958,
        141–2
    role as regulator of secondary education, 65
    Schools Board, 55, 100–1
    science graduates, 22
University Practising School (later
    University High School), 44

Vance, Canon G. O., 35, 37
Vasey, Mrs Florence (née Faul), 74–5, 153
Veal, Mildred, 153
vertical period, 100, 105
Victorian Certificate of Education (VCE),
    8, 179–80
    future of, 181–2
    public attitude to, 181
    results 1991, 181
    staff preparation for, 180–1
    see also Higher School Certificate (HSC);
        Matriculation